To Carole —
our dear
friend
Buddy!
Spencer

COUNTING CROWS

Stories of Love, Laughter and Loss

SPENCER HATTON

Dedication Page

This book is dedicated to my late son, Jed, who is the inspiration for "Counting Crows" and for so much more.

Proceeds from the sale of this book will go to the Bronwen Hatton Scholarship Fund at Central Washington University, in Ellensburg, Washington. Named in honor of my late wife who received a degree in special education from CWU, the endowed fund provides scholarships to future special education teachers.

Contents

BY LAND, SEA, AIR AND HORSE

FAMILY TIES

JIMINY CRICKET

A PRIDE OF SONS

DIFFERENTLY ABLED

IN SEARCH OF ANSWERS

EXIT LAUGHING

Foreword

There was a time, back in the mid-1970s, when journalists were actually revered, not reviled. Watergate had come into our vocabulary and a disgraced president had been driven out of office by the fine work of the Washington Post's Bob Woodward and Carl Bernstein.

During those halcyon days of print journalism, I made my move out of Durango, Colorado, an undergraduate diploma in hand and the backseat of my Datsun B-210 cluttered with books, a battered typewriter and an Army duffle bag bulging with clothes.

I drove north to Cheyenne, Wyoming, a desolate place even in the spring. But you have to start somewhere, so there I stood, outside the door to the human resources department of the Wyoming State Tribune. I knocked and entered. A very attractive young lady looked up at me.

"So you want a job in the newsroom," she asked after scanning my resume. I nodded. She smiled back. "You might be in luck."

She pointed down the hall to the editor's office. I had 70 paces to go before my future in journalism would be sealed.

Jim Flinchum stood up when I entered his glassed-in office. Tall and angular, he epitomized what journalism is all about — tough, serious, committed. He had earned his stripes at United Press International. Legend has it that one day he dashed into the Dallas UPI bureau and vaulted over desks and chairs, arriving at his Olivetti typewriter with fingers outstretched. That day in Dallas, President Kennedy had been shot. He cranked out a copy-ready story, all 300 words, in less than five minutes.

That's journalism — no glory, just seamless prose in the bat of an eye.

I handed him my resume. His eyes darted back and forth.

"Do you know anything about sports?" Flinchum asked. No friendly chitchat, no smiles, just business.

"Sure I do," I said, with a self-confident wave of my hand. Though I had never written a sports story in my life, I did like to play tennis and once had started as a defensive back on my high school's varsity football team. I figured those were worthy credentials.

"Have you ever been in a darkroom before?" he asked.

I hesitated for a moment. This is not an answer you take lightly, especially when you are out of work and have listed head grillman at McDonald's and Army medical corpsman on your resume.

I did own a camera and had taken several photos for the Durango Herald while I was finishing college. Surely those count. And how about the time a friend of mine showed me how to process film by dunking it in a vat of D-76 chemicals? That certainly took place in a darkroom.

I stared back and inhaled deeply the stale air that hung like thick automobile exhaust in the editor's office.

"Yes, I have," I said.

Flinchum's eyes dropped back down to the inked lettering on my resume.

"Can you start tomorrow morning?"

My heart skipped a few beats. I couldn't believe what I had heard.

Only later did I find out that Flinchum was desperate. His sports editor had walked out a few days earlier, forcing him to handle the sports page. And he hated sports. I was his ticket out of misery. Taking photos was an added bonus since his 72-year-old staff photographer could barely see anymore.

My first story for the sports section was a one-paragraph explanation about a high school track meet that had been canceled due to inclement weather. Though it was mid-April at the time, a blizzard had swept through Cheyenne and dumped six inches of snow, pushed along by 50-mph winds.

Flinchum pulled out the sheet of paper from my typewriter, glanced at what I had written and grunted: "This will do." That's the last sports story of mine he ever edited.

A year later, I loaded up my Datsun again and moved to Washington state, where I worked as a cop reporter and later as editor of the Skagit Valley Herald in Mount Vernon. Then I traveled across the Cascade Mountains to Yakima and the Yakima Herald-Republic where I served as city editor, responsible for coverage of local news. My career spanned another 27 years. My last job had a lofty title: editorial page editor.

During my years in journalism, I also wrote a column. Topics ranged from politics to sports to celebrities. My columns, too, included matters closer to home — about my family and the joys of raising two sons. I also wrote about what seemed the most impossible task of all — overcoming the grief of losing both a wife and a son.

Then on Nov. 11, 2006, just a few months after my 58th birthday, I married Leslie. This wonderful turn of events became, as most things do in my life, a rich source of material for future columns.

I have lined a bookshelf in my office with four thick notebooks filled with some 230 columns. With the hope of putting a book together after I retired in the fall of 2010, the challenge became what to do with all those newspaper clippings.

After organizing the columns into several categories — such as family, humor, profiles and commentary — a pattern emerged. Chapters began to take form. Photographs fell into place. I added postscripts to some columns in an effort to bring fresh details to what I had written. I inserted unpublished entries from my writer's journal to enliven my storytelling with raw emotions.

When I completed the first draft of "Counting Crows," Leslie gave it a thorough review. She proved to be an invaluable editor with a sharp eye for detail and narrative flow.

In the spring of 1975 when I first entered the offices of the Wyoming State Tribune, I never could have imagined that one day I would be holding in my hands a copy of my book, "Counting Crows." I just wanted a job back then. Better yet, I wanted a job where I could get paid for writing. My dream job.

Sometimes a dream does come true. It certainly has for me.

'HIT IT ELVIS' — A FRESH START

Beginning at the end seems the proper course to take when it comes to my roller-coaster ride through life.

And what better place to start than on the dance floor of a pub in Portland, Oregon, where I tried to impress my future wife, Leslie, with my rendition of the popular Irish Riverdance. It was a disaster but that didn't dissuade her a year later from marrying me at the Little White Wedding Chapel in Las Vegas.

So the journey begins.

This geezer can still bust a move, and that's no blarney

Dancing has very little to do with reality. When the music is loud and there's a crowd gyrating about on the dance floor, it's all too easy to think you're really better than you are, that you believe all those people staring bug-eyed at you are jealous of your moves when, in fact, they're really saying to themselves: "What's that bloated catfish doing out there?"

But illusions are hard to break, especially when the sweat starts stinging your eyes. A few songs later, you begin to see yourself as another John "Saturday Night Fever" Travolta, with one arm darting skyward, pointing to heaven as if anyone up there really cares you're grooving to "Stayin' Alive" by the Bee Gees.

Much to the dismay of those who actually can swing dance without slipping a disc in the vertebrae, I have returned this summer to the dance floor — with a vengeance. It must have something to do with my age — the more white hair I sprout, the more frantic I become to relive the days of my youth, when wearing a letter sweater in the high school hallways was considered hip.

The fact that I have absolutely no sense of rhythm doesn't keep me from dancing. In fact, that only heightens the thrill — like climbing a rock cliff without ropes.

My dancing exploits have taken me to the "Rock the Gap" event at the Yakima Greenway where my jump 'n' jive moves attracted not one but six women who joined me on the dance floor — probably out of sympathy. That was quickly followed by several visits to Grant's in the Glenwood Square where I banged elbows with kids who could easily have called me "gramps." And some, I think, did.

A couple of weeks ago, I took my Gene Kelly/Fred Astaire routine to the Moxee Hop Festival, where my feet pounded the portable dance floor for two hours straight with no visible bleeding and no harried calls to 911. That's success in my book.

But my most memorable dance moves were saved for a pub in downtown Portland.

Kells Irish Pub is a popular hangout for great Irish and Celtic music, and boasts of the West Coast's largest St. Pat's Day celebration. Sporting 16 beer taps, the pub also prides itself in its single-malt whiskeys and the presence of grown men parading around in kilts. Just don't laugh at them.

I heard about the pub while strolling around with my girlfriend, Leslie, in search of a place to hear some live music. We stopped by a restaurant that featured jazz, but the musicians could barely be heard over the din of clanking silverware.

I asked one of the waitresses about a nearby dance club. Her face blanched white.

"It's a meat market," she exclaimed.

Sizing me up, she concluded it wasn't a place for a card-carrying AARP member like me.

She mentioned Kells. You'll like it there, she assured us.

So off we went. When we arrived at Kells, there was a stream of people spilling out into the street. We squeezed our way past the Saturday-night revelers lining the 40-foot-long bar and reached a tiny dance floor tucked at the end of the building.

The pub had flown in an Irish band from San Francisco, and they were hot.

I scanned the sea of faces around me and couldn't spot anyone even close to my age bracket. A few looked at me with bemused delight, as if to say: "This geezer won't last long."

Undeterred by this youthful swarm crowding the dance floor, we maneuvered our way forward and strutted our stuff. I tried to do my best rendition of the famed Irish Riverdance I had seen on past PBS telecasts. My legs rocketed up and down, with my hands placed strategically on my hips.

But then we made a mistake. We took a break and stood near the bar to catch our breath.

That's when Bruce appeared on the scene.

He was with the band, and he swayed like a Douglas fir at 6-foot-4. He had tattoos down both arms and long, stringy black hair that clung to his sweaty face. He wore a big broad smile as he stepped toward us. His right hand reached out. I figured he was going to haul Leslie out onto the dance floor. Yeah, that would be a treat, I chuckled to myself.

His hand, though, stopped short. Instead, he had a grip on me. He was pulling me toward him. What's this all about? Does this guy want to dance with me?

Leslie laughed loudly, and those around the dance floor were whooping it up, too, even the guys in kilts.

Then a miracle happened. The bedraggled-looking Bruce stepped aside and up walked Helga.

If you have ever seen a Swedish model before, she was it: a statuesque blonde with a creamy smooth complexion and sensuous lips that seemed to purr, "Hi, fella." Well over 6 feet tall, she rose above me like a goddess ascending.

Dazed by the sudden turn of events, I did what any red-blooded American would have done. I took her two strong hands in mine and started to dance.

Cheers went up from those around us as I tried to spin Helga around. I succeeded twice, but only by hopping up on my toes and raising my arms toward the ceiling.

When the fiddle player strummed the final note, I bowed slightly and retreated to the bar where one onlooker exclaimed, "Nice moves, Pop."

Though Leslie and I continued to dance, I never saw the stunning Swedish model again. By midnight, my shirt was dripping wet. I looked like dirty laundry waiting for the spin cycle. I declared the evening over.

As I hobbled out the door, I wondered what John Travolta would have done. I know one thing for sure. He would still have been dancing with Helga.

August 21, 2005

Why rent a castle when you've got the King?

If you, along with the tabloid press, think Tom Cruise's wedding last weekend at a 15th century Italian castle was the "wedding of the year," I've got news for you. It wasn't.

Sure, a few million dollars will get you fitted for a Giorgio Armani Hand Made to Measure tuxedo and Cartier-designed rings to share with your bride.

But earlier this month, another wedding took place that offered as much of a spectacle and far more surprises than Cruise's made-for-Hollywood production.

Mine.

The moment of truth for me — when I thought my wedding might be the best — arrived early in the ceremony when the minister turned down the volume on Mozart's wedding march. An awkward silence ensued. That's when my blushing bride, Leslie, at the far end of the chapel, yelled out: "Hit it, Elvis."

On cue, the King, decked out in a flashy red sports jacket, grabbed a microphone and belted out "It's Now or Never" before a crowd of 45 wide-eyed wedding guests.

I couldn't have been happier.

If you want to get married in Las Vegas — and about 500 couples do each day — booking a date at the Little White Wedding Chapel is the next best thing to renting out a medieval castle on the coast of Italy.

I mean how can you pass up a 55-year-old chapel that has, among its brides and grooms, Frank Sinatra and Mia Farrow, Joan Collins, Mickey Rooney (two times), Michael Jordan, Demi Moore and Bruce Willis, plus Natalie Maines of the Dixie Chicks. Two years ago, Britney Spears sashayed down the aisle. Sadly, her marriage lasted only 54 hours. Sometimes even historic surroundings can't undo bad karma.

I must admit Cruise had a better view from his castle's promenade than we did from the Little White Wedding Chapel. Just outside the "Tunnel of Vows" (yes, you can get hitched at the chapel's drive-thru window), a tall sign reads: "Strippers." Below, in slightly smaller lettering, are etched these enticing words: "Nude Daily." We didn't know about the strip joint when we scheduled our wedding several months ago.

Leslie and Spencer show off their Elvis sunglasses and sideburns at the Little White Wedding Chapel

We picked a 5 p.m. ceremony on Saturday, Nov. 11, and chose from a long list of options the Romance Package. For $391 (Elvis was extra), we got a minister, 24 photographs, a bouquet for the bride, a stretch limo and unlimited access to the chapel's wedding planners. We made contact with five of them. Our most memorable was Jerry, who had been a Budweiser beer distributor for 25 years. How's that for qualifications?

With guests flying in from 12 different states around the country, the hours leading up to our appointed marriage got to be a bit hectic. Surprisingly, though, everything seemed to fall into place, probably due to the fact there were no rehearsals.

While Cruise and Katie Holmes held endless practice sessions, our rehearsal in Vegas consisted of taking an elevator to the second floor of the Crystal Chapel, where our minister greeted us. A veteran of nearly 2,000 ceremonies, he was a jewel.

The minister laughed when I handed him a sheet of paper detailing each step of the ceremony, including a list of songs Elvis should sing.

"No one has ever done this before," he exclaimed. "You have this wedding all planned out."

That prompted a quick reply from Leslie: "This was premeditated."

The minister doubled over in laughter.

As our guests settled into the red velvet love seats inside the Chapel L'Amour, I got my first chance to shake hands with Elvis. My son, Andy, who served as my best man, later referred to him as the "sweaty Elvis." There was a reason for that. This talented impersonator was busy that night, hopping from one wedding to another.

Then we got a nod from Roxanne, yet another wedding planner. The ceremony was to begin. Elvis straightened his jacket. Sweat trickled down his long sideburns as I hooked my arm around his.

"We're going down the aisle together," I said.

Elvis smiled and replied excitedly: "I hope Priscilla doesn't mind."

Later, after the dulcet tones of "It's Now or Never" faded away, Leslie and I exchanged vows that we had written together. I promised to love, cherish, honor and obey. She replied affirmatively to the first three, but balked at the fourth.

"I don't know about the obey part," she said, much to the delight of our guests.

We went on to promise to care for our two cats. Our vows ended with this heartfelt message: "I promise to remember life has no guarantees except one — that each day with you is better than a day without you. I love you."

There wasn't a dry eye in the chapel.

Then the minister had us repeat the vows he had prepared. He touched on all of the hallmarks of what a marriage should be — love, sacrifice, care and togetherness.

Of course, we wanted the ceremony to end with a bang, so we handed out song verses and asked everyone to join in with the sweaty Elvis as he concluded the ceremony.

After their vows, Cruise and his bride reportedly danced to "Songbird" by Fleetwood Mac. That's fine, but it pales in comparison to seeing my 87-year-old mother dance with Elvis as our chapel rocked to "All Shook Up."

Before heading to our reception at the Aladdin Casino, we gathered together at an outdoor gazebo across from the towering "Stripper" sign. There my son and I handed out Elvis sunglasses with fake sideburns to the wedding guests and took a group photo.

Really, does it get any better than this? Don't bother asking Tom Cruise. He hasn't a clue.

November 26, 2006

When owners get hitched, so do their cats

This is a tale of two cats.

Some days, it's the best of all possible worlds, with the two purring felines whisker to whisker, sniffing each other out. Other days, the fur flies and hisses echo down the hallway.

Life is, indeed, an experiment and so it goes with bringing together two cats under one roof. What's required are these: money, patience, more money, lots of litter and expensive drugs — for the cats, not you. Only after this arsenal is expended can you possibly hope for success.

Even when Leslie and I got married in November, everyone seated in the wedding chapel knew the toughest part of the nuptials would not be us getting along after I move out of my house into hers. No, it would be joining together my 5-year-old longhaired tabby with Leslie's 3-year-old shorthaired tabby.

My cat — named Sylvester after the cartoon character, or Sly for short — had the good fortune of being alert when my two sons and I were prowling the cages at the Humane Society in Yakima some five years ago. We had gone to the shelter because a friend had told us about a nice black-and-white kitty that was available. But by the time we had arrived, that cat had already found a home.

Determined to leave with a feline in hand, we checked out the other cats. I peered into a cage with three kittens all huddled together. That's when Sly poked her head up and stared at me with those emerald eyes.

"That's the one," I told the shelter attendant.

From a kitty I could hold in the palm of my hand, Sly has grown over the years to such proportions that my son Andy, while surveying her generous girth one day, declared: "She looks like a barge."

Now, from stage left, enters Leslie's cat.

She got the kitty three years ago from an animal shelter while visiting friends and relatives at the swanky resort town of Sun Valley, Idaho. To honor the place, she christened the kitty Sunny Boy.

The cat has lived a charmed life ever since. Really, how many shelter cats get a trip on a private jet from Sun Valley, stay overnight in a Seattle high-rise condominium whose neighbors claim lineage from the Nordstrom family, and then enjoy a front row seat on an Airporter Shuttle? That's how Sunny Boy traveled to Yakima. First-class all the way.

As the cat grew, so did its name, morphing from Sunny Boy to Sonny Bono to Bone-a-lator. But, for now, Bone will do. The cat is a marvel of aerodynamics. He defies gravity. Want a light switch turned on? Leave it to Bone. The cat can hit that chest-high switch with ease. Just don't expect him to turn it off.

One day, Leslie told me to shut the refrigerator door. I asked why, but before I could finish the sentence, you-know-who had leapt into the fridge. It took a while to pry him out from behind the milk carton. Weird.

So given Sly, the cargo ship, and Bone, the feline catapult, we had our work cut out. Getting married is one thing; negotiating a peaceful living arrangement between two distinctly different cats is another. We had to call in the experts.

After consulting several veterinarians and reading through a stack of pet articles, it became clear we had to unsheathe the credit card and get to work.

The list is impressive:

- New silver food dish and eight cans of fancy cat food, from salmon to turkey in gravy (this stuff only comes out when the two cats are together. It's called the "heavy artillery"). Ka-ching: $14.95.
- 30 pounds of litter, the stuff that clumps like cement. Ka-ching: $15.99.
- A third litter box for the kitchen area — just in case the overly excited cats can't reach their own litter box in time. Ka-ching: $34.99.

Sly   *Bone*

- A 3.5-pound bag of hairball-reducing dry food (cats and hairballs — the two are inseparable). Ka-ching: $10.49.

- A Feliway diffuser and spray bottle, a sort of aromatherapy for anxious cats. The stuff really works. Consider it feline Prozac. The scent sifts through the air, putting the unsuspecting cat in "la la land." Ka-ching: $77.98.

And don't forget the set of soft paws. It's the greatest invention since the Hula Hoop. They are little plastic caps that are super-glued onto a cat's claws. Since my cat was never declawed and Bone was, we had to make it a fair fight between the two combatants. So we got the caps stuck onto Sly's front paws. As an added treat, the soft paws come in a rainbow of colors. Leslie wanted blue. So blue it was.

After arranging for these essentials, we were then advised to keep the two cats separated. Lock the new cat up in a room, and throw away the key. This could last several weeks, the experts warned.

We took it a step further. Starting in early January, we kept Sly boarded up for nearly a month. She had crunchy dry food, water and an unlimited supply of cat-calming aromas. She only hissed and swatted at me for the first 82 hours.

Then we opened the door one day to Sly's room and let the cats approach each other.

At the first sight of Bone, Sly quickly retreated under the bed in her room. When Bone inched closer to her, Sly emitted a sound I had never heard before — a guttural rumbling reminiscent of a pickup truck's transmission going on the fritz. Then came a high-pitched hiss. Not a pleasant combination.

This went on for what seemed an eternity ... until one night when Leslie and I were watching the Academy Awards show in the living room. She wondered how the cats were doing. It seemed too quiet. So I went to Sly's room. There they were, like two old friends, curled up on top of the bed, only a few inches apart.

I could hear applause from the other room. The best actor award had been given out. What a shame. Sly and Bone could have won Oscars for their performance that night.

They deserved it.

April 1, 2007

What a moving experience

Experts place moving out of an old house and into a new one well within the Top 10 stressors to befall Homo sapiens in his or her lifetime.

What my wife Leslie and I encountered recently when we moved to a newer house in Yakima leaned more toward the bizarre. It involved FBI agents, hornets, a bloodstained pillow, destroyed property and a resolve never to move again for at least another decade.

Thanks to the sale of my late mother's home near Chicago earlier in the year, we were able to buy a new home before selling our older one. It's a nice predicament to be in.

However, after buying this recently built home off 80th Avenue, we were faced with a perplexing problem about what to do with our 25-year-old home in the Tancara subdivision near 56th Avenue and Tieton Drive: Should we haul the furniture to our new home or leave it behind to entice a prospective buyer into taking the plunge?

My wife voted for keeping everything at the old house. She's a pro at staging a home, so her vote was really the only one that mattered. In her eyes, everything has to be coordinated by color, size and shape. Paintings must match sofas that match lamp shades that match bathroom towels.

As a result, we ended up with white plastic furniture from our patio sitting in the living room of our new home. Very chic.

This also meant we had to sleep on a queen-size inflatable mattress. Sounds like a fun camping experience, but it isn't. An inflatable mattress doesn't allow body heat to dissipate during the night, so somewhere around 3 a.m. you wake up sweating profusely as if you're losing a bout with malaria.

Then there are the air-bladder-induced nightmares. I awoke one morning having dreamt I bit my lower lip. I looked at my pillow and noticed red streaks. I rushed to the bathroom and stared into the mirror. I had a gaping wound in my lower lip — exactly where my dream had foretold it would be.

We eventually did get some furniture at our new house. It was a loaner couch from our favorite furniture store. We placed it in the living room. We loved it. Its pale green fabric was soothing to the eye and comfy to the touch. My cat thought so, too.

"Did the couch come this way," I asked my wife the morning after it arrived. I pointed to tiny tufts of fabric atop the couch. The sound of her heavy sigh told me that wasn't the case. We both stared at Sylvester, my plump tabby cat, who's the only one in the household with front claws. Leslie's cat, Bone, had his removed years ago.

A few frantic phone calls later to the furniture store led to a brokered deal where we bought the designer couch at a reasonable price. All was forgiven. Again, money seems to solve a lot of headaches. Imagine that?

So between adding antibiotic ointment to my lower lip and having to clip the latest clumps of fabric from our "new" couch every morning, I was spending the rest of my free time at our old home prepping it for the open market. That meant cleaning our wooden fence in the front yard so the painters — yes, we had the entire exterior of the house repainted — could apply a fresh coat and persuade prospective buyers into thinking it's "good as new."

I had stripped clean most of the fence when I noticed the remnant of an old vine still stuck between two boards.

After several grunts and groans, I ripped it out and yelled to Leslie, "See what I got." I didn't notice that this old vine was attached to a hornet's nest on the other side of the fence. Out came a sortie of winged demons in my direction. I ducked and swatted with both hands, but a hornet — no doubt named Luke Skywalker — eluded my defensive moves. It landed on my chin and sunk its daggerlike spear into my flesh.

Again I yelled at Leslie but this time it was filled more with curses than celebratory cheers. A half hour later my chin had a chestnut-size knob bulging out.

Thanks to my wife's prowess as a "house stager," a buyer stepped forward in less than three weeks. It only required physical disfigurement to me and thousands of dollars spent over the last two years for a new bathroom, new roof, new shed in the backyard, new carpet in a bedroom and a new dishwasher.

Our move wasn't over just yet.

The new owners had taken out a mortgage from Banner Bank on Summitview Avenue. Money was to exchange hands on a Monday — September 21 to be precise. On that day, a bank robbery occurred in Yakima. Why do I mention this — because that was the very bank where the loan to buy our house was being processed.

Enter the FBI. Though no money was swiped in the botched robbery, Banner Bank essentially shut down for the day and with it our chances of finalizing the sale. Twenty-four hours later the deal closed.

While our move wasn't the most difficult on record, it did seem like it at the time. And to think, the new home where we moved is on Easy Street. How's that for a bit of irony?

October 25, 2009

CLOSE PERSONAL FRIENDS

Jim Gosney, a former columnist at the Yakima Herald-Republic, once coined a delightful phrase to describe chance encounters with famous people: Close Personal Friends or CPFs. These were, of course, far from close and not at all personal. No Christmas cards would ever be exchanged; no sharing of birthday greetings. But in that brief interlude with someone fabulously rich or People-magazine popular — whether it took place in an elevator or a locker room — a new relationship emerged. In other words, a CPF.

While these chance meetings with CPFs are prized memories for me, I doubt my newfound friends would say the same.

It's him ... the Dipper ... the Stilt

While serving as a member of the Army reserves for two weeks in El Paso, Texas, I witnessed one of those rare moments in sports — the debut of a superstar. However, it was no ordinary premiere. What follows is a column I wrote of that historic night while working as sports editor for the Wyoming State Tribune in Cheyenne, Wyoming.

Setting: The cavernous confines of the El Paso County Coliseum

Time and Date: 7 p.m., Wednesday, August 6, 1975

It was as if the Empire State Building had strolled onto the floor. Yet, surprisingly enough, no one seemed to care.

The Colossus moved with gifted ease. His arms, like giant willow branches, dangled carelessly at his side. Around him the grandstands filled with fans. Rumors about a record attendance swept through the stadium. Even so the big man on the floor went unnoticed.

Then he turned in my direction. An eight-foot high net rose up between us, but I could still make out the features on his face. The flecks of gold atop his head, the toothy grin, the close-cropped goatee. Could it be ... yes, it's him ... it's really him ... the Dipper ... the Stilt ... Wilt Chamberlain.

He stood a clear 7 feet 1 inch above the wooden floorboards. Reputedly one of the strongest men in organized sports, the 275-pound Wilt, now 38, dominated the pro basketball backboards for over a decade. His long list of achievements included a record 100 points in a game and 55 rebounds in another. Yes, he's the same man who even took time to play for a year with the Harlem Globetrotters, Wilt the Stilt. The very sound of his name starts the head to nod and the knees to buckle.

But for basketball buffs, it would be a bitter evening. Wilt wasn't in El Paso to dunk basketballs; he was there to spike volleyballs instead. Wilt became fascinated with v-ball a few years ago when, during the summer offseason, he and a herd of other enthusiasts congregated on the beaches outside of Santa Monica, California, to spike and dink the white pint-sized ball.

This fascination led Wilt down the sometimes rocky path of sports expansion. Early this year the International Volleyball Association (IVA) became something more than parlor-room gab and, to the surprise of many, fielded five teams for the May-August schedule. As expected Wilt was one of the founding fathers.

The big Dipper didn't stop there. With the threshold of success merely a cashier's check away, the millionaire basketball star decided to purchase the Southern California Bangers (an IVA franchise) lock, stock and coach. When buying the Bangers, Wilt also declared he would don a playing jersey once again.

Although in last place going into Wednesday night's game against the hometown El Paso/Juarez Sols, the Bangers, who suffered the first shutout in IVA history at the hands of the Sols one week earlier, were looking to Wilt for a reversal. From all the pre-game releases, Wilt's 12-foot high spiking range was seen as the key to both his own and the Banger's future success in the IVA.

The night's debut would be no cakewalk for the highly touted superstar. Wilt's only experience was on sand, not on the faster hardwood floors. Besides he had never even practiced with the Bangers before. The 7-1 behemoth admitted to the precarious nature of his position the day before his debut: "The coach runs the team. I am just a player. I will play as long as he thinks it will help the team."

The only other sound was that of the huge air conditioning fans overhead as the announcer sang out the names of the players. Soon the Bangers were out on the court, except for number 13.

"This is a monumental evening for the IVA," blared the loudspeaker.

"Oh, my gawd," groaned Wilt.

The fans rose on cue. Goliath broke into a trot.

The Bangers beat the Sols in the best out of five games, 12-6, 9-12, 12-9 and 12-8. The victory lifted the Bangers into fourth and dropped the

Sols into the cellar. Wilt's debut was a smashing or, more properly, a spiking success.

"Wilt played a super game," conceded the Sol coach Tom Beerman.

The Banger coach, Craig Thompson, was more analytical in his assessment: "He fit into the system, both defensively and offensively." The statistics bore out the young coach's statement. Wilt had 23 kills in 50 attempts for a .460 spiking percentage along with two stuff blocks and three saving digs.

"I really didn't expect to go the full route," said Wilt after the game. He leaned back in his chair and took a gulp of the locker room air. "I felt good."

Then there followed a pause. Into this calm strode the Banger coach. "Hey, Wilt. NBC is outside for an interview."

Ah, the shot in the arm the IVA has been looking for. Wilt bolted from his seat.

Gotta get that plane at eleven for L. A., chanted the Stilt.

Gonna make it Wilt, assured the coach, but first ...

A little girl stepped forward. Her father was a friend of a friend of someone in management. As if pleading for his daughter's life, the father asked Wilt: "Will you take a picture with my child?"

OK. Sure. Fine.

The girl's brother popped up with a Kodak Instamatic. Bare chested and with sweat still lacing his forehead, Wilt assumed the classic sports pose: hands poised, knees slightly bent, eyes half closed peering down at the fan.

Off went the flash.

"Not yet, Wilt. One more shot."

Hurry up, bellowed the Dipper, I've got to catch my flight.

The boy fumbled with the camera. Precious seconds ticked by in Wilt's head. Another flash and Wilt was out the door.

I was only a few steps behind the fleeing superstar but he had disappeared down one of the stadium's walkways. I wandered outside and returned moments later to the coliseum's inner sanctum where Wilt had just passed his opening night test in the IVA.

And there I found him. Wilt was in a familiar position — before the crowd, under the lights, dishing out his well-rehearsed spiel to a television interviewer. It was the same. Always the same. I had heard it in the locker room. And so had the fans heard it numerous times before from the other greats of the sporting world. We were there not so much to hear but to see, to make our unbelieving eyes really believe ... it's him ... it's really him ... the Dipper ... the Stilt ... Wilt Chamberlain.

The TV interviewer was still talking into the microphone when Wilt decided he had enough. He burst through the ring of fans and bounded out of the building. The coach was close by his side, whispering in the big man's ear, "Great night, Wilt, a great night."

And why shouldn't it have been great. Anything is possible in sports for everything has been done from Joe Namath in nylons to Mark Spitz on Hollywood Squares. Business as usual. The big name, the bigger story, the turnstiles drumming to the sound of spendthrift fans.

Yet the thought still stuck: no one seemed to care. Perhaps not even the little girl whose picture Wilt will never see.

Wyoming State Tribune
August 20, 1975

POSTSCRIPT: The short-lived International Volleyball Association folded in 1979. Chamberlain was its president and was enshrined in the IVA Hall of Fame. Wilt the Stilt died in 1999 of congestive heart failure. He was 63.

Queen Mum's charm graced a nation

The plastic cup splashed with water as the boy grabbed it. His forehead and cheeks were smudged with grit from playing nonstop in the gym. He swallowed the water in a single gulp and wiped his mouth with the sleeve of his shirt. He smiled a toothy grin and dipped his head slightly, "Ta, Queen Mum."

The hands that had held the throne of England together in the face of King Edward's abdication in 1936 had just served up lukewarm water to a child of Deptford. The Queen Mother had arrived, that familiar face festooned with one of her feathered hats, and everyone in London's most poverty-stricken community had come out to greet her, including me.

The Queen Mother was the patron of the settlement home where I was working that summer in 1969 as a member of a three-month volunteer exchange program. But at 20 years of age, I was filled more with eager wanderlust than with passion for being a social worker. I preferred to spend my nights in the theater district of London, not the dark, dank hallways of the settlement home.

But I wouldn't have missed the Queen Mother.

She was making her yearly visit to the drab four-story brick building that served as a child and recreation center and meeting hall for the inner-city community of Deptford.

It's easy to see why the "Queen Mum," as Londoners called her, would pick Deptford for her patronage. England's poor had embraced the Queen Mother as one of their own, and nowhere else in London could you find a more impoverished following than in Deptford, where gangs of "skin-heads" roamed the streets and families huddled in two- and three-room tenement flats, which offered little heat in winter and no relief in summer.

I was the only American among the six volunteers working there at the time. One of the more colorful helpers was a young police officer, a bobby, who was required to spend nearly a year doing community service. He chose the settlement home because he thought it was the easiest work he could get. Though he fancied himself a ladies' man, his successes were marginal at best.

His spirit, though, never flagged. So I wasn't surprised to see him approach the Queen Mother that night. When he squeezed her hand, I caught him giving her a wink. The Queen Mother must have seen it, too, for a pained expression crossed her face. This stalwart of the English royalty had seen it all, even flirtatious winks from young bobbies.

That wasn't the first time I would come face to face with the Queen Mother. I must have set a Guinness Book of Records that summer for a vagabond American coming in contact with England's upper crust. Not only did I greet the Queen Mother at the settlement home, but I also got to shake her hand a month later at the Royal Palace.

Our group of American volunteers — about 40 in all — along with other exchange students and workers from the states were invited to meet the "Mum" and her court for tea. It was no ordinary gathering. The aristocracy was in full bloom, with dukes in starched collars and duchesses dripping with jewelry. A fellow volunteer, who also worked in one of the poorer sections of London, remarked to me, "Now I see why we Americans had the Boston tea party."

For some unexplained reason I got on famously with the Lord of the Exchequer. What the Lord Exchequer found most fascinating about me was my first name.

"Have you met Lady Spencer yet?" he asked excitedly. I barely got a chance to shrug my shoulders before he had spun around and worked his way through the crowd. We ended up in front of a friendly looking lady. Lady Spencer, I presumed.

Did we talk of Vietnam and the anti-war protests sweeping the globe? No, Lady Spencer couldn't wait to tell me about her thimble collection. Her husband, Lord Spencer, confirmed it was the world's largest. So Lady Spencer and I had what the English would refer to as a chinwag about thimbles, a topic I knew little of then and even less now. The Queen Mother soon appeared. Conversations ceased immediately. The lords and ladies, for whom their very existence rested with the Queen Mother, bowed in deference to her presence.

After reaching the rarefied age of 101, England's beloved Queen Mum died in her sleep several days ago.

Myth and reality often clash when wealth and power merge. Gone are the days when newly elected presidents like Jefferson and Adams would have to wait in line for dinner after their inauguration. Today we are all too eager to confer royal status on our elected leaders, and bow to those with wealth or fame. Imagine then those who are truly of royal blood.

So I am not surprised that 400,000 waited in line to view their beloved Queen Mum one last time. I'm sure among them was the police officer I once knew back at the settlement home. I can see him now, no doubt his hair streaked with gray and a few deep creases lining his face.

But he would still have that roguish look about him. I bet he even gave the dear old lady one final wink as he walked by. Even in death, royalty never loses its appeal.

April 14, 2002

Sorry about the sprockets, Lady Bird

If somebody asks to grease your sprockets, just say no.

I didn't, of course, and that miscue has dogged me for decades, ending what could have been a budding friendship with Lady Bird Johnson, one of America's more beloved and respected first ladies, who died earlier this month at the age of 94.

This all took place after I had entered the Army in May 1971, when war protesters were still flocking to Washington, D.C., and President Nixon was still sending troops over to the Agent Orange-laced jungles of Vietnam.

After going through boot camp in Fort Lewis, I ended up as a medical corpsman at Fort Sam Houston in San Antonio, Texas. There I helped out in the eyes, ears, nose and throat clinic where we took care of the active and retired military along with their dependents.

One day, the colonel who ran the clinic said the main hospital needed an extra corpsman and asked if one of us could help out. Naturally no one stepped forward. That's the Golden Rule of the military — don't volunteer for anything, unless it's for an early release. But I wanted a change of scenery, so I raised my hand.

When I arrived at Brooke Army Medical Center, I was greeted by what I thought was a friendly enough major. At least he didn't cuss me out when I met him. My assignment that day seemed simple enough — run the elevator. But my passenger was no ordinary military dependent.

"The first lady will be here at 1400 hours sharp," the major told me. He had a glint in his eye, a way of telegraphing to me that this was very important. I kept up a steady string of "yes sirs" that seemed to appease him.

Then he asked me if I had been cleared by security. Since I wanted to meet Lady Bird, I fibbed and said "sure." Next came the edict: "Don't talk to the first lady and definitely don't talk to the Secret Service. They mean business." The major cracked a grin when he said this.

Several more "yes sirs" brought the conversation to a close. But he did leave me with a very clear command — make sure the first lady gets to the fourth floor and stay there for her hour-long appointment.

So I stationed myself at the front of the elevator and waved off anyone who tried to enter, even a two-star general. That's heady stuff for a private first class.

The clock inched toward 2 p.m. At the entranceway, three or four men in suits stepped inside. The lobby took on an eerie silence. Then she entered, smiling, the former first lady, the one who had banished sleazy roadside billboards from our nation's highways.

The Secret Service stepped in first, followed by Lady Bird. She stood to my left. What struck me was how pleasant she looked, quite unlike her image on television. Maybe that had more to do with the person always standing next to her, LBJ, who sadly had the mug of an aged bloodhound.

"Do you know where we are going?" Lady Bird joked as I pushed one of the buttons.

"I hope so," I replied, unwittingly violating the major's order not to talk.

Moments later the doors opened to an empty fourth floor, cleared for her arrival.

The first lady took a step forward and then paused. "See you later, young man," she said. I waved, and then noticed a Secret Service agent shaking his head. So much for esprit de corps.

I pushed the "stop" button on the elevator, and began my vigil. It didn't last long. A voice came on the elevator's small speaker: "Please come down to the first floor."

Thinking it was some high-ranking officer, I complied. I was disappointed to find another private first class staring at me when I arrived.

"I have to grease the sprockets," he informed me. "It's annual maintenance."

He showed me what looked like official documents.

No way, I told him. I have the first lady using this elevator.

"It's only going to take 20 minutes," he replied.

To this day, I don't know why I agreed. It might have been the fact the guy had the same miserable rank as I did. Maybe I figured he would be done in 20 minutes. Of course, it never takes 20 minutes. That's another Golden Rule in the military — hurry up and wait.

So up to the top floor we went. He greased the sprockets and I watched the clock tick away. At the 35-minute mark, sweat began to slick down my back.

"All done," he exclaimed.

I jumped back in the elevator and headed to the fourth floor.

The doors opened to a terrible sight: Doctors strolling the hallway in white coats and little kids skittering about. Uh-oh, I said to myself. This isn't a good sign.

When I dropped down to the first floor, the major was there to greet me, his jaw jutting out a few inches away from where the elevator's steel doors had been. This time he did cuss me out.

Then his expression changed. Blood drained from his face.

"Were you drafted?" he uttered through clenched teeth.

"Yes sir," I eagerly replied.

The major shrugged his shoulders. What's the point, he surely thought. I was another LBJ legacy, a curse to the military. I was a draftee.

He spun on his heels and left me there, alone in the space where Lady Bird had once stood.

I decided to ride the elevator one more time. It seemed like the right thing to do.

July 22, 2007

My good buddies, Al Pacino and Kurt Vonnegut

I don't like to boast about it, but Al Pacino and I are close personal friends.

Now you are probably wondering why would a nice guy like me hook up with a brash method actor like Pacino who — let's face it — has taken on some pretty weird movie roles. What's with "Dog Day Afternoon" when he played a crook who's trying to finance his gay lover's sex-change operation by robbing a bank? Not what you would call a Disney role.

But Al is really a down-to-earth guy. He likes to have fun, and to make fun of others.

I know. That's what he did to me.

We met a year ago this past spring. I was in the Big Apple with a group of Yakima Herald-Republic reporters. We were there to receive a George Polk Award for our coverage of the deadly Thirtymile Fire. At an early evening reception for the awards, we struck up a conversation with one of the judges.

Since it was dinnertime, I asked him if he knew a good place to eat. He looked at his watch — it was around 8 p.m. — and offered to take us on a tour of New York's finest.

It was a pleasant spring night, so we walked the long boulevards to what New Yorkers call Restaurant Row, a stretch of eateries in the heart of the theater district. The first restaurant we came upon was Joe Allen's. It's the spot to go to in the city. It's always packed, but we got there just after the curtains had gone up on Broadway. So we took a chance. We poked our heads in the front door, and to everyone's surprise, snagged a table smack dab in the middle of a very cozy dining room.

After settling down at our table, I excused myself and headed outside so I could call my sister. She lived outside the city and I hadn't been able to connect with her, except for her irritating answering machine. A reporter followed me. He wanted to check out the street scene and grab a smoke.

So I pulled out my cell phone and dialed up my sister. Behind me, a shiny black Lincoln Navigator pulled up and parked alongside the curb. Just then, I heard my sister's voice. I yelled into the phone: "Hey, how are you?" I gave it my best Brooklyn accent, too.

Well, I tried to carry on a conversation, but the reporter kept trying to interrupt, tugging at my coat sleeve. After ending the call, I turned to him and gave him a jaundiced eye — you know, the kind that should stop anyone, even a pushy journalist, in his tracks. But that didn't stop him.

"Didn't you see him?" he asked excitedly.

Who?

"Al Pacino."

The Godfather?

Yep, in living color. Apparently the guy in the flashy SUV was none other than Al, aka Michael Corleone, Scarface, Serpico. It turns out that at the very moment I started chatting with my sister, Al was standing next to me. He heard my explosive salutation and couldn't help mimicking my slaughtered New York accent: "Hey, how are you?" The reporter confessed Al did a better job of imitating me than I did of myself — if that makes any sense.

I remained skeptical. So we trundled on back into the restaurant to get a confirmation. There, in the back of the dining room, a mere 20 feet from our table sat *the* Al Pacino. And sitting next to him? His longtime sweetheart, actress Beverly D'Angelo.

I smiled wistfully at him trying to make contact. He glared back, giving me his version of a jaundiced eye. I froze in my seat. Don't forget, I said to myself, he knows the Mafia.

That, ladies and gentlemen, is how I became a Close Personal Friend of Al Pacino.

As you can see, there are several key elements to being a CPF. A chance meeting is essential, along with the celebrity status of the person to whom the Fickle Finger of Fate has drawn you in close proximity. Brevity also can't be overlooked. Too much exposure to a "person of stature" can lead to some disastrous results. Actual friendship is one. Another is making a fool of yourself.

Naturally, that's what usually happens with me, as it did a mere 16 hours after Al and I became linked as CPFs. I had another encounter with a celebrity. And this guy is huge for those of us who dabble in ink.

Kurt Vonnegut.

He's my generation's version of Mark Twain. He even looks like Twain, with a mop of unruly hair, bushy eyebrows and a mug that screams "irony" (that's a word writers love to use).

Vonnegut makes a point of attending the formal George Polk ceremonies, since he is one of the advisers for the awards. And sure enough, as a group of us from the Herald-Republic was chatting away with each other at the noon reception, in walked the inimitable Vonnegut.

We all shook hands, most of us hyperventilating with superlatives like "You're my most favorite," and "I can't believe I'm shaking your hand," to the one I unloaded: "Slaughterhouse-Five is a classic."

Vonnegut seemed to wince with pain at the praise. He's had enough of that. The author of 14 books and recipient of countless accolades doesn't need us to stroke his ego.

But that didn't stop me. I just kept blabbering on, all to my utter shame and embarrassment. I noticed he was taking particular interest in a story by the Indianapolis Star that was on display. The newspaper had won one of the George Polk Awards.

"Have you ever been to Indianapolis," I asked.

Now that was a dumb statement. I totally spaced out the fact he is an Indianapolis native. But he was nice to me in his reply, figuring my stupidity was not contagious.

"So what have you been writing about lately?"

Again, I had forgotten that two years earlier he had told the world he was finished, kaput, done with the written word.

Writing is for young bucks, not for old people like me, Vonnegut said. I could tell he had aimed that comment at me as well, since he kept staring at my white hair.

Thankfully, lunch intervened and we parted company.

"Well, see you later," I blurted out.

This time he really did wince with pain. I should have realized that CPFs should be seen, and never spoken to.

It was only later that I realized I could have really hit it off with Vonnegut. That's when a longtime friend reminded me about a play review I had written about Kurt's brother. Back when I worked at a newspaper in Mount Vernon, Washington, in the late 1970s, I had actually seen Kurt's brother Walt perform in a musical for the Anacortes Community Theatre. It would have been a perfect entree into a conversation with Kurt.

But I blew it. I had a brain-freeze. That's what happens when you try to turn a CPF into a PA, a Personal Acquaintance. Take my advice — stick with the fleeting moment. It's better that way. Just ask Al Pacino the next time you see him.

May 25, 2003

B.B. King sings where other legends danced

Neither gale-force winds nor bad knees could keep B.B. King off center stage. By sheer force of will, King stiffly walked across the stage last weekend at the Maryhill Winery and wowed, as he always does, a cheering crowd of worshippers that included me and my wife. We were among the 3,000 or so sitting in chairs or picnicking on the grassy terraces of the huge outdoor amphitheater.

At 82 years old, King is the epitome of a living legend. Who would have imagined the son of a sharecropper would one day be regarded as one of the most influential musicians in American history. He wears this mantle of fame with humility.

"You are so wonderful coming out here tonight to see me," he crooned into the microphone as cheers rose up. Then he launched into one of his signature tunes, "Blues Man," which telegraphed a clear message about who this giant of a musician is all about: "I'm a blues man, but I'm a good man, understand."

Having battled diabetes for some 20 years, King no longer gyrates across the stage. Even though he's firmly fixed in a chair, that still doesn't stop him from showing off some flashy dance moves. With trumpets blaring behind him, King kicked his feet high into the air and flailed his arms about as if he were a puppet on a string.

That's the way he was six years ago when he played at Legends Casino in Toppenish. He wowed the crowd back then, too, and showed off his singular talents on his black custom Gibson guitar — yes, the famed "Lucille."

Last weekend, though, he did less playing and more storytelling. He talked about growing up dirt poor in Mississippi and about having to go to separate drinking fountains, with one marked for whites and another for blacks. One day, he said, he snuck over to the fountain with the "whites only" sign on it and took a sip.

"Guess what? It tasted just like the water for blacks," he said with a big grin. Applause rained down on him.

The great blues guitarist might not have known it at the time while singing his most recognized tune, "The Thrill is Gone," but he's not the only legendary figure to have passed by this scenic ridge that overlooks the Columbia River Gorge. Far in the distance, beyond the stage, where the Deschutes River spills into the Columbia, two of America's most celebrated explorers once pushed their dugout canoes, perhaps scrambling up to this very spot — where I sat watching King strum his guitar — so they could get a better view of what lay ahead.

Back in late October 1805, Meriwether Lewis and William Clark had their hands full as they led the Corps of Discovery toward the Pacific Ocean. From this vantage point near Maryhill Winery, they would have looked down at a far different Columbia. It would have roared loudly, a wild and turbulent river, free from manmade dams. What faced Lewis and Clark was 55 more miles of terrifying rapids that started with the Celilo, the Great Falls.

In his book about the Lewis and Clark expedition, "Undaunted Courage," historian Stephen E. Ambrose writes about the moment when the explorers came upon the rapids at The Dalles, where the river tightened to less than 45 yards in width. Clark was appalled by what he described as "the horrid appearance of this agitated gut swelling (water), boiling & whorling in every direction."

Realizing it was impossible to portage the heavy dugout canoes, the explorers had no choice but to run this set of rapids. After unloading their equipment, including the highly prized journals and scientific gear, the Corps of Discovery climbed into the canoes and paddled toward the frothing whitewater. Ambrose pegged the rapid by today's standards as a Class V — in other words, a rapid that's impassable for even modern-day canoes.

But the explorers charged ahead anyway as hundreds of Indians lined up along the riverbanks to witness the disaster they were certain would befall the white men.

Despite plunging down what amounted to a waterfall, Lewis and Clark survived, without incident. Later, at night, the Corps of Discovery gathered around a large campfire where Private Cruzatte played his violin, and there they danced under a sky filled with stars, much to the delight of the Indians and two weary explorers, Lewis and Clark.

We, too, danced under the stars as B.B. King played his last song, not realizing some 203 years ago others had done the same.

The next morning, as we were leaving the Shilo Inn hotel in The Dalles, Oregon, my wife and I noticed B.B. King's bus parked at a nearby exit door. So we waited. It took several hours but the blues guitarist finally emerged.

"Get the camera," Leslie called out.

As she draped her arm around B.B. King's shoulders, I clicked the shutter. But King wasn't smiling. In place of his infectious grin was a frown. Perhaps it was the wheelchair that he was in. For someone who has performed more than 15,000 concerts over a span of five decades, being wheeled around is not what a living legend would prefer.

We thanked him, and as we were walking away, Leslie turned and said, "I hope you keep playing forever."

That brought a smile to the face of America's most famous blues guitarist. He entered the bus laughing.

July 13, 2008

Herb Peterson: Much more than the McMuffin guy

Few outside of the Santa Barbara area in California had heard much about Herb Peterson until late last month, when the 89-year-old died. Then his name became the talk of the nation and the world, with stories about him on CBS, Fox and CNN news and in newspapers as far away as China and England. He even earned a two-minute spot on National Public Radio's "All Things Considered" and an immediate entry on Wikipedia's website.

On Tuesday, hundreds will pack the All Saints by the Sea church in Montecito, California, for a memorial service and sing his praises.

His claim to fame, though, has nothing to do with sports or the movie industry, nor does he have his name etched on a Nobel Prize. But what he invented has touched just about everyone in the U.S. and has changed the way Americans eat breakfast. Herb Peterson invented the Egg McMuffin. The fast-food world, and certainly the fortunes of McDonald's, have never been the same.

To me, though, he will always be Herb, mom and dad's friend who did his best to laugh the loudest at my dumb antics and off-the-wall jokes. I knew him while growing up in Northbrook, Illinois, a northern suburb of Chicago. Our families went on several trips together, including a skiing trip in the early 1960s to Fish Creek, a small town in northern Wisconsin, where we traversed down the frozen slopes of Nor-Ski Ridge.

My earliest memory of Herb goes back to the fall of 1957, when I was 9 years old. We were over at the Petersons for dinner, but the real excuse was to hunt the night sky for the greatest prize of all — catching a glimpse of Sputnik, the Soviet satellite that was the first to orbit the Earth. We were not alone. Across the nation, families were hauling out lawn chairs and dusting off binoculars, waiting for that moment when Sputnik would cross the heavens, its reflected light winking back at us.

Herb Peterson holds up an Egg McMuffin
Photo courtesy of McDonald's

So there we were, my dad and Herb and us kids, lying on our backs, our eyes scanning the inky blackness of night.

"There it is!" I cried out. Actually, we both yelled at the same time, Herb and me. After Sputnik had passed out of sight, we all stood up, brushed the dew off our clothes and headed inside, wondering what the future of orbiting satellites would mean for all of us.

A few years later, I remember seeing Herb at what turned out to be a critical moment in his life. I must have been 13 or 14 at the time, and was on the commuter train traveling with my dad to downtown Chicago. It was quite the experience being on a commuter train back in the early 1960s. The cars were packed with white-collar workers wearing black suits and narrow ties, heading off to jobs at banks, law offices, accounting firms and insurance agencies. Most wore hats and everyone had a briefcase.

Herb, though, didn't run with the herd. He was on his way to "Hamburger U." It's the headquarters of McDonald's where Herb was studying to become a franchisee of the burgeoning drive-in restaurant chain. He had become fascinated with McDonald's and had come to know its founder, Ray Kroc, while he worked as vice president of the company's advertising firm. In fact, Herb coined McDonald's first national advertising slogan: "Where Quality Starts Fresh Every Day."

So there I was sitting with my dad. He had his briefcase in his lap and a newspaper propped up in front him. Everyone else did, too. Then in popped Herb, lugging along a stack of files and folders. Immediately, the long lines of newspapers dropped and a chorus of voices called out: "How's it going at Hamburger U, Herb? You haven't flunked out, have you?" Herb cracked a few jokes and the train car rocked with laughter.

That's when I realized Herb was in a class by himself.

And then it happened. Herb was taking his family and moving to Santa Barbara to open up a McDonald's restaurant, where he would end up owning six. The last time I saw Herb was on a warm summer's night, as the setting sun slanted through a row of elm trees.

We were having dinner at a country club and Herb had stopped by to say goodbye. Of course, country clubs are a bit strict, especially when it comes to proper attire — white shorts and shirts on the tennis courts, no jeans allowed, jackets required for men at dinnertime. So into this setting gamboled Herb wearing, of all things, a bright lime-green suit. He smiled and waved to us as he left. He walked triumphantly across the club's putting green, disrupting golfers in midswing and causing a young teenager (that would be me) to dish up one final salute — a belly laugh.

A few years after arriving in Santa Barbara, Herb put his genius of marketing to work. Up until the early 1970s, McDonald's had only sold food for lunch and dinner. That was about to change when Herb transformed his love for eggs Benedict into a new breakfast treat. To cook the egg, he fashioned a Teflon ring that could be used on a hamburger grill. He then added grilled Canadian bacon, substituted hollandaise sauce with a slice of cheese and placed the concoction on an open-faced English muffin.

Herb didn't quite follow company rules. He developed the Egg McMuffin in secret, and apparently got reprimanded by the corporate office. But Kroc knew he had a winner in Herb and the newly branded Egg McMuffin. Thanks to Herb's breakfast-in-a-bag concept, breakfast sales now account for one-third of McDonald's revenues.

Too often I hear the phrase: "Good guys finish last." I have never believed it for a moment, and Herb Peterson is proof of that. I still don't know about the lime-green suit. For him, though, it was a perfect fit.

April 20, 2008

V.I.P.

Celebrities may rule big-budget movies and reality TV shows, but they pale in comparison to those whose fame rests, not simply on good looks, but on inspiring others through their good works.

These Very Important People bring hope and vitality to a community. Luckily I have met many during my life.

Really, what an outrage it would be if the only calculation of a life well lived is the number of hits you get on Google.

Bill Robertson: A colorful life enjoyed to the fullest

Even Stephen Sondheim, the great composer and lyricist, would have agreed: Let Bill Robertson live.

And that's what happened when Sondheim's musical, "A Little Night Music," opened at Yakima's Warehouse Theatre. Dorothy "Bill" Donelson Robertson, who was in her early 80s at the time, accepted the role of Madame Armfeldt. It's a part that requires a little singing and a lot of sitting.

As the play winds down and the score for "Send in the Clowns" is reprised for the last time, the final scene reveals a lone figure on stage, Madame Armfeldt. Confined to a wheelchair, she is supposed to slump over and die.

At least that's the way it ended when I saw the play performed in Chicago.

But not in Yakima. Here, endings are rewritten, especially when the spotlight is on Bill Robertson. Apparently on opening night, some of the theatergoers, unfamiliar with the darker side of the play, feared Bill had actually expired when she slumped over in her chair. Frantic calls to the box office alerted producers to the disquieting revelation that they may be facing a public relations nightmare. So they wrote the death scene out of the play.

In a miracle only Yakima residents would appreciate, for the rest of the play's performances Madame Armfeldt remained wide-eyed and alert, with a smile often appearing ever so gently upon her lips.

And Bill lived on, until 10 days ago when she died following a stroke.

In life, Bill never shied from the spotlight. She always was ready to share a laugh, contribute one of her hundreds of paintings for a good cause, or swing across the Capitol Theatre stage as she did for a fundraiser without a care in the world, her straw hat firmly affixed atop her head, a statuesque figure who seemed so calm, so self-assured, handsome in an astonishing way for a lady who had lived every bit of her 95 years.

She led a charmed life by any standard, not so much because of the obvious wealth that she so happily doled out in her later years, but because of the people whom she touched with her sweet disposition, from the two husbands she loved so dearly to the strangers she left with a smile and a skip in their step.

Bill married her high school sweetheart, Tiny Donelson. For Bill, Tiny was her first date. For Tiny, Bill was the first woman he had ever kissed. How natural that the two would not use their formal names of Dorothy and Lloyd. Too stuffy for them, too pretentious for a couple who shared a rare, romantic love for each other.

The romance lasted nearly 53 years — until 1981, when Tiny died.

At that time, the wife of Ted Robertson, owner and publisher of the Yakima Herald-Republic, also passed away.

Bill and Ted were longtime friends, so it seemed only natural that soon they would share their lives together in a newfound marriage and live in a home high atop a hillside overlooking Yakima, the community they would so generously support, donating to the Yakima Valley Museum, YMCA, Yakima Greenway path and Children's Village, recently built for children with special needs.

Through both marriages, Bill found a way to open her world to all of Yakima. She was the city's unofficial "welcome wagon," accepting hundreds of people, friends and strangers alike, for tea and storytelling, for fashion shows and parties.

When Tiny and Bill purchased the 13-room, two-story H.M. Gilbert mansion, it had been abandoned for more than 10 years. After another decade spent restoring the home to its Victorian splendor, they turned the mansion into a popular tourist attraction. Once Bill took more than 700 people on a tour of her home. How many of us could boast of so many guests in a day, let alone a lifetime? After Tiny's death, Bill donated the home to the Yakima Valley Museum.

However, the role of being the convivial host did not end when Bill closed the doors on the Gilbert mansion for the last time. At the sprawling Robertson ranch-style manse in the West Valley, Bill kept the welcome flag flying high, eager to take pictures of each guest, showing off her home while gingerly skirting around the outdoor pool where Ted had painted, for all to see, a scantily clad mermaid.

Bill never had a mean word to say about anyone — at least not within hearing range. And she never tired of laughing with others, or at herself. Maybe that's why she wore so many hats, no matter what shape or size.

Once in 1957, while showing off the latest in fashion for the wives of real estate agents, Bill wore an enormous hat fashioned in the shape of a green and white bungalow. Fastened to this chapeau, which flopped precariously atop Bill's head, was a sign loudly proclaiming: "For sale, Cheap!" The Herald-Republic's society editor at the time gushed with praise for Bill's routine, proclaiming she "had her audience in stitches, handling comic lines and situations with a finesse that smacked of smart nightclub fare."

Even before Bill had become renowned for her hats and as Yakima's consummate philanthropist, Bill had been an artist. Bill had argued she was nothing of the kind. She said she just liked to draw a lot.

And she did, all the time and on every surface imaginable, on walls, on toy boxes, across cupboards, around doors, and in vibrant colors and sweeping landscapes filled with wide-eyed children with tangled curls and a menagerie of animals, from penguins and monkeys to rabbits playing hopscotch.

Her paintings of flowers were legendary, and prolific, often donated to charities for auctions or raffles. Murals, too, had become her trademark, with scores of wall paintings being completed decades before Toppenish — now the "city of murals" — ever knew what a mural was.

One of Bill's proudest moments came during a project in the early 1960s when she accepted the job of painting murals in the lobby at Yakima Valley School in Selah. The state-run institution has long served as a sanctuary for some of the most severely disabled children in Washington. Before taking the project, Bill confessed she had never known a child with special needs.

It was nearing Christmas when Bill drove up to Yakima Valley School. With paints and brushes clutched tightly in her hands, she entered the building with her head bowed, fearful of what she might see.

But as her friends and family were reminded this past Tuesday during a memorial service for Bill, though childless in marriage she had always shown an unconditional love for children. It never wavered, not even there.

Perhaps she didn't notice at first, but Bill was not alone when she started to paint. She had an audience of one. Her name was Jeannie. She sat there in her wheelchair, unable to speak, her body contorting in uncontrollable spasms but soon calming to the rhythms of Bill's brush strokes. After a while, Bill talked to Jeannie, describing what she was painting, about the rabbits and the long-necked giraffe, and the children with happy faces.

One day, Jeannie made a sound. "Ootiful," she said softly. "Did you say 'beautiful'?" Bill exclaimed. Jeannie's body agitated wildly.

Beautiful, indeed.

In the Christmases that followed, Bill became a regular visitor of the school and revealed to Yakima yet another legacy of her boundless affection for life enjoyed to the fullest — wheeling children around the lobby and laughing playfully, captivated by the look in their eyes, a look more vibrant than anything Bill had ever painted before.

July 11, 1999

Mitch Weary: Preacher's gone, but his music lives on

Though his name may fade over time, Mitch Weary's music, the songs he drove into the hearts of those fortunate enough to hear him play and sing, will resound — for generations to come.

That is the power of music. It overwhelms and conquers both the meek and the mighty. It reminds us of our creative genius and how quickly it can disappear, like the sound that fades on the final note of every song.

Often its expressive power settles in the person who's performing. And it's this vision of a smiling Mitch Weary that will be forever a part of the memories for those at Greater Faith Baptist, Bethel A.M.E., Morning Star Worship Center, Mount Hope Baptist and Yakima Evangelical. Although he preached and prayed in those churches, the best part was when he played gospel music, filling the sweetened air of the sanctuaries with hope and reconciliation. He made heads to sway, feet to shuffle, hands to clap and, whenever possible, souls to soar.

He had the gift.

But that's the power of music. And nowhere was it more evident than on the day of his funeral two weeks ago. The pews were filled and aisles overflowed at the Greater Faith Baptist Church in southeast Yakima as a community came together to say goodbye.

I sat downstairs in the church with my wife and 200 others. We were part of the overflow crowd. Distant from the pulpit, we stared at a big-screen television and sang with the church choir, standing up when they did and weeping when the eulogies were given.

I didn't really cry much until Weary's choir director from Davis High School, Roger Stansbury, told of the day some six years ago when Weary held his hand and together they prayed — Weary the preacher and

Stansbury the cancer patient — both seeking strength from each other. Now Stansbury stood as a survivor, and beyond him lay Weary in a coffin, victim of a heart attack a week earlier. He was only 47.

Weary married his wife Dianna nearly 23 years ago in the same church where his funeral was held that afternoon. He leaves behind three sons.

Yes, we all wept that day.

The day after the funeral, I attended an evening service at Englewood Christian Church in Yakima. It's called "Connections" in honor of the late Rev. William Sloane Coffin, who would invite musicians and anyone else walking down the street near his Riverside Church in New York City to come inside for music and a few words of prayer and benediction.

So it is with this service at Englewood. It's where music becomes the core of the ministry at the church's informal gathering. Besides a piano player, saxophonists may show up along with flutists and drummers.

Though I hadn't been to Connections in weeks, I wasn't surprised to hear Mitch Weary's name spoken on that Sunday evening. The preacher with a song in his soul had made his own connection with everyone in that sanctuary. One lady told about the time Weary and his wife had traveled out to White Swan and spent a day in the schools, delighting students with their gospel singing and even getting teachers and parents to join in the chorus.

Then Bart Roderick spoke. He's the piano player at Connections and a longtime school choir teacher who has played alongside some of the top names in the music industry. He recalled a time when Weary had brought together a disparate group of singers and performed the familiar African American gospel song "Precious Lord, Take My Hand." It was Dr. Martin Luther King's most favorite song, and often the civil rights leader would ask the famed singer Mahalia Jackson for a solo performance as a way to rev up the crowd.

So that night, our choir of 15 or so voices sang "Precious Lord," ending with the final verse: "Take my hand, precious Lord, lead me home." I doubt we replicated Mahalia Jackson's virtuoso, but we tried our best. That was good enough, for we all knew that this was the way Weary would have wanted it. That's how he taught others. Not to be perfect, but personal. Just try your very best.

We will deeply miss Mitch Weary. Our community has lost a gifted musician and a gentle spirit.

But the music — no, that will always be with us, like a dear friend.

March 29, 2009

Cindy Peterson: Her name stands for strength, compassion

I wear two wristbands.

The purple one has the word "Hope" on it, showing support for the American Cancer Society and its drive to find a cure for cancer. The other is yellow and has the distinctive "Livestrong" logo carved across it, a testament to bicyclist Lance Armstrong's miraculous recovery from cancer and his later triumphs at the Tour de France.

I still have room for a third. It would be blue, and I know the exact word that would be etched into the smooth rubber. A name with only five letters, but recognizable to those in the Yakima Valley who are cancer survivors.

That name?

Cindy.

Cindy's name speaks of courage. Of resolve. Of love of family and devotion to friends. And when necessary, a knack for bringing a smile to a fourth-grader who's simply had a rotten day.

Her full name is Cynthia Darlyne Peterson, but for all those who were lucky to cross her path and for the hundreds of cancer patients who felt her warm hand gently touching theirs, she was Cindy.

You could always count on her to be there walking stride for stride with other cancer survivors at the annual 24-hour Relay for Life held in Yakima. Cindy was there at the very beginning, 21 years ago. Once, she served as honorary chairwoman of the event. As the years slipped by, everyone expected to see Cindy at the survivor's walk that begins each 24-hour relay at noon Saturday.

But last year, for the first time, that ceremonial walk began without her. On June 1, two days before the relay was to begin, Cindy died at age 55. She left behind her husband, Dan, one of the most affable doctors you could ever meet, a son, Jeffrey, and a daughter, Jennifer.

Through 25 years, nearly half her life, Cindy battled cancer. Her breast cancer spread relentlessly, to her lungs — though she had never smoked — to her liver, to her bones.

First, Cindy had repeated surgeries to stem the spread of cancer. Then came the chemotherapy treatments, becoming more frequent after 2000 when cancer had metastasized throughout her body. Despite the devastating toll these treatments can take on a patient's physical strength, Cindy always kept her spirits up. Those around her marveled at it.

Especially those at Cottonwood Elementary School in the West Valley School District. That was Cindy's second home, where she served for 15 years as the school's secretary.

Even during her toughest regimen of chemotherapy, Cindy would schedule the treatments on Thursday so her worst days would fall on the weekend. That would allow her to return on Monday where her incandescent smile would brighten everyone's day and would so overshadow her cancer that many students over the years never knew she was sick.

Really, who could have guessed back then, while she chatted with teachers and students and munched on one of her favorite treats, red licorice, that another round of chemotherapy awaited her? Who could have guessed?

When a student at Cottonwood would step into the office not feeling well, Cindy would stop whatever she was doing and zero in on that child.

"And like magic, she would know exactly the right words to say to bring a smile to their faces," Sarah James, a Cottonwood teacher and dear friend of Cindy, told me recently.

It's hard to imagine Cindy had a closer friend at Cottonwood than James. Naturally, when James gave birth, Cindy was at her side. They also worked together more than 15 years ago to help map out the construction plans for Cottonwood.

"We had lots of shared smiles and lots of problem-solving in getting the new school started," said James, who will be at the Relay for Life this weekend walking for the Heart and Spirit team that Cindy had championed for years.

Whether it was raising money at the relay or raising the spirits of breast cancer patients through the cancer society's Reach for Recovery program, Cindy had always been a steady presence for others, offering a consoling word, a shoulder to cry on, or in one case, the ultimate gift that only a mother could give to another.

In the early morning hours of June 2, 2004, Nancy Sides, a co-worker of Cindy's at Cottonwood, learned that her 22-year-old stepson, Dustin, had died in Iraq. Though Sides told everyone she didn't want visitors, Cindy knew she had to see her.

When she arrived, Cindy held in her hands a necklace with a Gold Star — the symbol of sacrifice that long has been given to mothers who have lost a child in combat.

"She was so concerned that I would not receive one since I was Dustin's stepmother, that she had to bring it to me," Sides wrote in a memorial website set up after Cindy died. "She knew that Dustin was my son in my heart since he was 2 years old. I wept at her thoughtfulness and her insight on how much it would mean to me."

The relay ends at noon today when the luminary bags, lining the track at Zaepfel Stadium, will be put away — their white parchment lovingly marked in ink and crayon with the names of cancer survivors and those who have died. Cindy's name will be among them, but her memory will not be silenced for long.

On Friday, her husband will stand before a gathering of West Valley High School seniors and present a $1,000 scholarship in Cindy's name. The scholarship was set up a few months before Cindy died, allowing her a chance to tell others the kind of recipient who should get the monetary award. It doesn't go to a straight-A student or a top athlete or a national merit finalist. They get enough financial help.

No, the Cindy Peterson Scholarship will go to a student who is often overlooked — the one with good, but not spectacular, grades from an ordinary middle-income family. Someone solid. Someone strong. Someone who makes others smile.

Just like Cindy, who has brought a measure of grace to all of us.

June 3, 2007

Bob Clem: The reason we didn't buy resin

First, there was the ashfall from Mount St. Helens to deal with.

Then there was Dr. Hana Claus and his nemesis, a furry creature with big ears. But let's not get ahead of ourselves. Let's begin where every story about Mount St. Helens does — up to your eyeballs in ash.

Several weeks after the mountain blew a hole in the stratosphere, Dr. Hana Claus arrived from Chatsworth, California, and proclaimed himself the savior of the city. It was clear to everyone living here that Yakima needed saving after being buried under a blanket of volcanic ash — some 600,000 tons of the stuff.

What this latter-day Pied Piper of ash had up his sleeve was a special resin formula that would seal the grit under domes of rigid plastic until the St. Helens residue could be turned from a nettlesome problem into a handsome profit — yes, into toilet bowls.

The city welcomed Claus with open arms as this impresario of plastic resins paraded around ashtrays made of ... well, ash. With bathroom fixtures dancing merrily in his head, Claus promised more — new jobs, new production facilities and a new tax base for a city that wallowed in a sea of gray for as far as the eye could see.

Claus had an inexhaustible supply of the ash thanks to municipal crews dumping tons of it onto city property at 40th Avenue and Powerhouse Road, which is now home to the soccer fields of Chesterley Park. He even promised the city he would pay for the ash at 1 1/4 cents per pound.

It seemed too good to be true.

But leave it to the news media to put a wet blanket on things and raise doubts about Claus, the human "resin-ator."

Reporters couldn't find anyone who thought highly of Claus in California. As a matter of fact, experts in the resin-plastics business hadn't even heard of the supposedly renowned research chemist.

So when Claus showed up for a news conference to tout the virtues of his "Poly II" formula, he took a grilling from the media, especially about his business and education background.

Claus exploded with rage. He lashed out at the reporters and claimed the government had advised him not to divulge any information about himself. The reason? Death threats. Furthermore, the government deemed his credentials and his patented resin "top secret."

Then with a flourish worthy of an Academy Award, an infuriated Claus swept his hand across the table in front of him, sending microphones clattering to the floor. He stormed out, leaving the assembled crowd slack-jawed.

Well, almost everyone. In the back of the room stood Bob Clem, who wasn't at all amused by what Claus had just done.

"You sonofabitch," Clem muttered under his breath. "I've got you."

If anyone could spot a charlatan, Clem was your man. He wrote the book on being a fake. Clem, who retired this winter from his job as manager of the Yakima Air Terminal, had once operated an advertising agency and, by virtue of his fertile wit and impeccable stage delivery, he had been able to secure speaking engagements at some of the most prestigious conventions in the country. His job was to make fun of those in the audience by pretending to be someone whom he clearly wasn't. He had played a vast array of roles, from a stern English headmaster to an Australian heart surgeon.

He always left the crowd laughing at themselves. And that's what Clem meant to do with Claus and all of those who thought he was their man.

Claus, sadly, wasn't even a convincing crook, Clem admits. He certainly didn't look the part.

Photos taken 25 years ago show a frumpy-looking, middle-aged man whose stooped shoulders gave way to a protruding gut. His face held little humor thanks to a pair of beady eyes that peered out from beneath a crown of slick, shiny black hair. The only thing that was remotely distinguished about him was his well-trimmed beard and mustache.

And Clem might have allowed the dour Dr. Claus a "free pass out of Yakima" had he not heard about a demonstration Claus was to perform shortly after the ill-fated news conference. Worse yet, Clem had also learned the city of Yakima was about to hand Claus a $50,000 check for his "Poly II" formula.

Something had to be done. So Clem & Co. sprang into action. Cups of coffee were slurped; calls were made. Someone headed out to the fairgrounds to pick up a few costumes. A six-door stretch limo was lined up. Several hulking behemoths were conscripted. The stage was soon set.

With reporters, city officials and curious onlookers gathered among the mounds of ash at 40th and Powerhouse, the limo arrived minutes before Claus was to begin spraying his secret concoction. Frightened by the commotion, Claus beat a hasty retreat to a nearby vantage point.

From there, he witnessed quite a show.

Behind the wheel of the limo sat a chauffeur decked out with a derby hat. Out popped two turban-headed bodyguards brandishing palm fronds, followed in hot pursuit by a belly dancer and four mean-looking thugs wearing pith helmets.

Then from the inky black darkness of the limousine emerged a 6-foot-tall rabbit, Samurai sword in hand. The furry animal proclaimed to those within earshot, "Call me Esther Rabbit."

Well, that might not be the exact quote. But Esther, whose voice had the distinctive ring of Bob Clem, had many other one-liners to dish out.

"I'm deeply upset that somebody would come in and try to take my act," the rabbit exclaimed. "I've had this town staked out for years, and it's mine. Mine! You hear that?"

Esther's plump foot thumped madly on the ground, causing a pillowy cloud of ash to lift into the air.

Then the rabbit pulled out a spray can, the kind a gardener would use on a bouquet of dandelions.

"Quiet, ladies and gentlemen ... let us spray."

With that, the enormous rabbit squirted mist upon the ash. The demonstration had its desired effect — nothing happened.

With that, Esther and the rabbit's retinue returned to the limo and drove off, leaving a swirling trail of ash in their wake.

Claus returned moments later, trying to pick up where he had left off. He produced two wooden boards topped with ash supposedly hardened by his secret "Poly II" formula.

Few, though, cared to see his handiwork. His bubble of fame had burst. The rabbit had stolen the show.

To this day, Clem still gets a good laugh out of the antics of Esther Rabbit and Dr. Hana Claus. At least once a year, a writer who's working on yet another Mount St. Helens manuscript will call and ask Clem, "Hey, did that really happen?"

Of course it did, Clem replies. It's certainly more believable than turning a pile of volcanic ash into a toilet bowl.

May 15, 2005

Mary Skinner: Bringing a gift of joy to so many

I never saw a day when the sun didn't shine on Mary Skinner. Even in the long, bleak months of her cancer treatment, she found a way to make you feel better about yourself.

Maybe it was the way her face lit up when she met you, or those eyes of hers that danced about whenever she would talk. And she was a talker, so those eyes were never still.

For Mary, every day meant she had a chance to lend a hand, share a greeting, befriend a stranger.

That gift of joy she brought to so many is now gone following her death Thursday morning after a three-year battle with colon cancer. Her passing comes less than three weeks after the death of Hal, her husband and constant companion.

Mary certainly made an impression when she showed up at our newspaper following her election victory in 1994.

The first Latino elected to the Legislature from the Yakima Valley, Mary arrived brimming with excitement. In tow was her fellow House Republican Jim Clements, who also represented the 14th District. Jim came with an agenda; Mary came armed with a basket of freshly baked muffins. When I tried to decline the treats, Mary pulled out a tub of butter and a knife. How could I resist?

So as they chatted about the upcoming session, I stuffed myself with the oven-warmed muffins. The fresh food worked its magic. Each time I tried to ask a question, crumbs would explode from my mouth. So I just sat there and listened. Through this culinary finesse, Mary had found a way to muzzle a journalist.

During her next 14 years in Olympia, critics would often complain that she was too nice, too easily swayed. Not enough backbone, I heard once.

She showed her grit when it counted most. Like the time she refused to back down on the issue of abortion during a turbulent time in 1997 when House Republicans held a majority. She was among only a handful of GOP lawmakers who supported abortion rights. A bitter battle ensued when she voted against a ban on "partial-birth" abortions. But she held her ground.

That showed toughness. She also proved her mettle when she pushed for "Anton's Law," a requirement for additional car-safety restraints for children older than 3.

It was named for Anton Skeen, a bright and bubbly 4-year-old boy who died in 1996 when the car he was riding in rolled over along Interstate 82 south of Ellensburg. Anton slipped out of his seat belt and was thrown from the vehicle. Anton's mother and father had both worked at this newspaper. The day he died, Anton was to have visited our newsroom with his mother.

Mary fought for that legislation, and it became law in 2000, making Washington the first state in the nation to require the added booster-seat restraints. Within five years, the federal government passed its own law.

So much for having no backbone.

I never really forgot about those muffins she had brought to our newspaper. So a few years ago, when Mary was in the throes of another round of chemotherapy, I decided to make her and Hal a homemade supper of baked Parmesan chicken. It was one of my late wife's favorites when she was going through her cancer treatments.

When I drove up to their home, I didn't know what to expect. I hadn't seen Mary in weeks. I feared the worst.

Hal greeted me at the front door and led me into the living room. After I settled into a chair, I could hear Mary's voice from down the hall. She sounded good, I thought.

Then she entered the room, talking a mile-a-minute with her arms waving wildly about. It was vintage Mary. Cancer had not beaten her just yet.

That's when I first met their cat Caramellow. How Hal and Mary loved her. The cat had showed up one day in the backyard of her mother's home. Hal described the feline as "emaciated, flea-ridden, unkempt and hissing." Though they thought she was a kitten, they were told she was 7 or 8 years old. She was also deaf and had only one tooth.

But into their lives Hal and Mary welcomed her, and how Caramellow flourished.

In 2007, Hal and Mary wanted to tell everyone what Caramellow meant to them. After dropping Mary off in Olympia for a committee meeting, Hal drove all the way back to Yakima so he could have his photograph taken with Caramellow for our special section, "Pets and Their People." For 20 minutes, our photographer worked with Hal to get just the right pose. I was there, too, cheering the two on.

Last year, Hal called and left me a phone message. He was weeping. Caramellow had died. He wanted to tell me, and to let me know how much Mary had loved the cat.

I already knew. I had seen it in her eyes.

February 8, 2009

Dale Carpenter: From the heart to a special friend

How many ways can you say, "I love you"? More than 440, and counting. It helps if you're Dale Carpenter.

The messages of love to Dale have come from as far away as Addis Ababa, Ethiopia, and the sunny beaches of Hawaii, and from nearly every soul in between. Since Dale underwent surgery to remove a brain tumor 13 days ago, an expanding community of family, friends and acquaintances has come together to express their love for this 59-year-old dynamo of altruism. Pre-Valentine messages have crowded more than 29 pages at CaringBridge. The count of those who have paid a visit to the website is staggering — some 6,000 hits, equal to the combined populations of Zillah, Cle Elum and Tieton.

Julie, Dale's daughter, provides updates on a journal and typed in the first message on the site's guestbook:

"I just got home and started your Web page. You're going into surgery tomorrow and I can't even believe it. It seems so surreal. But I want you to know that I feel peaceful. I know you'll be in great hands tomorrow, with the neurosurgeon, assistants and aids, but most importantly, God's. I love you very much and I'll see you in the morning. I know it won't be the last time."

Then the avalanche of messages started flooding in — whether it was a joke, which Dale himself is never in short supply, or a helping hand, which Dale has always extended.

"Our love, thoughts and prayers are with you during this difficult time," a friend wrote. "We know that our Lord has you in His hands."

Dale Carpenter

"What do you mean you have a brain tumor," another writer joked. "I didn't think you HAD a brain ... just a gigantic HEART, like ALL HEART!!"

Then there was this note, which captured a common theme about Dale: "You are one of a kind — so intensely loving and funny. ... What a gift you are to all of us."

Dale is Mr. Everything to the Yakima Valley despite his hectic schedule at work as general manager of Yakima Theatres and at home, where he and his wife Marci have raised their daughter and two sons, both with special needs.

His desire to help others is inexhaustible and his skills at accomplishing projects are remarkable. Little wonder that when he once served as chairman for Yakima's annual March of Dimes walk he was one of the top fundraisers in the nation. Yes, he's that good.

Perhaps even more important than his gift of volunteerism is a steadfast, unflinching loyalty to his friends.

I'm happy to say I'm one of them.

So as only a good friend would do, Dale called me from his hospital bed.

"I don't want you to hear about this from anyone but me," he said.

A few days earlier he had told me about cracking a rib after taking a bad fall when he slipped getting out of the bathtub. So when Dale said he was in the hospital, I assumed it was due to the busted rib.

"No, it's not that," Dale said. He cleared his throat, and spoke slowly: "They found a tumor in my brain."

Dale didn't want any weeping, though my wife Leslie and I did later. He wanted to face his surgery and the treatment that lay ahead with resolve and, of course, with humor.

"It's the only way I'm going to get through this," he said.

The next afternoon, less than 24 hours before his surgery, Dale was in rare form when we arrived for a visit.

He talked a mile-a-minute as if it would be the last time. That's what he feared. His neurosurgeon had warned him the operation might affect his speech.

"If I can't talk, I don't want to go on living," Dale said, half serious. "Please cut my throat if that happens. Will you do that?"

I told him it would be too messy.

"You will be fine," I said, my fingers crossed.

The next day as he was being prepped for surgery, Dale couldn't resist getting in one last joke. When asked if he was allergic to anything, he said, "Yes."

The operating room staff waited anxiously for his reply.

"Carbide blades from Walmart."

Laughter echoed through the room. Dale said he just wanted to loosen them up before the operation.

Sure enough, Dale woke up Monday evening after the surgery talking non-stop. He apparently spoke a little Russian and requested a gallon of morphine. Typical Dale.

There will be no shortage of challenges in the weeks ahead. The tumor is malignant and will require a regimen of radiation and chemotherapy to reduce its spread.

The good news is it took only three days after the surgery before Dale returned home.

"I'm so happy he's home and recovering," someone wrote after reading Julie's latest update. "Heaven is hearing this community's choir of prayers."

Dale never wants to be the center of attention. I have no doubt he will hate this column. But he also must realize that the goodness he has brought to so many people can't be forgotten, or go unnoticed.

For this Valentine's Day, love is more than a bouquet of roses. It means telling someone that you care: Dale, we love you.

February 14, 2010

BY LAND, SEA, AIR AND HORSE

Travel stories tend to follow a familiar path, offering prerequisite tips on where to stay, what to eat and how to get there.

That storyline has never interested me. Instead I like to take a different tack, spicing up my journeys through life with a heavy dose of heightened drama and self-deprecating humor. For me, traveling is more about exploring your foibles than about poking around the nooks and crannies of a medieval castle.

A bit rusty but never forgotten

Old friends come in all shapes and sizes.

Sadly, one of our family's closest friends has begun to show his age. No longer does he have the zip and drive of his youth. He lurches instead of leaps. His joints are a bit stiff, too. If you listen hard enough, you can definitely pick up a squeak or two.

It's the rust spots, though, that worry me the most.

My friend is no ordinary sidekick. He's a 1971 Volkswagen Camper Van, and after two decades of trusted companionship, he's no longer at my side, or in my driveway for that matter.

Suddenly, my identity is in tatters. My white camper van and I were once inseparable. Often I was recognized not for who I was but for what I drove: "Oh, yeah, you're the guy with the camper van."

Why do I care so much for this rusting hulk of metal whose engine is held in place by a few bolts and can be replaced by a four-cylinder rebuilt costing less than a riding lawn mower?

Maybe it's the water-stained curtains that hang across the rear window. Or the heater that ices up the windshield in December. Perhaps, it's the metal coat hanger — a symbol of defiance — that attaches the license plate to the front bumper.

Whatever the reason, it seems I have always been destined to own a VW van.

My maiden voyage in a van came decades ago while growing up in the Chicago area. I remember my Uncle Bruce, a man who wasn't afraid to stand out in a crowd, at the wheel of one of the very first vans produced by Volkswagen. I was propped up in the passenger seat as we headed to an elementary school to pick up my cousin from a dance. A group of teens approached us and started to laugh. Back then, in the late 1950s, conformity ruled. VW vans just didn't fit in.

Gripped by a mixture of fear and humiliation at being spotted by others, I slunk low in the car seat. My uncle was unfazed, and roared off into the darkness, the muffler spewing smoke and that distinctive whining sound which only VW vans can produce, a noise akin to a poorly built washing machine forever stuck on the spin cycle.

It was then I realized VW vans make a statement.

It wasn't until later, just before I was drafted into the Army in 1971, that I again had a chance to ride in a VW van. This time a good friend and I had decided to hitchhike from Salt Lake City to his hometown of Cleveland. An ambitious task, but not so foolhardy as it would be nowadays. Remember, it was when hippies thrived and Vietnam was hot, peace symbols were in, and hitchhiking was considered a noble calling.

After several rides that brought us near the Colorado border, a two-toned red and white camper van pulled up beside us. The driver, his long hair gathered in back with a beaded leather strap, motioned for us to jump in. We opened the side door and found we were not alone. Four others were inside. We somehow wedged our bodies into the van and off we headed, ever so slowly, to the foothills of the Rockies.

Dusk was approaching when we finally reached a beautiful meadow, its green grass surrounded by mountain peaks. "We're sleeping here," our driver said, inhaling the fumes from his hand-rolled cigarette. He confessed he never drove at night in the mountains. Too disruptive to Mother Nature. So he pulled the camper van onto a dirt road. There we slept, beneath the stars, our trusty steed, the VW camper van, at our side.

Yes, I guess you could say destiny rides a VW. That's certainly been the case for me.

So it seemed only natural, 10 years later, to hunt down a VW camper van for my own family. That urge to fulfill my destiny led me to Champagne Motors, a very small used car dealership north of Seattle.

The two guys, who owned the used car lot, were certifiable ex-hippies. The only camper van they dealt with was the 1971 German-made Westfalia model, the kind with a pop-top, an icebox, sink and a full canvas tent that attached to the side. They preferred it to the later versions, which offered peppier, higher-powered engines.

How could I resist the temptation? So I swapped my burnt-orange Datsun for a white camper van. Who needs power when you have a four-speed stick shift to divert your attention? I can safely boast that I have never passed another car on the open highway unless I was heading down a steep hill, had a favorable wind at my back and the car I was overtaking had somehow blown a cylinder head. Truly the stars must be aligned.

You certainly don't head over the mountains for weekend jaunts to Pike Street Market or the Seattle Symphony. Mountain passes are only attempted in emergencies, such as earthquakes or volcanic eruptions. Or when you have to move your family, as I did 19 years ago when we hauled our belongings from Mount Vernon to Yakima. Since then, I have never attempted to take the van over Snoqualmie Pass.

But that came to a gear-crunching halt earlier this fall when my 21-year-old son, Andy, a junior at Western Washington University in Bellingham, took over ownership of the family heirloom, which has a modest 163,000 miles under its fan belt.

When it came time to head back to school in late September, we packed the trusty VW camper van with all of my son's worldly possessions — two electric guitars, an amplifier, computer and television set. It turns out the worst part of the five-hour trek to Bellingham wasn't Snoqualmie Summit but rather the steep slope rising up from the Fred Redmond Bridge on Interstate 82. Andy took that incline in second gear, topping out at a cruising speed of 28 mph.

The last time I saw my piston-driven friend was several weeks ago. I had snared two tickets to the Mariners playoff game against the Yankees. My son was to meet me at the parking lot in the Northgate Mall along Interstate 5. He had no desire to take the camper van into the swirl of Seattle's downtown traffic.

I got there early and waited at the edge of the parking lot. I stared down the road at the long line of cars. A BMW streaked by followed by one of those ponderous-looking Lincoln Navigators, its high-gloss shine nearly blinding me.

Then I saw something white. It jostled along the roadway, swaying up and down, its license plate still hanging by a single wire. I waved, as if to myself, and a hand from inside the camper van waved in return.

An old friend never forgets.

November 11, 2001

POSTSCRIPT: The VW Camper Van is no longer a member of the family. Proceeds from its sale in 2007 paid for a new couch, which proudly sits in our living room, providing far more comfort than the van ever did.

Sick of waiting out flight delays

Twenty-four hours and four time zones. That's what it took to see my mother in Chicago.

It all began quietly enough several weeks ago at the Tri-Cities Airport in Pasco, Washington. My wife Leslie and I arrived a comfortable 90 minutes before takeoff.

After we boarded our SkyWest jet bound for Salt Lake City, the first leg of our trek, I noticed the cockpit door was still open even though all of the passengers had settled into their seats. What's with that?

The captain came on the intercom.

"There's a warning light on the control panel," he began in a friendly tone. "We are going to check it out. It should only take a few minutes."

If these warning lights are anything like the ones I once had in my vintage VW camper van, they don't mean a thing. They blink madly for a few minutes then — poof — they're gone. So I relaxed and retrieved from my backpack a few magazines and my iPod.

Then came that voice again.

"I've never had this happen before," the pilot declared. "We don't have any hydraulic fluid."

While I don't profess to be an expert about planes, I do know one thing — you need hydraulic fluid to get the landing gears up and down. Without it, you will end up like a pancake — sans butter and syrup.

So we were asked to deplane. It was a grim walk down the gangplank to the air terminal for we all knew what awaited us — the dreaded rebooking process. It's a ritual at airport ticket counters that brings out the worst in people.

Remarkably there were no temper tantrums, though one young mom confessed this was her second day at the Pasco airport and she was getting a bit tired of the decor.

While waiting in line, I overheard the airline attendant tell a passenger he was being rerouted through Las Vegas. Now that's a way to turn a summertime traveling disaster into a memorable outing. Bring on the Elvis impersonators and the yard-tall margarita glasses!

So I casually slipped the word "Vegas" into my conversation when handing the attendant our tickets. She smiled politely.

"How about Atlanta?"

Yes, that's where we were headed — but only after flying to Salt Lake City for a 4½-hour layover. We had suddenly become another statistic in this summer of airline delays that have set all-time records, infuriating thousands of passengers with lost luggage and nowhere to go.

After a butt-numbing three-hour wait, another SkyWest jet pulled up to the Pasco air terminal. When we boarded, I asked the stewardess if there was enough hydraulic fluid. She laughed.

Then a minute later I screamed. I discovered something was missing from my backpack. My iPod. I had left it in the seat pouch where airsick bags are stuffed.

The stewardess didn't bat an eye. She had been through this before. She waved to one of the baggage workers on the tarmac and told him to check seat 10D on the fluidless plane parked nearby. Just as the door to our plane was to be closed, the baggage handler returned with a Ziploc bag containing my highly prized iPod.

"Boy, are you lucky," a nearby passenger remarked.

Well, that luck played out quickly after arriving in Salt Lake City.

We ended up at the Squatters Pub for a bite to eat. It's a place made famous not for its awkward name but for the beer it dispenses — a Polygamy Porter, a full-bodied ale that some slick advertiser claims is so good you can't have just one. I doubt the Mormons appreciate the humor.

I chose instead a chilled glass of chardonnay and headed to the airport restroom to take out my contact lenses.

I washed my hands and popped out my right contact. But when I flipped out my left one, it slipped in my fingers. I looked down and saw the contact had broken in two.

So there I was, in the airport restroom, angry and tired and now legally blind.

When we arrived in Atlanta at 5:15 a.m., I had begun to adjust to wearing my eyeglasses. My wife and I trudged into the air terminal. We came upon a row of panels showing upcoming departures. Among the 80 or so flights, all were on time except for one flight. Chicago. Delta Flight 1626: CANCELED.

But we didn't panic. What's the point? I called Delta's 800 number and learned that the airline had rebooked us on an 8 a.m. flight. Not bad. Only an additional hour layover. That would make an even 10 hours sitting in air terminals.

When our new flight started boarding, Leslie and I looked at our seat assignments — Row 1, seats C and D. Our seats were in first-class. Finally something had gone right.

The seats were luxurious. Leslie leaned back and sighed contentedly. Then from the cockpit we heard an alarm go off.

"Right engine fire. Right engine fire."

Instead of dashing off the plane, we looked at each other and laughed. It was part of the safety checklist the pilots were going through. Nothing to worry about. Just another blinking light.

As we taxied for takeoff, the stewardess asked in a cheery voice what I wanted. Why not, I thought to myself.

"A Bloody Mary, please."

September 9, 2007

Paris may be hip, but Vern's got a bass boat

Just for the record: Paris Hilton and I were at the same restaurant on the same night.

It's also true we never saw each other. That's the price of being a celebrity. Sometimes you never get a chance to rub shoulders with the common folk.

Paris (yes, we always refer to celebs by their first name) was attending the grand opening for the Yellowtail, an upscale sushi restaurant where the service is brisk, a dollop of Alaska King crab costs $25 and the music is hypnotic — like a jackhammer to the ears.

Yellowtail is definitely hip. Yakima certainly doesn't have an equal. Then again, we don't have the location that the Yellowtail does — inside the Bellagio, a five-star casino and resort on the Las Vegas Strip.

Naturally, Paris didn't come alone to the Yellowtail. That happens with celebrities. They move in packs. Charlie Sheen, of the CBS comedy show "Two and A Half Men," was there along with his new wife Brooke (news flash: she's pregnant — an announcement that hit the Hollywood blogosphere and tabloids several days earlier). "Desperate Housewives" actress Eva Longoria also made an appearance, as did singer and actress Shar Jackson, who gained instant fame four years ago after being jilted by Kevin Federline in favor of another celebrity icon, Britney Spears.

Although my wife and I never got to see any of these celebs (most came later in the evening), we did catch a glimpse of one star who strutted his stuff down the red carpet. As cameras flashed in strobe-like frequency, a chorus of "Who's that guy?" rose up among us onlookers.

"It's the Fez," someone cried out.

Yes, none other than Wilmer Valderrama stopped and preened for the paparazzi. He played Fez in "That '70s Show," which aired from 1998 to 2006. The 28-year-old Latino actor is now an accomplished screenwriter, director and talk show favorite, having done stints with Jay Leno and Oprah. He also had a famous sit-down with radio host Howard Stern where apparently Valderrama described his physical prowess with assorted female celebs. That made quite a splash in the tabloids.

While others in our group of gawkers waved at the star, I decided to take a different tack.

"Hey, could you get me some sushi," I hollered.

The Fez didn't hear me. But two muscular bouncers did. They glared at me with steely eyes that telegraphed a simple message: Make one move, buddy, and you're going down.

I didn't realize how hazardous this celebrity business could be. It's exhausting stuff, standing along roped walkways for hours and cheering on scantily clad young ladies as they try to cajole their way onto the invited guest list. And then there's the research you've got to do — keeping up on their latest reality shows, arrest warrants, infidelities, broken marriages.

Republicans had me believing this celebrity stuff was all of Barack Obama's doing, but now they have their own freshly minted diva who can field-dress a moose — Alaska's Gov. Sarah Palin. And yes, everyone calls the vice presidential hopeful by her first name. That's how you know they have celebrity credentials.

My star search in Las Vegas didn't end at the Yellowtail. My wanderings eventually took me to the rocky shores of Lake Mead.

Being an avid fisherman, I had always wanted to land a striped bass. So for my 60th birthday, which we were celebrating in Sin City, I decided to book a fishing trip on Lake Mead, the world's largest manmade reservoir that's loaded with striped bass.

I scanned the Internet and located a professional fishing guide. He had a great resume — a touring bass pro who organizes fishing tournaments. He also possessed a Coast Guard license, one of the first ever issued to a guide in Nevada.

His name: Vern Price.

I called him Vern. Yes, he's another celebrity, at least among bass anglers. He has done television shows and is on speaking terms with angling hall-of-famers like Bill Dance, Shawn Grigsby and Hank Parker, whom Vern says is the nicest guy you could ever meet.

Spencer with a Lake Mead striped bass

This fishing venture required me to get up at 3 a.m. It was still dark when I met him at the Laker Plaza outside of Henderson. He had a cigarette dangling from his lips. By the time we had reached the boat launch, he was on his third.

He didn't say much. How could he. He was lighting up all of the time. Anyway, the guy's a professional bass angler. Words are a waste of time.

We hit Lake Mead in a blaze of glory. He cranked up his Nitro bass boat, equipped with a 250-horse-power outboard, and whizzed across the inky lake, reaching a top speed of 67 miles an hour. What a blast.

Vern headed to a spot where a flotilla of 30 boats was bobbing about. We were all waiting for the striped bass to do their thing.

Sure enough, as if an imaginary starting gun had gone off, the water around us exploded with fish. The striped bass were in an eating frenzy, attacking tiny shad and our floating lures with reckless abandon.

Four hours later, Vern and I were exhausted. We had landed and released 42 striped bass.

After paying Vern a hefty tip, I realized a rare thing had happened. This celebrity had actually delivered on a promise. "You want a striped bass for your birthday, and I'll deliver," Vern had pledged.

I doubt Paris Hilton could do that. Sure she may be a tad bit more attractive than Vern, but when it comes to tying a knot — as in an improved clinch knot — onto a Zara Spook lure and tossing it 20 yards to a surfacing striped bass, I'd put my money on Vern any day.

And that's exactly what I did.

September 14, 2008

Starring in a poolside cruise revue

Taking a cruise to an exotic location has nothing to do with comfort.

Oh sure, you are treated like royalty. You have scores of trained staff cleaning your rooms three or four times a day, even depositing a piece of dark chocolate on your pillow at night. But when you are stuck in the Atlantic, with only the rolling seas to keep you company, the mood can suddenly turn ugly.

The reason I found myself in such a predicament was my sister's 60th birthday. We wanted to celebrate her memorable B-day in style, so we decided a family cruise to the tropics of Bermuda would be ideal. Our entourage included my sister, her husband, my 86-year-old mother and my son.

Our ship was the 1,100-passenger Norwegian Crown, loaded to the gunwales with lobster tail, French champagne, chocolate truffles and poker chips — the essentials for a seven-day cruise.

All was going well until the return trip to New York City. When at sea, passengers become a captive audience, and believe me the cruise director takes full advantage of that. There isn't a moment that passes without some form of competitive entertainment being arranged. It's hard to resist. You find yourself signing up for talent shows and trivia contests, getting a bid number for the art auction, packing the casino for slot machine tournaments and checking your credit rating to see if Texas Hold 'Em fits into your retirement plans.

And don't even think about enjoying a quiet game of bingo. It's pure cut-throat as passengers try to be the first to black out a card and win a free cruise.

But I didn't care for any of that, even declining the buffet of chocolate and champagne that was offered. I decided instead to head out to the pool for some down time.

Easing myself into a lounge chair, I soon struck up a conversation with several ladies sitting nearby who said they were part of a Shriners' group from the Philadelphia area. Curious about these folks who champion hospitals for the less fortunate and who wear funny-looking fezzes and drive miniature cars in parades, I asked how many were in their group. One hundred and eight came the reply. I gasped. One of the ladies pointed to an elderly gentleman across the pool from us. He's the Grand Potentate, she said.

Before I could make any wisecracks about the Shriners' weird fedoras, the ship's cruise director appeared before us with a microphone in hand. I winced with pain. Something bad was about to happen.

"Guess what," she said. "We're going to have the sexiest-legs competition. Are you ready?"

Despite hearing only a smattering of applause and encouragement, the cruise director charged ahead. As I feared, it was a competition for men only. Entries were encouraged. Several wives shoved their husbands forward. The Grand Potentate got drafted. That forced a laugh out of me, not a good move on my part, since I was within earshot of the cruise director.

"If you think it's so funny, why don't you come up here," she said, pointing an accusing finger in my direction.

The female Shriners thundered their approval, as did my sister and son who had also joined me at the pool. What could I do?

So up I went, standing alongside the oddest assortment of men I've ever been associated with — except perhaps for the time in 1971 when I stood in line with other draftees in the Army and was ordered to strip down to my boxer shorts.

I groaned back then, and I groaned again when the cruise director, in a voice dripping with devilish delight, described how the competition would be held. All of us male contenders had to dance around the pool and do whatever it would take to sway the opinions of three hand-picked judges. That meant, she said, taking off our shirts and performing "suggestive" dance moves.

There were six of us competing, and naturally there were six awards to be handed out. Besides the sexiest legs, the other prizes were for the strongest legs, hairiest legs, chicken legs, whitest legs and legs with the knobbiest knees.

The first competitor put on a display worthy of TV's "American Idol." He immediately ripped off his shirt to reveal abs of steel and bulging biceps. This mesomorph performed all sorts of lurid moves in front of the three women judges, swishing his posterior only inches from their faces. How in the world could I match that, I thought grimly to myself.

But that was nothing. Moments before the loud disco music came to an end, he stopped and performed a back flip into the pool.

My heart sank and my knees began to wobble.

Next came the Grand Potentate. I knew I didn't have a chance against him. Not only could he sway to the music, but also one of the judges was with the Philly Shriners. The fix was in, I muttered under my breath.

Eventually, the spotlight shifted to me. The loudspeakers pumped out a throbbing beat and I began my dance moves, which consisted of madly swinging my arms from side to side like a deranged ape and pounding my feet on the wet ceramic tiles encircling the pool. Not to be outshined by the Grand Potentate, I tore off my shirt to the horror of my son standing nearby, exposing skin that hadn't seen the sun in years.

Laughter swept over me.

I continued to gyrate around the pool and even kissed a baby along the way. Near the end of my ghastly routine, I grabbed a woman's leg and compared it to mine. What a sight — my gnarled and pockmarked limb next to her smoothly shaven and tanned appendage.

The crowd roared in delight.

Well, as predicted, the Grand Potentate earned the sexiest-legs honor, and the guy with the back flip garnered the strongest-legs award.

Then the cruise director came over to me. What does this guy deserve, she asked the throng of passengers.

The crowd replied as one voice: "WHITEST LEGS!"

For my effort, I was given a plastic water bottle and a yellow sash, the kind that beauty pageant winners wear. Mine read: "Mr. I Need A Tan."

After the contestants had dispersed and a new competition had begun, this time for the hairiest chest, my son offered these words of consolation: "Well Dad, at least when someone asks you what's your most embarrassing moment in life, you won't have to think about it. You'll know."

Who would have guessed a trip to Bermuda would have given me that moment.

June 12, 2005

Ride 'em, buckaroo

Imagine the vast expanses of the Yakima Training Center and then multiply that by 10, and then add to the mix about a million prickly cactus plants and a rattlesnake under every rock.

That's the terrain I faced when I gingerly settled into a hot leather saddle. It was cinched around a head-shaking, wild-eyed horse that had never been ridden before. Never.

As the horse kicked up its back legs, a chorus of cowboys roared: "Go get 'em, city slicker." Their weathered hands wiped away a tear or two as their laughter rolled like thunderclaps along a windswept arroyo.

These hard-bitten cowboys, rarely given to wild antics, were busting a gut at my expense.

I was a natural target. I was the ultimate tinhorn, the kid from Chicago who couldn't tell the difference between a mare and a Morgan, and had no idea how to saddle either.

Among the many jobs that I have held in my life — from a Holiday Inn desk clerk to a social worker in London — being a buckaroo in the desert wastelands of Arizona ranks as the weirdest of all.

For reasons I have yet to fathom, I ended up in the tiny town of Parker, Arizona, some 40 miles south of Lake Havasu City, with a traveling companion whom I had met while hitchhiking out West. It was in the early 1970s and I was several months away from getting my draft notice from the Army. So I figured, "Why not?"

I confess, though, Parker was not what I had expected of a Wild West town. It had only one saving grace — the Colorado River, which ran beside it.

Parker also had a Dairy Queen, a cafe that served terrible coffee and a gas station. I actually pumped gas there for several weeks. Not a bad job, except for the fact I kept forgetting to put the gas cap back on the cars that drove off. I ended up with a collection of six or seven caps before I left.

That's when I met up with a rancher who had more than 50 head of horses, donkeys and mules. He convinced my companion and me to help him out. So I figured, "Why not?"

The guy's spread was nothing to brag about. The 60-year-old rancher, who had been a welder most of his life, had a single-wide trailer where he lived with his wife. A swamp cooler atop the aged trailer provided the only reprieve from the sweltering desert heat.

Nearby, four corrals built of rough-hewn wood held an odd collection of horses, from American paints and thoroughbreds to a lone mustang he had roped from a roaming herd of wild horses. I was hired for room and board to help care for this hodgepodge of animals while the rancher did some part-time welding work.

One day, the rancher stopped by a friend's house and picked up a young, untamed horse. That's where I came in. The rancher wanted me, the city slicker, to be the first to ride the horse.

Now that may sound really dumb now, but back then, when I was barely 22 years old, it seemed like a good idea — "Why not?"

This was also the time I discovered what the term "rank" meant when paired with the word "horse." For the rider, it's never a good match. Unless you're competing in a rodeo.

So a few days later, with three or four cowboys positioned around an empty corral and my friend urging me on, I slowly put one foot in the stirrup and swung over onto this "rank horse." Nothing happened. The horse just stood there and snorted.

"Is this a good sign," I asked. The next sound I heard was my friend slapping the right haunch of the horse with a leather strap.

Whack!

That got the horse's attention. Off we went round and round the corral, the horse bucking crazily and the peanut gallery — all seasoned cowboys — whooping it up. Meanwhile I hung onto the horn of the saddle for dear life.

Then my friend got the brilliant idea of opening the corral gate.

Seeing an escape route, the horse charged past the dislodged gate and broke into a headlong gallop — the kind I once saw on television with Roy Rogers heading into the sunset. But this time I was atop that galloping horse with no idea when the ride would end, or whether I would still be there to witness it.

Some 30 minutes later, the horse and I limped back to the corral with my left leg a pin cushion of cactus quills and my cowboy hat lost somewhere in a ravine. I had tamed the horse, but not through any skill on my part. Credit sheer exhaustion.

That was the only horse I ever broke. The rancher finished his welding job, and my traveling companion and I soon left Parker on separate paths. We never saw each other again.

Nor did I ever return to Parker. Sometimes it's best to leave memories of past conquests closed shut — like you would a corral gate.

April 19, 2009

Trip to Maui and Freedom, on the road to Hana

"A hippie is someone who looks like Tarzan, walks like Jane and smells like Cheetah."

— Ronald Reagan

On the road to Hana, Freedom lives.

When my wife Leslie and I met Freedom, he was seated serenely on the front steps leading to his wooden yurt. It's set deep in the tropical forests of Maui near Twin Falls, one of the prized destinations along the island's picturesque and rugged eastern coastline.

The balding 47-year-old hippie was wearing paisley shorts and a dark T-shirt emblazoned with portraits of his hero, Jerry Garcia, the late Grateful Dead impresario whose concerts in the '60s once featured "acid tests" as a way of popularizing the use of LSD. Below Garcia's bearded mug were the words: "Legalize pot."

Welcome to hippie heaven.

It appears Freedom also experienced his own brand of acid test. He had apparently spent 17 years of his youth on the lam after being charged with the illegal sale of drugs, including LSD. Only through the intervention of his mother was Freedom allowed to walk free. We were told he later inherited a million dollars through a trust fund, which he parlayed into the purchase of some 40 acres with towering coconut palms and red-dappled plumeria trees.

Freedom never budged from his perch on the stairs, even when a passing shower raced by overhead. While his home seems like paradise, with yellow globes of passion fruit swaying in the breeze like so many Christmas ornaments, Freedom confesses it's not ideal. He pointed to a trail, crowded with tourists who wander by his property. Not much privacy. And then there are the fly-overs by federal helicopters, checking for illegal marijuana grows.

Still, Freedom seemed content. He leads an uncomplicated life, which is at the core of what being a hippie is all about. It also helps to have an abundant supply of cannabis readily available. That's what put the "wowie" in Maui, right?

Walking down the sidewalks of Pa'ia — a small town that serves as a starting point on the road to Hana and Freedom's backyard — is like being time-warped back to the halcyon days of San Francisco's Haight-Ashbury district. Lots of long straggly hair and handmade, wildly colorful clothing. Not a Tommy Bahama shirt in sight (except for mine).

We eventually traveled the entire 52 miles from Pa'ia to the nondescript town of Hana. Though guidebooks extol the virtues of the drive by calling it a trip through the Garden of Eden, I beg to differ. It's like taking a roller coaster ride — for two hours straight. The 600 curves and countless one-lane bridges are reason enough to stay in your condo, not to mention the local drivers who use the road as a Motocross speedway.

What we did find on the island were fabulous sandy beaches. It's easy to fill a day with snorkeling among the coral reefs in search of exotic fish and the occasional sea turtle. At a beach along the southern shores of Maui, I nearly got swallowed up by a turtle. It floated underneath me, its enormous olive brown shell brushing up against my stomach.

While that's the closest I ever want to get to a 300-pound green turtle, getting to shake the hand of a bona fide hippie was even more unexpected. It's refreshing to see there are devotees of the '60s counterculture revolution still hanging around, giving renewed meaning to what my generation of baby boomers had accomplished — turning marijuana into a growth industry and chiseling out a slogan that will surely stand the test of time: "Make love, not war."

I could tell from Freedom's weathered face and sunny grin that he hasn't met a person, or a hookah pipe, he didn't like. Indeed he's ready for any occasion. Next to the yurt, under a large canopy, he has set up an expansive, open-air kitchen while his backyard deck features an odd luxury for the tropics: a hot tub.

Like a proud papa, Freedom becomes giddy when talking about his outhouse. It features a high-efficiency, self-contained composting toilet that can handle 200 flushes a day. Why so many?

"I have big parties," Freedom replied.

Indeed he does. Freedom holds "potlucks," welcoming anyone who wants to show up. The emphasis, I would venture to guess, is on the pot and not the macaroni salad. Freedom's guest list has included one of his neighbors, actor Woody Harrelson. No word about Oprah, Carlos Santana or Willie Nelson. They also own homes on Maui.

We met Freedom through Jesse, my wife's 32-year-old nephew. He's tall, thin, with long curly hair, which bounces wildly about his shoulders whenever he runs in his flip-flop shoes. He has lived on Maui for the past six years or so. He takes care of a rundown cottage near Twin Falls and often sets up a tent on Freedom's plot of paradise. Jesse doesn't hold a steady job. He has no health insurance and complains of several teeth that he wants yanked out. While driving to Freedom's house, he claimed his goal in life is to conquer boredom. Good luck with that.

Remarkably Jesse travels a lot. Earlier this summer he was in southwest Washington to attend the 40th annual Rainbow Family gathering, which attracted nearly 20,000 peace activists, spiritualists and hippies to Skookum Meadows in the Gifford Pinchot National Forest. The yearly get-togethers serve as a defiant statement against mainstream society and the rough-and-tumble realities of capitalism. Jesse says peace and harmony prevail, and so does freedom.

Yes, it turns out even at a Rainbow Family gathering, all roads lead to freedom.

And as we discovered on our trip to Maui, Freedom also comes with a Jerry Garcia T-shirt and a 200-flush guarantee.

November 6, 2011

With plenty of unsolicited help, Slovenia beckons

Waking up in the middle of the night has a host of root causes for those of us with thinning hair. The culprit could be, as in the case of Charles Dickens' Scrooge, an undigested bit of beef.

My problem, though, is more distant. Ever heard of Slovenia? I never did until one night last summer, at 2 a.m. to be precise, when my wife, Leslie, bolted upright in bed and exclaimed in a voice loud enough to be heard in nearby Union Gap: "I want to go to Slovenia."

Really, how do you frame a reply when, moments earlier, you had been pleasantly dreaming about sinking a 60-foot putt on the 17th hole at Apple Tree Golf Course?

"Where the hell is Slovenia?" I asked.

As I learned later, Slovenia lies in Central Europe between the southern Alps and the Adriatic Sea and boasts a slew of tourist attractions: baroque architecture in the capital city of Ljubljana, hillsides studded with vineyards and picturesque Lake Bled, which comes complete with snowcapped mountains, forests and a medieval castle.

Sounds too good to be true, right? Leslie found out about Slovenia while watching one of her favorite cable network shows, HGTV's "House Hunters International." In the episode she saw last summer, a young couple from a busy city in England were searching for a second home they could renovate as a summer getaway. They had their sights set on northern Slovenia. Leslie found the countryside stunning and the Slovenes remarkably friendly.

After a night's sleep lost over her European epiphany, I figured I had to act swiftly. My idea of foreign travel was a fly-fishing trip to British

Columbia, not a 26-hour plane ride to a postage-stamp-sized country with ties to the former socialist republic of Yugoslavia.

I decided to hatch a plan. I would try to find people eager to trash-talk Slovenia. Only then would I be able to dissuade Leslie from traveling to a place that prides itself in this corny tourist slogan: "I FEEL sLOVEnia." Very cute. So why do I FEEL NAUSEAted?

Sadly, my campaign to discredit Slovenia didn't start well. Three days after Leslie's early-morning wake-up call, I opened up the Sunday New York Times, and on a whim, turned to the Travel Section. My eyes scanned down the front page and fixed on a word printed in large type: "Slovenia."

Good grief, I muttered to myself, the Times has a travel story on Slovenia. What are the chances of that happening? Leslie saw it as divine intervention. I saw something else. Picture Satan holding a pitchfork.

A few weeks later, we took a side trip to Windy Point winery nestled high in the hills above Parker with a stunning view of the Yakima Valley. After settling down for a sip of wine, I noticed two men and a woman taking pictures of each other. I offered to photograph all three of them with Mount Adams in the background. They were delighted.

Again, the fates stepped in. One of the men had a thick European accent. Leslie couldn't resist. "Have you ever been to Slovenia?" she asked. I hoped his next words would be a cascading torrent of vitriol aimed at the puny country. No such luck. He was ecstatic.

"It's a wonderful place," he exclaimed before launching into a 10-minute tribute to the joys of traveling through the Slovenian countryside.

I began to panic. I've got to turn this around, I told myself, or else I'll be forced to spend $3,500 on plane tickets and fly to the other side of the world. I came up with another scheme. I would try to sap her enthusiasm about Slovenia by bombarding her with other, more familiar destinations like Rome, Paris or London.

So last month I signed us up for a special series of travel workshops put on by the guru of European excursions, Rick Steves. The Edmonds native is well-known in the Pacific Northwest for his popular PBS series, "Europe through the Back Door." He has his headquarters in downtown Edmonds, where the workshops were held.

Our first workshop featured traveling to England. Seemed like a perfect diversion. Before it started, Leslie checked out a table crowded with travel books and opened a thick paperback about Eastern Europe. One of Steves' tour guides peeked over her shoulder and said excitedly as Leslie flipped to a chapter on Slovenia, "Oh, I've been there before. It's a beautiful country. You have to go." Doomed again.

In the early afternoon we headed back to our hotel in downtown Seattle through a blinding snowstorm. Another ominous sign for me. I suggested we relax and enjoy a glass of wine at a bar next to our hotel. We were soon joined by a group of six or seven kitchen staff from a nearby restaurant. A young man, who sat next to me, asked what had brought us to Seattle. I told him about the travel workshops. "Yeah, my wife wants to go to Slovenia," I laughed. "I mean really, isn't that crazy?"

A guy sitting a few chairs away piped up: "Slovenia? I've been there. It's a great country." It turns out his father's grandmother lives in the outskirts of Ljubljana. Last year, he and his dad traveled there and were treated like royalty. He ended his story with the now familiar refrain: "You've got to go to Slovenia."

So much for enjoying a glass of wine.

Later that night, we walked to a Nordstrom store so Leslie could buy some cosmetics. A young woman in her mid-20s greeted us and started up a conversation. Leslie told her about our trek to Edmonds. I couldn't resist. There's no way, I thought to myself, that a young woman dishing out expensive cold cream would know anything about Slovenia. So I asked.

"Yes, I do," she said smiling. "My roommate spent a year there as a foreign exchange student. I can't wait to go there myself."

That's when I threw in the towel. So next year, we are planning to visit Slovenia. I wonder, though, what are the chances, among a population of 2 million, that a native Slovene will wake up in the middle of the night and exclaim, "I want to go to Yakima."

I'm not holding my breath.

February 12, 2012

FAMILY TIES

Growing up the youngest of three children, I developed a close relationship with my brother, Jay, who was only 15 months older. We shared the same friends and the same interests, especially playing baseball. I confessed to my brother on his wedding day that he was my best friend, and I meant it.

So when he died on his birthday at age 45, my world fell apart. While standing outside the church where his memorial service was to be held, I sobbed uncontrollably when I saw the urn carrying his ashes. A half hour later I delivered his eulogy. Somehow words replaced tears and I talked of happier times when we were young.

These are the stories of my family, and the memories that will forever bind us together.

Family took the Galaxy to fair far, far away

Whenever you take a family road trip across America, there always comes a time when you kick the dirt and mutter under your breath, "This was a mistake."

Rarely does this epiphany unfold after the first night. But that's what happened to my family in the summer of 1962. We had left the tree-lined suburbs of Chicago with all of the fanfare of an Admiral Byrd expedition, our tent trailer bouncing behind us, with horns blaring and confetti — ripped from that morning's Chicago Tribune — filling the air. Our destination: the Seattle World's Fair.

That first morning on our camping trip, though, almost did us in. I should have known something was wrong when I slammed down the trunk lid and the first words out of my mother were, "Where did I put the keys?"

First rule of the road: Never, ever, put your car keys on a suitcase in the trunk of your car when you're camping.

Second rule: Never, ever, let a 13-year-old near anything that locks.

So here we were in the middle of nowhere, in a state park amid the cornfields of Iowa, with our only set of car keys buried deep inside our spanking new Ford Galaxy, as irretrievable as a gold icon in an Egyptian crypt.

For some reason, my mom didn't put me in shackles. She probably figured I was getting enough grief from my older brother and sister. I didn't know who said it, but the phrase "Oh, you twerp" seemed to echo in my ears.

We tried banging on the trunk for starters, thinking that maybe in my simple-minded exuberance to get the trip going I hadn't pushed hard enough.

No luck.

But the banging on the car and my caterwauling of grief did accomplish something. Several park rangers overheard the commotion and stopped to see if we needed help.

For some strange reason one of the rangers was an expert on Ford Galaxies.

"You can get at the trunk through the back seat," he said firmly, much to everyone's amazement.

Easier said than done. Back then, there were no such novelties as fold-down seats.

Luck, though, was on our side. With the help of a Phillips screwdriver that we found wedged between two seat cushions, we were able to unfasten the back seat. Sure enough, there was an opening to the trunk.

But only a skinny rat could fit. Naturally, all eyes fell upon me, a "rat fink" if there ever was one. So I crawled up to the V-shaped opening and wriggled my way into the trunk. I reached out with my right hand, blindly groping for the keys. If I knocked them off the suitcase, we were sunk. Then I felt something metal. "I've got 'em," I yelled.

From goat to hero in the span of one hour. What a way to start a road trip.

That wasn't the only calamity of our expedition. We encountered dust storms, hail and lightning, winds that reached tornado-like velocities, a snow flurry in Montana and an overheated engine that quit at the top of Longs Peak in Colorado, forcing my brother and me to serve as traffic cops.

We also visited the nation's most fabled national parks: Glacier, Yellowstone, Grand Teton, Crater Lake and Yosemite.

When we arrived in Washington and drove to the shores of Lake Roosevelt and Grand Coulee Dam, the thermometer hit 105 degrees. Welcome to the Evergreen State.

Though my recollections of the World's Fair are a bit sketchy, I do remember the Monorail and peering out over Puget Sound from high atop the wind-swept Space Needle. While I don't recall the floating city of the future where humans in the Year 2000 were supposed to wear plastic underwear and munch on goodies made from wood waste (that's definitely for low-carb dieters), I do remember chewing through a Mongolian steak served up at the Food Circus.

While visiting a friend of the family there, we decided to head out to the backyard after dinner and gaze upon the Seattle skyline. Music seemed fitting for the occasion, so my dad's friend put on a recording of Harry Belafonte singing live in Carnegie Hall. With Belafonte belting out "Day-O, He Say Day-Ay-Ay-O" and the Space Needle lit up like a Roman Candle, I couldn't help but find the world a wonder to behold, so impossibly grand, especially for a 13-year-old who still had San Francisco and Yosemite to conquer.

Somehow my family survived the seven-week ordeal, no thanks to our Ford Galaxy, which seemed to overheat at the slightest hint of an incline. We even survived my sister's nightly ritual. Regardless of where we were, whether it was in a Grapes-of-Wrath-era, dust-choked KOA campground or at the foot of the majestic Grand Teton, my 16-year-old sister would put her hair up in a mass of knobby plastic rollers. Every night.

I also had my little quirks, too. Near Death Valley, I picked up a steer skull. My dad called it "desiccated," his way of trying to improve my vocabulary. Dousing it with a can of pop, I christened the skull "Farfel" and used it to attack my brother.

Such are the fond memories of a family road trip.

While travelers today have digital cameras and a family website to capture their exploits, in the early 1960s the only high-tech gadget we could get our hands on was a Polaroid camera. We took hundreds of Polaroid shots that summer and pasted them in a thick scrapbook, setting off each photo with a witty caption.

Though over the years the pictures have turned a coffee-colored brown, that scrapbook is one of our family's most prized possessions. Whenever we get together, invariably the scrapbook comes out of hiding. Laughter quickly fills the room.

Thankfully these memories find a way of surviving adulthood. Sometimes, as with me, they lead you to a place thousands of miles from your boyhood home.

And to think, it all started from inside the trunk of a Ford Galaxy.

June 20, 2004

Losing is easy when you're used to it

There's something tranquil about losing. Especially when it happens all of the time.

What's the point of winning anyway? What do you really get for capturing the World Series crown? Flat champagne and a nasty headache. Face it. After winning there's only one direction — downhill, that inevitable fall from grace.

Trust me. As a diehard Chicago Cub fan for the past 45-odd years, ever since sentient feelings began to crackle through my nervous system, I have welcomed defeat, knowing it will eventually come.

And really, what's wrong with losing the seventh game of the National League playoffs? It's not that Cub fans are accustomed to unfurling pennants. It's been nearly a century since the Cubs last won a World Series. We have made defeat the national pastime, not baseball.

To follow the Cubs is a solitary act of defiance, sprinkled with highs and buried by lows. Wednesday night was no exception. You sit there alone with your thoughts, staring blankly at the television screen as the Marlins hurl themselves atop each other in a celebratory mosh pit. You are a Buddha with a blue Cubs' hat on, contemplating nothing in particular because if you do, the veins in your neck might explode.

Yes, to be a diehard Cub fan, you must accept the slings and arrows of outrageous fortune, accepting the interference of a hapless fan on a foul pop fly with a shrug of the shoulders. Yes, even with a smile.

But to enter the diehard ranks, you need to fulfill one very important task. You must make a pilgrimage to the hallowed shrine, the Valhalla of Cub misery — Wrigley Field. It's sacred ground. I wouldn't be surprised if the Holy Grail is stuck somewhere in the green ivy in right center field.

Growing up in the Chicago area, I spent many afternoons watching the Cubs getting caught in rundowns, leaving runners in scoring position and bringing in a relief pitcher who promptly would load up the bases on three straight walks, only to hit the next batter and bring in the eventual winning run. How do you script losses like that?

Wrigley Field is like no other. It's smack dab in the middle of a bustling city, the one Carl Sandberg called "hog butcher of the world." It's squeezed amid tenement flats, bars and Vienna sausage stands.

It's not one of those cavernous modern-day sports complexes with acres upon acres of parking, a million seats and an electronic scoreboard that does everything except tell you the score. At Wrigley, the scoreboard is hand-operated, you can't fit the city of Yakima in its bleachers, and the best parking spot is in an alleyway. That's baseball, folks. No silver lining, no pampering, nada.

I first stepped into Wrigley as an 8-year-old back in the 1950s. It was a sensory explosion. Back then, before smoking became a federal offense, you were greeted by a thin cloud of cigar smoke that wafted gently over you. It was like being blessed by holy water, except this time it came courtesy of a well-chewed Roi-Tan.

Then there's the green. What a vision, like seeing Dorothy's Emerald City for the first time. The outfield grass was so finely manicured it looked fake.

But the ivy. Ah, that's the coup de grace, the showstopper. I marveled at its beauty. What a tapestry, what a tangle, what a way to get a ground-rule double. Only at Wrigley.

Finally, there's the fabled catwalk in the corner of left field. It runs for 20 feet or so and serves as a gangway between the outfield bleachers and the grandstands along the third-base line.

One Cub player, in particular, loved that catwalk. He was Ernie Banks, one of the great shortstops of all-time and the Cubs' most famous ambassador of goodwill. To the dismay of the opposing pitcher, Banks would take his familiar stance at home plate, his wrists cocked in an oblique angle, and then "nine-iron" a low, inside fastball out of the park, just far enough to reach the catwalk in left. There, it would rattle around in the fenced walkway until some lucky fan would clutch it in his hands and raise it up for everyone to see. Banks owned that catwalk.

Jay and Spencer stand outside Wrigley Field

Going to Wrigley, of course, is more than just notching another loss on your infielder glove (yes, I always took mine to the games). It's about the memories.

One of my best times at Wrigley happened when I was 10 years old. I was there with my big brother Jay, and it was a doubleheader. Our last-place Cubs faced their bitter rivals, the Milwaukee Braves.

The stadium was packed, as it always was when the Braves came to town. We were forced to find a seat in the upper deck, the first time we had ever ventured into Wrigley's Stratosphere.

We sat on the stairs and watched as the Braves sent Warren Spahn to the mound. Henry Aaron and Eddie Matthews were also in the lineup, all future Hall of Famers. We answered back with our only superstar, Ernie Banks at short. It was hardly a fair fight.

Sure the Cubs lost two that day. Spahn threw a shutout and Aaron went deep. But who cared. We thrilled at the chance just to be there, gulping down an Orange Crush or two and tossing peanut shells into the sultry summer air.

My brother is no longer alive, but the memories still are of that day years ago. It's my piece of Wrigley that will always be with me. If I close my eyes, I am there, just the two of us, our knees knocking together, high in the upper deck, a step closer to heaven, where the ivy never fades and where Ernie Banks just might swat one to the catwalk in left, the ball falling gracefully like a dove descending.

October 18, 2004

My big brother, the very best

There is something about Jay you had to love.

Whether it was his booming voice or his infectious laugh, Jay was always there to brighten your day. When you came in contact with him, he became a wonderful affliction. He was always the first to start a conversation and he was always the one to deliver the last word, the final point of exclamation that rattled your ears and your senses. Strangely enough, he had you coming back for more.

There was always something about Jay you had to love. Yes, even his fascination with mirrors. I can't recall a time that Jay ever passed by a mirror without stopping at least once to check the slant of his hair or the color of his suntan.

To a younger brother, Jay seemed a bit vain. But he always balanced his vanity and God-given good looks with an equal dose of charm and humor. Always humor. Never forget the humor.

I remember back in the mid-60s, during the time when a mop-haired foursome from England invaded the states, Jay would have a unique way of introducing himself to strangers. He would take an exaggerated pose and ask, "Who do you think I look like?"

Invariably the reply would be, in an all too eager voice: "I know. One of the Beatles — George Harrison!" That was Jay, my brother, the rock star.

Yes, there was much about Jay you had to love. Simply put, he was the best big brother you could ask for. He never once let me down; he never once hurt me, either by words or in deeds. He was always there at my side while we were growing up — helping me out at school, cheering along the sidelines as I fumbled my way through high school football — and yes, even once arranging a blind date. The date was a disaster, but never our affection for each other.

Even at a young age, Jay had an air of confidence

We were more than brothers; we were the best of friends. Separated by only 15 months, our lives seemed to blend together. His friends were mine, and mine were his. He always invited me along and I, in turn, would welcome him on my many misadventures, including a wild bicycle trip when I was 15. Jay hated bikes, but he agreed to be my companion on a trek that took us from the outskirts of Port Washington, Wisconsin, to our family cottage in Door County. We weathered headwinds, flies, honking cars, dinners that consisted of canned beef stew, and a monstrous rainstorm that washed away our flimsy tents.

You can see there was a lot about Jay you had to love. And now it is up to us — his friends and family — to keep his loving spirit alive.

I have two sons, Andy and Jed, and cherish them as much as Jay did his wonderful daughters, Alexa and Cory. My 12-year-old Andy is a big brother like Jay. Jed is 7, and is a very special child who needs constant care and attention. When talking to Andy about helping his younger brother, I always mention Jay's name.

"Be loving and caring," I tell Andy. "Always be at your brother's side and never let him feel alone.

"I know how important it is to have a good, big brother. I had the best, the very best. He is my big brother, Jay."

Eulogy delivered at my brother's memorial service on Saturday, June 13, 1992

For Father's Day, give Dad what no one else can

Before you put the finishing touch to Father's Day by wrapping up that fancy variable speed drill inside last Sunday's comic section, you should also consider slipping in another gift that only you and your father share.

Memories.

They should be about an event or a pivotal moment grounded deep in your childhood, at a time when both you and your father finally figure out it's all right to be seen together, that you no longer think of him as "my old man" but rather as someone you may actually respect.

For lack of a better term, let's call them "primal paternal memories." That makes them sound kind of important, as they should be. For a Father's Day gift, rekindling the emotions of a primal memory is far superior to anything Craftsman could devise for its line of power tools. Face it, gifts that resonate from the heart are far superior to anything that dips to the bottom line of your Visa card.

Now when you first attempt to retrieve a primal memory, the exercise may lead you to some sort of outdoor activity or sporting event. That's understandable since fathers usually relate best to their children when there are crickets chirping in the background or a vendor yelling out, "Get your cold beer here."

My dad and I had several such points of reference. However, that doesn't mean my dad yearns for the mountains. Like many who claim the mantle of fatherhood, my dad preferred sitting behind a desk to the rigors of building a campfire. A genius when it comes to scholarly pursuits like reading Russian history and debating the finer points of anti-trust laws, my dad

— an attorney who commuted daily to downtown Chicago — had little time for the fatherly pursuits of pitching tents and reeling in 30-pound muskies.

However, there was one magical day when my dad and I threw caution to the wind and headed out together for a day at the ballpark.

It was back in 1964 when I was a sophomore in high school. The Cubs, a team that has given new meaning to the phrase "perennial losers," were having another banner year and were firmly ensconced in last place. That day they were pitted against the Los Angeles Dodgers, a World-Series caliber team and one of the most successful franchises in all of professional sports. It was a lousy matchup but my dad had promised to take me to a game, so there we were, two lonely figures in a stadium of empty bleachers cheering on a team of second-rate underachievers.

At the bottom of the ninth inning, the game was reaching its inevitable conclusion. The best relief pitcher in all of professional baseball — the dreaded lefthander Ron Perranoski — had taken the mound. To this day, his name still sends shivers down my spine. But Dad and I hung tough. With two outs, we cheered as an error and two walks filled the bases.

Then Ellis Burton stepped up to the plate. A collective moan issued up from the few fans who had stuck it out. Everyone knew that Burton, who had already struck out twice, didn't have a chance against the fearsome lefty.

I hung my head in defeat and prayed for rain. "Don't give up hope," my dad blissfully advised.

Perranoski reared back and threw a laser-beam fastball. I couldn't watch.

Then I heard a sound that seldom occurs within the friendly confines of Wrigley Field. The crack of a bat against a ball. My dad yelled wildly. Burton had connected. The ball sailed on a line drive into the empty left field bleachers.

Mighty Burton had cleared the bases to win the game. For a brief moment, life seemed simply wonderful.

Yes, this comes close to "primal," but a Cubs' win doesn't quite pass the test. It certainly can't match that bizarre summer's day when I was 9 years old.

It was a time when my dad could do no good. Every child goes through this period of denial and distrust. Some, sadly, never come out of it.

That day, 39 years ago, was a typically hot, muggy soup that Midwesterners call summer. As usual, two of my buddies and I were playing baseball in my backyard. I was ready to take a cut at a fat-looking pitch when a terrifying scream ripped through the air. It had come from across the street. In a few minutes, our quiet neighborhood was abuzz with activity, with grownups running back and forth, sirens blaring and cop cars screeching to a halt.

From the bits of conversation we had picked up, it seems that a wild, exotic animal had bitten its new owner. The beast apparently looked like a cross between a boar and a badger and had the ferocity of a rabid wolverine.

Regardless of its size, the most distinguishing feature of the beast was its razor-sharp teeth. The owner proved that point by showing how the animal had bitten a chunk of flesh out of his leg.

Our ragtag trio nudged closer to the victim of the animal attack and got a clear view of the man's gnawed leg. We gasped. Blood drained from my face and my hands began to shake.

"You kids get inside," a neighbor hollered. The man, his torn T-shirt soaked with sweat, was wielding a shovel for protection. That sent us scurrying for cover, back into my garage where we regrouped and tried to stoke up our courage.

"What are you scared about?" inquired my closest friend as he seized his pocketknife from his back pocket.

I grabbed a baseball bat and out we went into the sunshine, hoping against hope that we wouldn't be the first to find the beast with razor-sharp teeth.

As we headed across the street to prowl around a neighbor's collection of garbage cans, a kid came running full speed up the street, his black sneakers flapping against the blacktop.

"It's cornered," the boy screamed excitedly and continued on, a modern-day Paul Revere spreading the good news about the beast's capture.

We all hurried down to where a chorus of voices was congratulating the hero of the day. Hands thudded against his back; a police officer shook his hand. I pushed my way through and stared up at the center of all the attention.

My dad smiled back. "Hi, son."

I stood next to my dad that day and felt proud to be his son. That feeling has never stopped.

I'm sure the years have blurred some of the details. The beast was probably not as ferocious as I had imagined. But a primal paternal memory doesn't have to be like a documentary film. It has to feel good, though, and mean something to you.

So when you get through fiddling with the buttons on that new variable speed drill on Father's Day, try sitting down with your dad and begin by saying, "Hey dad, remember when ..."

He'll get the picture.

June 15, 1997

Turkey Day memories: The way we whirred

I doubt the Food Network's celeb Rachael Ray has ever served up a turkey disaster. You know the kind — the Butterball that's still frozen when you yank it out of the oven.

For her, this Thanksgiving will unfold like clockwork, even when whipping up a pot of pumpkin soup and roasting to perfection an herb-crusted tom turkey the size of a small beached whale.

In contrast to Ray's flair for flavor and impeccable timing, my family's feasts when I was young were kind of mundane — gooey cornbread stuffing, frozen green peas with pearl onions and green Jell-O embedded with miniature marshmallows.

Despite our lack of culinary panache, that never stopped us from venturing back into the kitchen each November, a bulb baster in hand, knowing full well we would fail again to turn a broiler pan of greasy turkey residue into silky, succulent gravy.

For the most part, our failures had little to do with cooking.

As dining-room diva and former prison inmate Martha Stewart has taught us over the years, it's not so much what you cook that matters. It's how you accessorize the dish. That's the key. Decorate a green bean casserole with sprigs of fennel and boughs of holly, and who cares if it tastes like mush (ours often did).

This was particularly true one Thanksgiving years ago, when I was 10 or 11. At the time, I had marveled at my dad's ability to carve the turkey. Well, actually, more like his inability. He never knew how to approach a turkey while armed with a knife. He especially had a hard time poking through the bird's crusty skin.

It would have helped if he had sharpened the knife beforehand. But he never did.

Enter the Hamilton Beach electric knife.

When word circulated in our neighborhood about the wonders wrought by this newfangled gadget, my dad couldn't wait to buy one. And what better time to demonstrate its sharp, serrated cutting edges than at the Thanksgiving dinner table.

I remember hearing the whirring sound of the electric blades as dad powered it up for the first time. It's a sound that haunts me to this day.

To satisfy invited friends and relatives, Mom had cooked a massive bird, some 20 pounds or so. Dad started immediately with the easiest target, the drumstick. It sheared off like a small limb from an oak tree.

So far, so good.

Dad then poised the twin electric blades over the supple flesh of the turkey breast. I held my breath. This was the true test. He thumbed the "on" switch and the blades began that agonizing sound. Meat flew in all directions, except onto the plate below. The prized white turkey meat, which should have fallen off in thin layers, showered down like pencil shavings.

"Oh, my God," Mom exclaimed.

My dad, of course, couldn't hear her because of that demonic whirring sound of the blades. He merrily kept on shredding the turkey, until a rather large mound of meat had piled up in front of him, easily covering the plate and spilling over onto the polished veneer of the credenza.

When Dad had finished eviscerating half of the bird, he held up the electric knife and struck a triumphant pose, much as young King Arthur must have done after he unsheathed Excalibur from its rocky crypt.

But this was no Camelot. The heroic scene quickly faded when a chunk of meat flopped to the carpet below. Luckily, our springer spaniel, Oliver, was there to gulp it down.

Though Mom didn't talk to Dad for several days after the carving incident, there was one saving grace. For the meal, Mom had whipped up a batch of instant potatoes. She loved lump-less mashed potatoes and figured Betty Crocker's "new and improved" instant spuds were the answer.

The finished product did, indeed, look like mashed potatoes, and there were certainly no lumps. Its consistency, though, was that of Elmer's glue.

Little did Mom know at the time, but these pre-fab potatoes were a stroke of genius. When rolled together with Dad's shredded turkey, it made a dollop-sized sphere perfect for swallowing. And oddly enough, the balled-up mass of meat and preservatives tasted OK. Even Oliver wanted seconds.

It has been decades since Dad turned turkey into sawdust and Mom made paste out of potatoes. They are both gone now. Dad passed away 10 years ago and Mom died last November, two weeks before Thanksgiving.

When cleaning out our family home near Chicago earlier this year, I came across a cluttered drawer in the kitchen. I found an old gravy bulb baster. The plastic bulb had cracked. It had long outlived its usefulness. I tossed it into a garbage can.

I reached deeper inside the drawer and uncovered something cold and steely — the twin blades of Dad's electric knife. Why would Mom have kept these? But there they were, the white plastic darkened by age but the serrated edges still sharp to the touch.

I held the twin blades high in the air and watched the light from the room shine off their silver skin. Then I tossed them, like the bulb baster, into the garbage. Memories of past Thanksgivings should be carried in the heart, and not in the hand. That much I had learned over the years.

And one more thing. Don't forget to sharpen the carving knife.

November 23, 2008

In praise of my father

My Dad had such a warm and caring heart, that's probably why we always called him "Easy Ed" — he was easy to love, easy to talk to, easy to share a laugh with, and easy to rekindle memories about.

That's what I want to try to do today.

One of my Dad's most favorite places in the world was at the family cottage, on the rocky bluffs overlooking Ellison Bay in Door County, Wisconsin.

During our many trips there, when a storm would blow in from the North and rain clouds would force us to batten down the doors and windows, Dad and Mom and Kathy and Jay and I would sit in front of a roaring fire in the fireplace, and ponder the imponderables.

On a number of occasions, when the conversation would begin to wane, Dad would bring up for discussion a lifelong goal of his — writing "the great American novel." Dad insisted it would be easy to write, all you really needed was an eye-popping title for the book — after that, everything else would fall into place.

✼ ✼ ✼

Well for Dad, the beginning chapter of his career in the legal profession surely fell into place neatly.

At Evanston High School, Dad literally sprinted to the head of his class with a full head of steam, gaining academic honors and a state track record along the way.

At Amherst College, Dad burned the late-night oil in his studies, despite the best efforts of his fraternity brothers at Phi Gamma Delta to entice him away with invitations to toga parties and other soirees of a disreputable nature.

Mom and Dad at their wedding on Feb. 27, 1943

After later earning his law degree from Northwestern University, where his father had been a professor emeritus in the school of dentistry, Dad hit the ground running in his new field of juris prudence, stopping for a few years in Washington, D.C., to clean up the federal government before coming back to Chicago — for good.

He joined a group of attorneys who later formed one of the most prestigious law firms in Chicago, and the nation — Jenner & Block. His close friend and fellow partner in the firm, Addis Hull, fondly remembers Dad as the "heavy hitter" for Jenner & Block. I guess you could call Dad the Sammy Sosa of his day.

Just look at his resume. Dad specialized in three extremely challenging aspects of the law.

The most troublesome was labor relations, where he did battle with some very tough customers — labor unions. You've got to remember, back 40 years ago, labor unions were much stronger, and meaner.

Dad once mentioned to my sister Kathy about one of his more contentious labor negotiations. It had a very auspicious start. Dad told the labor bosses he wanted them to put everything on the bargaining table. And they did — literally — filling the tabletop with revolvers.

Dad also specialized in the administration of trade associations — which Addis Hull explained is a nice way of saying they tried to set prices — and in anti-trust litigation.

His greatest moment occurred when he stood before the U.S. Supreme Court to argue a case on behalf of National Brick. This was Dad at his very best. As senior attorney on the case, he had an array of attorneys working on the final, oral arguments.

On the night before Dad was to go to court, a final draft was completed, and Dad sent all the attorneys back to their hotel rooms to get some sleep. But not Dad. Early that morning, a mere five or six hours before he was to address the nine justices, Dad tore up the arguments and rewrote them — completely.

Did he win? You bet he did. Was there really any doubt?

✷ ✷ ✷

The hallmark of Dad's success at work, and in life as well, was his unflappable loyalty. This, of course, extended to his clients.

Once, when the Dairy Association hired him, margarine and skim milk were outlawed from our household. Only under the cloak of night were we able to sneak in tubs of Miracle Whip margarine.

His affiliation with the Pet Food Association resulted in a long list of dogs that gobbled up pet food by the bowlful. The most famous of our canines was Oliver, a hyperactive springer spaniel who, to this day, is still regarded as a member of the family. There wasn't a curtain left standing in our house that Oliver didn't leave his mark on.

And then there was Dad's longtime client, Chris Craft boats. This relationship cemented Dad's long, torturous love affair with powerboats.

Dad loved boating. Sadly though, the boats did not reciprocate that affection.

First off, "power boat" was a misnomer. Although Dad was proud to extol the virtues of his twin-screw diesel inboard engines, rarely did both of them work in tandem.

And on the few times they did both run, even worse calamities awaited us on board. There wasn't a jetty or a reef in South Florida that Dad didn't get to know — up close and personal. On Lake Okeechobee, I understand they have even named a portion of the lake after him. It's called simply, "Ed's Eddy."

Unlike Papa Hemingway who would return from his African safaris with the head of a gazelle or a rhino to mount on the wall, Dad would return from his expeditions down Florida's intercoastal waterways with hunks of twisted metal that once served as propellers.

Mom and Dad always wondered why they were greeted so warmly by the mechanics at the marina where they kept their boat. Why wouldn't they? The mechanics knew their Christmas bonuses were guaranteed.

While Dad did have his fling with golf and tennis, and even took a few ill-advised schusses down the ski slope, I think his most adventurous foray into the world of manly endeavors was deer hunting.

Now here was someone supremely ill-suited for the blood-lust sport of hunting. My Dad had the sweetest, gentlest disposition of anyone I have ever known. He made St. Francis of Assisi look like Attila the Hun.

However, under the prodding of his close friends, Dad took up the sport of bow hunting.

Our backyard soon became the practice area for Dad and his merry men of archerers. They purchased only the finest of equipment. But remember, this was long before the days of compound bows. Back then, the bulky fiberglass bows were not only impossible to shoot straight, they also took two grown men to string.

I remember one time — with a great deal of fanfare — Dad and his cohorts arranged a 10-foot high stack of hay bales and over this, down one side, they hung a target made out of burlap. It had the menacing outline of a bear on it. So here we were, the kids, staring intently at our dads as they let fly their arrows at the bear target. The burlap, though, must have had an especially tight weave in it, because each time an arrow would happen to hit the target, and that wasn't often, it would bounce off.

This spectacle got us kids to wonder — if our Dads couldn't stick an arrow in a bale of hay, how did they ever expect to bring down a deer?

Thankfully, I can say my Dad never did.

Each time he would return from a deer-hunting trip, he would be smiling from ear to ear, empty-handed except for his bow and a quiver full of arrows.

I wonder if their hearts were really into the hunt. My uncle, Bruce Lippincott, who also went on these deer escapades, shared with me the other night his insights as to why the hunting trips were so unsuccessful. These are his words, not mine:

"When you put brandy in your tea in the morning, you can't really expect to get many deer."

✪ ✪ ✪

If you didn't already know by now, Dad had a way with words. He always punctuated a conversation with a well-worn phrase that he would pull out of his encyclopedic memory bank. There was one that always stuck with me, and it's one I often mention to my sons whenever I'm dispatching worldly advice.

"If you can't boost, don't knock."

For Dad, that said it all. Dad never had a harsh word to say to anyone. He exuded optimism from every pore.

Even during his long five-year stay at Whitehall nursing home, when the strokes had left him blind and weakened him so much he was unable to sit up on his own, he would always greet you with a smile and with an exuberance in his voice that brightened the room you were in.

Dad understood the value of words, the way they connect with people, the way they heal wounds and embolden spirits, the way they wash away tears with a smile.

That brings me to the words he spoke in 1943 — 55 years ago — when he said to my Mom, "I will love and cherish you forever, in sickness and in health, till death do us part."

What a remarkable love story Mom and Dad wrote together, a love built on trust, commitment and sacrifice.

What greater proof of this love could there be than what Mom and Dad shared during the past five years. Each afternoon, Mom would visit Dad at Whitehall. They would share ice cream and popcorn together, listen to mysteries by Dick Francis on the tape recorder, enjoying the closeness of each other and the many memories they shared — a richness beyond wealth and measure.

My Mom said it best: "We simply enjoyed each other."

What a wonderful book my Dad has written. It's not the Great American novel he probably had envisioned while watching the embers fade from view as they rose up the chimney in the cottage at Ellison Bay.

The book is his life, and it's better than anything a novelist could have imagined.

It's a book I'm not ready to put down.

Not now.

Not ever.

Eulogy delivered at my father's memorial service on October 27, 1998

Remembering Dad a birthday tradition

After you turn 21, celebrating a birthday gets a bit tedious. After turning 60, what's the point?

I prefer spending my time fishing. That's what I will be doing today for my 63rd birthday — trolling for walleye.

However, if I were to hold a birthday bash for myself, the guest list of other 63-year-old baby boomers would be quite impressive. Comedian Billy Crystal would be on the docket along with famed Broadway star Bernadette Peters, who could perform a Stephen Sondheim song, "Send in the Clowns." An appropriate tune for me.

I would definitely send an invite to former Vice President Al Gore and Secretary of State Hillary Rodham Clinton. Hard to imagine these two presidential contenders are both 63. It's a small world, isn't it?

And reporting my birthday party to millions of viewers across the world would be CNN's quintessential reporter, Wolf Blitzer. It's comforting to know that Wolf and I are not only kindred spirits in the profession of journalism — I'm retired, he's not — but we also include 1948 in our Facebook profile.

A birthday celebration, though, is much more than chitchatting with best-selling writers like Stephen King. By the way, he's 63, too.

For me, this particular birthday triggers memories of when my father was 63. His life couldn't have been better back in early 1980. He was a well-respected attorney, specializing in corporate law for a firm in downtown Chicago. Six years earlier he had argued a case before the U.S. Supreme Court, and won.

On April 11, 1980, I phoned him in Florida where he and my mom were vacationing. I wanted to tell him the big news: I was a new dad.

My son, Andy, entered the world at 2 a.m. that day at the University of Washington Medical Center following an emergency delivery. He was a preemie and weighed a mere 3 pounds, 2 ounces. He was 15 inches tall, an inch short of the length of a college football.

When I called, Mom answered the phone.

"You have a son," she replied in bewilderment.

I corrected her. "No, Mom, you have a grandson."

But her voice was muted. Something wasn't right. Then she told me Dad was in the hospital. He had suffered a stroke.

"This can't be true," I blurted out. But it was. Both my newborn son and my father were in intensive care units at the opposite ends of the continent at the same time.

Distant memories seem so vivid, so real. It's as if you can reach out and touch them. So it is with the memory of a summer's day when I was 10. We were at our family cottage near the top of the Door County peninsula in Wisconsin. My grandfather had built a log cabin on a bluff overlooking the emerald waters of Green Bay. It was a warm July afternoon and I was playing in the water, teetering on the rocks that lay below, their surfaces scrubbed smooth by glaciers thousands of years ago. That summer, the Midwest had suffered a terrible drought, leaving the water level at near-record lows. It had exposed our wooden dock and left our small sailboat marooned on the shore.

I decided to open up a channel so we could pull the sailboat safely out into deeper water. I started tossing the rocks on either side of me. It was a slow process. Some of the rocks were large and my hands were small. That's when Dad arrived, his baggy swimming trunks flapping in the breeze.

We worked together that afternoon, dredging a safe passage for the sailboat. Sweat ran down his face.

I smiled back at him.

"I'm going to call it Channel Seven," I said proudly. We both laughed. It was the news network that Dad always watched when he was at home.

We finished Channel Seven and I sailed the rest of the summer, aiming the prow of the small boat toward the west and the setting sun.

My son stayed in the hospital for more than a month before being released. He never returned again. Sadly, my dad returned many times.

Slowly, the strokes robbed him of the use of his right arm. Then he lost his vision. Finally, doctors had to amputate one of his legs below the knee.

The culprit was arteriosclerosis, a hardening of the arteries. The real fault, though, lay in the choices Dad had made over the years. He was a smoker. He would go through three packs of Marlboros a day. He would have a cigarette with coffee in the morning and a cigarette with bourbon at night.

The human body can take only so much insult, and finally Dad's body broke down.

After his leg surgery, he was placed in a nursing home. He lived there for the next five years until his death in 1998 at the age of 82. For 18 years Dad had battled the effects of his smoking, and his family suffered alongside him.

Though his body was ravaged, Dad's mind was as sharp as ever. When visiting him, I would help push his wheelchair down to a cafe the nursing home had set up and there we would enjoy a hot fudge sundae together. Dad loved his chocolate.

One afternoon, I wheeled Dad into a large television room where a dozen or so other nursing home residents were seated. A few were slumped over, taking naps.

I left him there and as I walked down the hallway, I could hear a nurse ask the residents which television station they wanted to watch.

A single voice rose up, loud and distinct. It was my dad's.

"Channel Seven," he called out. "Channel Seven."

I closed my eyes and, for a moment, I no longer heard the footfall of my shoes on the linoleum tile. Instead, I heard the sound of water splashing through the rocky channel Dad and I once built years and years ago along the shores of Green Bay.

Keeping alive that sweet memory is how I wish to celebrate my birthday. Especially now, on the day I turn 63.

August 28, 2011

Bringing Mom home for a final loving touch

I had never given my mother a foot rub before. It's something I had never really thought about.

But with mom lying motionless in the intensive care unit last month, it seemed the time had finally come.

After she underwent emergency surgery for a ruptured intestine at Glenbrook Hospital near Chicago, doctors had given her little chance of making it through the first night. I couldn't even kiss her on the forehead; there were too many monitors in the way.

A few days later, though, mom's condition improved. They took her off the mechanical ventilator and — miracle of miracles — she breathed on her own. Doctors, though, worried about internal bleeding, infections and her heart, which was growing weaker.

I told them not to give up hope for my 88-year-old mother just yet. She's made of stern stuff. Even after being diagnosed with lung cancer earlier in the summer, she never stopped seeing friends and playing duplicate bridge.

What's more, she wants to go home. And when her mind is made up, I reminded the doctors, she usually gets her way.

For my older sister and I, what we wanted most was for her to be comfortable and free of pain. The doctors and nurses said they would do their best.

So I figured I would do my part, and that meant a foot rub. It was the least I could do for my mom. She'd always been there for me. She had nursed me through my own brush with death when I battled pneumonia as a 5-year-old. She held my hand then, stayed with me during the long nights and soothed my hot forehead with a cool, damp towel.

"Is it all right if I give you a foot rub," I asked. She nodded yes.

I lifted up the covers at the end of the bed and freed her feet of the tight plastic stockings used to ward off blood clots. I squirted out a thick gob of lotion and rubbed my hands together to warm the liquid. I then pressed my hands against her cold feet and gently rubbed the white lotion into her skin.

Her blood circulation, especially to her feet, was miserable following the surgery. Her toes were purplish, and the big toe on her right foot had blackened.

I continued to work the lotion into her thin, wrinkled skin. Slowly. Gently.

I wasn't the first in my family to do this. My son Andy started the ritual seven years ago when his mother lay in bed, dying from cancer. He would arrive with a towel and a big bottle of lotion and would rub his mother's feet for what seemed an entire afternoon.

My foot rubs didn't last as long.

As I worked the lotion in between her toes, I wondered about all the places her two feet had taken her during the past eight decades — to England, the Bahamas, Greece and Russia. I wondered about the countless times she had visited her favorite spot in the whole wide world — a log cabin her father had built along the bluffs of Ellison Bay in Door County, Wisconsin. She would never walk its rocky beaches again.

Nor would she dance. I remembered the time after she and her friends had returned to our house following a night of revelry. With Benny Goodman's tune "Sing Sing Sing" playing loud on the stereo, mom danced the Charleston to the delight of everyone — including her young son, perched high on the stairs, laughing at her madcap antics.

Yes, I had to rub those feet.

It's hard to weigh the value of time. So much is lost just waiting for something good to happen, and when it does, it goes too quickly. Being able to give those foot rubs was a gift. It was a gift, of course, from my mom.

The gift she gave to herself was going home. And she succeeded in that, too.

Three weeks after undergoing surgery, my mom returned to the two-story, wood-frame home she had lived in for the past 54 years. It rises among towering oaks on a quiet street in Northbrook, a northern suburb of Chicago.

She often said how she loved the way sunlight filtered through the windows, especially in the family room. So that's where we told the hospice workers to place her bed — in the room where she had celebrated birthdays, high school graduations, my sister's wedding and so many Christmases. It's also a favorite spot for her 19-year-old cat, Tigger.

Taken by ambulance, mom returned home on Nov. 10, a Saturday afternoon. Longtime friends and neighbors stopped by to hold her hand. She chatted with her three grandchildren. And yes, I gave her another foot rub.

But by the following afternoon, she had become unresponsive. Her eyes were now closed.

In the early evening, after still more of mom's friends had come and gone, my sister was holding one of her hands while I held the other. Hoping to rouse her, I said out loud, "mother," followed by "grandmother." Her eyelids never flickered.

Then I uttered a word that my son Jed had made up. Though words did not come easily for my autistic son, he had fashioned a great one for her: "Grand Mom-Mom." So that's what I used.

Mom squeezed my hand.

A moment later she heaved a sigh and breathed her last.

December 2, 2007

A sophisticated lady

Three weeks after undergoing emergency surgery, Marian Hatton died November 11, 2007, at her home in Northbrook, Illinois, surrounded by her family as her favorite song, Duke Ellington's "Sophisticated Lady," played in the background. She was 88.

Known for her keen skills at bridge and her smile that blossomed into an infectious laugh, Marian kept friends close and her family even closer, always eager to take trips to exotic locales such as Yugoslavia and the Panama Canal and always ready to dine out, from no-frills taverns such as Charlie Beinlich's to the white tablecloths of Skokie Country Club.

Spencer, 2 years old, Kathy, 6, and Jay, 4

She was born on April 7, 1919, in Evanston, Illinois, to George and Blanche (Spencer) Sollitt. She attended Smith College in Northampton, Massachusetts, graduating in 1941 with a degree in bacteriology, one of the first that the college had ever granted.

While at Smith, she met Edward Hatton who was attending nearby Amherst College. They shared wedding vows on Feb. 27, 1943, and eventually moved to Northbrook, a suburb of Chicago. There they became involved in community activities, hosted neighborhood parties and raised three children — Kathy, Jay and Spencer.

Always the adventurer (she climbed Longs Peak in Colorado as a child), Marian tackled one of the most daunting challenges a mother can face — she single-handedly traveled cross-country with three teenage children, hauling them along with a pop-up tent trailer to the Seattle World's Fair in 1962. Though her youngest child Spencer locked the car keys in the trunk on the family's first day on the road, Marian persevered, cooking campfire meals over a gas stove and taking the kids horseback riding in the Rockies.

Even when she was in her 80s, Marian never stopped traveling, enjoying cruises with her family to Bermuda and to the outer reaches of Alaska, where she rode in a helicopter and landed on a glacier outside of Juneau.

Yakima also became a favorite destination, where she visited her son, Spencer, and her two grandsons.

A year ago, Marian ventured to Las Vegas for Spencer's wedding at the Little White Wedding Chapel where she danced with Elvis ("I thought he was dead," she proclaimed) and raised a toast to her son and his new bride, Leslie.

Marian was involved in numerous civic organizations including the Evanston Junior League, Infant Welfare Society and the League of Women Voters, for which she served as president. She excelled at duplicate bridge, volunteered at the Northbrook Public Library, took part in a book club for nearly five decades and was a loyal member of the Chicago Botanic Gardens and the Chicago Symphony. She also played golf and tennis, and became a dedicated teammate on the curling team for Skokie Country Club.

Despite being diagnosed with cancer earlier this summer, Marian kept up her daily routines, filling out the Chicago Tribune's crossword puzzle each morning, tuning to "Wheel of Fortune" and, at five o'clock sharp, preparing her favorite drink — vodka on the rocks with an anchovy olive.

As a testament to her independence, just two days before she underwent emergency surgery, Marian drove to a duplicate bridge game and trumped everyone.

"She went out a winner," declared Ann Brundage, a lifelong friend, bridge player and college classmate from Smith.

Indeed she did.

My mother's obituary was published in the Yakima Herald-Republic on November 25, 2007

You make the call ... to Mom

Calling my mother on Sunday morning had become a ritual ever since my dad died more than a decade ago.

When Mom answered the phone, her first words would always be the same: "How's the weather out there?" Familiar words spoken with a familiar voice.

Today, it will be different. This will be my first Mother's Day without my mom. She died last November. I can't even get a dial tone at her home near Chicago. The phone line Mom had used for 54 years is now disconnected.

I'm just glad last year's Mother's Day was so special. I didn't even have to call. I was there in person. My wife Leslie and I spent five days treating Mom to dinner at her favorite restaurants and buying her the quintessential Mother's Day gift — a colorful hanging plant for her backyard patio.

Before leaving, I took a group photo of us, our three smiling faces peering at the screen of my digital camera as I tried my best to frame a portrait. That was the last shot I would take of my 88-year-old mother. Two months later she would be diagnosed with lung cancer and photographs would become a thing of the past.

I'm lucky we had that time to share together.

I know of others — one is far too many — who never call or see their mothers, not even on Mother's Day. They have been out of touch for weeks, for months. Maybe it's because an angry word was spoken in haste, or a perceived wrong was never forgiven. The reasons don't matter; the results do.

Don't get me wrong. Mothers can drive their children crazy at times. It's why they're mothers, right? I remember my older sister back in high school having bitter arguments with Mom about the friends she was hanging out with.

Leslie, Mom and Spencer

One night, after another yelling match, my sister smashed a drinking glass against a wall and stormed out the front door, vowing never to return. It was great drama for my brother and me, but my sister's flight lasted only a minute or so. It was winter, and bitterly cold outside. She returned, her head hung low.

Those were tough times, but years later, my mom and sister would become best of friends.

Even when we do reach adulthood, mothers still find fault with how we are handling our lives. They always wonder whether you will ever get a job and move out of the house. Then when you finally do land a job, they complain it's not good enough for you. Or worse yet, that you will be a miserable failure.

I went through all of that with my mom. She said hurtful things — there's no question about that. Life is filled with these painful moments. But I never held them against her for long.

Not even during the heady days in the late 1960s when I was attending college in Meadville, Pennsylvania. Back then the Vietnam War had turned the country inside out, and had turned sons and daughters against parents and students against institutions. Yes, we thought we had all the answers. I wrote polemics against higher education and the irrelevancy of our upbringing, and would hand out these rambling commentaries to fellow students and faculty.

During these days of protest, I remember my parents visiting and Mom staring at me in utter bewilderment. "How long have you had that mustache?" she asked. It's a question she would raise for the next decade or so until she finally gave up, realizing I would never be the clean-shaven son she had expected.

This strained relationship, though, didn't stop me from remembering her 50th birthday. She had traveled with Dad and several other couples to Spain for a whirlwind trip in 1969. Though I couldn't reach her by phone, I wanted to send her something special, a peace offering of sorts.

So I headed down to a florist near the college and told the clerk I wanted to send a bouquet to my mom. I hauled out a world atlas, and together, we plotted where my mom would be on April 7. She had left Madrid and was headed for a small town in the middle of nowhere. I asked the clerk if it was possible to get the flowers there. She smiled. Anything's possible if you truly want it, she said.

Late in the afternoon, on her 50th birthday, my mom walked into her room in a small hotel in the middle of Spain and found a vase of bright spring flowers. She held the flowers in her hands and cried.

That was my best call ever.

But really, any call is the best call if it's the first in a long time. Not much has to be said. The important thing is the act, the putting aside of past differences, and above all, forgiving yourself. That's the hardest part — forgiving not only the things your mom might have said or done, but to forgive yourself for how you reacted. Forgiveness has to begin at home, in your heart.

The late Rev. William Sloane Coffin, a social activist and modern-day prophet, once wrote, "Love measures our stature: the more we love, the bigger we are. There is no smaller package in all the world than that of a man all wrapped up in himself."

So for those of you who are no longer in touch with your moms, whether the distance has been a week or a lifetime of regrets, take the first step. Make the call. Or arrive in person, as I did last year, and greet her with the best gift of all — your smiling face.

We do not know what tomorrow may hold, but we do know what silence and separation will bring — a chilling of the heart. Who needs that? Life is hard enough without losing a mother who is still alive.

May 11, 2008

JIMINY CRICKET

When Bronnie and I exchanged our wedding vows in the summer of 1979, I never imagined that 21 years later she would clutch my arm and plead with me, "I want to die."

After more than eight years of battling ovarian cancer and with doctors ruling out surgery to clear a blockage in her intestine caused by the disease, Bronnie no longer had the strength to fight. In the summer of 2000, she asked me to let her go. Not now, I said, not now. But how could I say no to this, her final wish?

And when she breathed her last, I faced another agonizing question: How would I say farewell?

Late Fragment

And did you get what
you wanted from this life, even so?
I did.
And what did you want?
To call myself beloved, to feel myself
beloved on the earth.

By Raymond Carver, writer and Yakima native.
He wrote this poem shortly before his death from cancer.

I have kept a writer's journal for more than four decades. It's where I seek refuge and try to make sense out of life. What follows are six entries from that journal. They cover the days and hours leading up to the death of my wife, Bronnie, at a time when making sense out of life was the furthest thing from my mind.

Fishing from heaven

Bronnie speaks so softly these days, you need to have the chair pulled up tight next to her or stand at the head of the bed, your back arched and your head poised over hers.

Last night I had the chair pressed tight against the bedrail. I cupped my hand in hers. I asked her what she wanted. I always ask this right before I leave the hospital.

But this time she asked for something other than a cup of chipped ice.

"I want to talk to Gom."

And what do you want to tell her, I asked.

"To keep the bait fresh."

It's Bronnie's way of telling me again that the struggle is over, that she is ready to let go of this firmament and be released. She keeps mentioning this image of her grandmother Gom, who lived to be 102, and the time she was a kid fishing for tiny perch with Gom on Kangaroo Lake in Wisconsin. It's a mantra for her.

Bronnie mentioned it again today. She talked of her obituary notice this time.

"I want it to say that I went fishing with Gom, and I went to be with my mother and father and my brother Jim."

She also said she wanted to give thanks to all of the people who made it possible for her to live so long. But there's one word she doesn't want in the obituary. That word is courage.

"I just wanted to live," she said through muffled sobs.

I tried to think about how I was going to compose my wife's obituary, and the tears too fell from my eyes and splashed across Bronnie's scalp.

Fishing with Gom, that's all I could come up with. For now, that will have to do.

August 2, 2000

Heading home

It's two months to the day that we brought Bronnie to the emergency room for what appeared to be just another annoying, temporary blockage in her intestines.

This afternoon, we will bring her home to die.

To prepare for her trip home, one of her great nurses from 2 East at Memorial Hospital showed me how to inject Bronnie with a dose of Valium through one of her ports. It took four injections to deliver the much-needed pain medication so her chills could fade and sleep sweep over her. My medic training from 30 years ago is of little value now. However, I was able to keep a steady hand and not commit any major snafus.

It's another busy day — but they are all filled with many dramas, each of the 60 days since Bronnie entered the emergency room.

And there is no question that Bronnie wants this to be her final act, the last soliloquy in her play. Again last night at the hospital, she pleaded with her doctor that she wanted to go. She kept pressing him on the point, and asked how her life would end and when. Her doctor couldn't answer either of those. He wasn't about to order a lethal load of morphine for Bronnie to use, and because of that, he couldn't say what would claim her life. It could be pneumonia; it could be one or more of her vital organs shutting down due to lack of nutrition. Bronnie wants death to come in her sleep. But even that, her doctor could not promise.

There is only one thing we know for certain. The end will come. It clings to her like a dark, enveloping shadow. Nothing of substance, but a fear that causes her to shake with chills and forces me to flush her veins with Valium. I am a weak opponent, but I refuse to give up the fight. Her life is still a miracle I want to embrace, to brush away the tears that slip down her cheeks, and to kiss her forehead a hundred times to prove life is still worth loving even now, even as she fades from my touch.

August 17, 2000

There are many downs, and only a few ups

Midnight began with a Zofran for nausea followed by a Valium for pain, the first that Bronnie had taken since she had come home. It seemed like a turning point, a place that leads only down to something vast and unknown, a path that leads only away, not toward anything. And so I gave her the Valium and the night passed.

In the morning, the nausea became worse and worse. At 9:30 a.m., another Zofran was given, and at 10:30 a.m. the second salvo of Valium.

Bronnie thought I should phone the doctor who's on call. I told her I would, but what good would it do? The doctor may not be familiar with your case history, and even so, there's not much a doctor could do. A home visit would not be in order. Pump in more medication would be the advice, I argued.

Bronnie relented. A look of resignation passed over her face.

"I guess it's going to be like this," she said, her voice trailing off.

I hoped it would not, but who could say. We have never been down this road, even if there's a road to follow. It's like coming up to a forest meadow at night, and suddenly the moon, whose silver beams of light had once guided you, goes dark behind a bank of clouds. You stumble across the clumps of grass and lose your footing as the ground drops from beneath your feet. So we walked into the meadow that morning searching for light and found only darkness.

But light did peak through. In the afternoon, just after Bronnie said she would have to take another shot of Zofran to stave off her nausea, she had another bounce. She didn't want to take the medication. So she tried to concentrate on something else. She asked to look at a box of old letters and mementos. She came across several of Andy's "signature" cards that he had drawn for Mother's Day and for her birthday. Bronnie's mind shifted away from the Zofran and focused on her son.

Ah, that was the light. Sonlight, spelled with an "o."

August 27, 2000

Another decision sealed with tears

It had been building for the past two or three weeks. At some point, we had to decide about Andy and whether he was going to Western Washington University for the fall quarter.

Naturally, I ruminated about it endlessly, trying to figure out the best time and situation in which to ask Andy and then, by far the more difficult of the scenarios, when to broach the subject with Bronnie. She had made it clear from the very beginning of this tortured summer that she wanted Andy back at school, no questions asked.

But then she didn't expect to be living this long. Bronnie thought she had reached the edge of the precipice several times before, especially when the blood swooshed out of her stomach and filled the suction bottle. Now, she had reached a plateau of sorts, taking fewer medications. Last night, we went through the evening without a Zofran or a Valium, a first in a long while.

That doesn't mean Bronnie is gaining strength. The skin on her arms and legs hangs in folds that remind me of my grandmother when she was in her 90s. Bronnie's body is chewing up her muscles in a relentless effort to gather strength in whatever way possible. Since Bronnie is receiving no nutrition, the only place to suck up reserves is to consume the very body tissue that once was the storehouse of all her vitality.

With Western starting in a little more than two weeks, I had to get the process going, with or without Bronnie's blessings. I figured it would be better talking to her if I were able to lay out all of the options first. Then we could ask for her blessing. Because it was clear Andy wanted to stay home. He said so when I finally put it to him at the dinner table last week. I had called from work earlier in the day to talk with someone at Western. It was several days before the Labor Day weekend and no one was around. I was told a dean would be calling back. He had some highfalutin title like "Dean of Student Judicial Issues." I was assured he was the one to talk to about Andy's situation.

Andy didn't need me to list the options. He wanted to be home. Period.

So I kept calling Western. Finally, late Wednesday, just as I was giving Bronnie a dose of Zofran, the phone rang. I let the answering machine snare the call. I figured it was another Kiwanis Club member calling up about an imminent delivery of more food. They have been performing this act of mercy for the past three weeks. But it wasn't. Instead the voice echoing from out of the dining room was none other than the dean from Western. Bronnie heard the voice and began to ask what it was all about. I didn't answer and rushed to the phone.

I grabbed the cordless receiver and hurried to the upstairs bedroom where I could keep the conversation out of Bronnie's hearing range. In our talk, which lasted a good 10 minutes, I relayed to the dean what was going on at home. He went through the options that Andy could take, everything from taking a reduced course load to dropping out entirely and then reapplying for the winter quarter. That's the option I said we wanted to take. He then began telling me about the death of his mother.

"I guess it's much different for sons, losing their mother," the dean said. It took him months to get over the loss, he said.

The sadness still lingers. I could tell in his voice. He agreed keeping Andy out of the fall quarter was the best thing, the only option that made any sense.

And that's the way I presented it to Bronnie the next day. But I wasn't the one who brought up the subject. She knew something was afoot following the previous evening's phone call.

"Let's talk about Western," she asked us after summoning Andy and me to her bedside. "What do you want to do Andy?"

Andy was clear, softening his voice to make what he had to say persuasive without being too emphatic.

"I want to be here with you, Mom."

Her eyes filled with tears as we talked about foregoing the fall quarter and reapplying for the winter term. The tears slid down the bony ridge of her cheeks as I handed her several tissues to dry her face. I, too, started to cry as Andy wrapped his arms around her and told her, in a voice that broke your heart, "I'll do anything for you, Mom."

What Andy wanted was to be at his mother's side, to the very end. Bronnie relented. She knew she had no choice. When Andy left the room to get her a glass of cold water, she turned to me and asked again, how long will she live.

"What if I live till the winter term begins," she asked me. "I don't want to live that Iong." She paused, and pleaded with me, "l won't live that long, will I?"

How often does a husband say to his wife of 21 years: "No, you won't live that long. You are getting weaker each day."

I looked up at Bronnie and thought I saw relief in her face.

It will end, but as I could tell from my conversation with the dean from Western, the memory of that ending lasts forever.

September 8, 2000

Watching Jed go by

I wonder what thoughts crossed Bronnie's mind Tuesday morning as she lay there in her rented hospital bed, the sound of the oxygen machine whirring away as air pulsed into her nostrils through a long, snaky plastic hose. What was she thinking as she watched Jed standing nearby, his backpack in hand, and then the front door swinging open to the outside world where a school bus waited to take him to the first day of a new year at Eisenhower High School.

Jed bounded out the door, a sight Bronnie probably couldn't see since her field of vision was blocked by a nightstand crowded with bottles of body cream and glasses half filled with water. She might not have wanted to see it anyway for it would have meant she was witnessing another routine in her life taken from her, never to be replaced, never to be re-enacted — that fleeting sight of Jed as he scurried toward the open portal of the yellow bus, his heavy backpack swaying from side to side in rhythm to life that waited for him outside of our house, far from view, so far now from Bronnie's caring touch.

I wonder what she thinks when scenes like this play out beyond her reach but within the range of her hearing. With all of the morphine that is being pumped into her, the sounds must come out disconnected, jumbled in a bedlam of Jed's constant chatter and the patter of my over-solicitous encouragements, "Good job, Jed. Atta boy, get your socks on."

It's the life Bronnie was once accustomed to, and we play it out each day for her despite the medications coursing through her veins. Her mind is so muddled at times she can't figure out what she just said moments earlier. But then she will have an interlude of clarity where everything makes sense and she can recall distinct details of the past.

Another pulse of morphine from the automatic pump will wash that clarity away and she will doze off again, her eyelids sometimes stuck half-way open, causing her gaze to stay fixed somewhere beyond your face as you strain to bend down closer to her, her breath hot against your cheek, her forehead cool to the press of your lips as you kiss and say, "I love you," again and again, repeating the refrain as if it has a saving grace to it.

I wonder what she thought when we forgot Jed would be arriving early from his first day of school and she spied the bus before anyone. Maybe she felt panic-stricken at first. I hope she felt there was still a purpose to her life. Clearly there is, if nothing more than to keep me moving straight ahead instead of veering off on another project, which is where I was, up-stairs screwing in another piece of hardware to Jed's new armoire.

"The bus is here," Bronnie exclaimed in as loud a voice as she could muster.

Jed scampered back into the house, skipping past Bronnie's bed in the living room where her days and nights are spent. Bronnie hardly has the strength to reach the bathroom once a day. Luckily she was making that trip yesterday afternoon for if she hadn't, Jed might still be out in the bus waiting for his dad, who should have known better. Instead, as always, he relied on his mother to see him through.

How we will miss her unerring touch. I wonder if that thought, too, haunts her as she lay there hearing Jed munch on a bowlful of pizza Combos, his treat for the first day of school successfully brought to an end, a passing of a ritual that Bronnie will never see again.

From what I heard later when talking on the phone with his special education teacher, Jed had a great first day. From all accounts, it was prob-ably his best first day ever.

For Bronnie, though, it was more misery. She didn't say so, but I could see it in her eyes. The vacant stare had given way to one of sorrow, deep sorrow at seeing the family she had raised pass by her — footfalls receding down a darkened hallway, soon silent, so far removed from the joy of that first day of school for Andy, years ago, when she was a young mother, free to believe in tomorrow, free to believe there would be another first day of school, and another and another.

September 9, 2000

Calling out for Jiminy Cricket

I am numb from head to foot. The days seep through the thin cloth of reality, so slowly if you pay much attention to it, the whole process ceases and you are standing there, staring at a photo or a word she had scribbled down, and wandering off in your mind to a time when she was still alive, desperately hanging on as I am now, to the shreds of memory that are now all that remain.

It was two Saturdays ago, on the night of October 14, when I knew the end was near. I just didn't know how close it was.

I was in the kitchen trying to wash the dishes. I was watching the Washington Huskies football game. I had gone into the living room to check on Bronnie and cool her face with a wet towel. She had become increasingly disoriented, not making sense of the surroundings and not really responding to anything I was saying.

That night, though, seemed worse for some reason. Andy had gone out that night to a movie with some of his friends. So I was alone with Bron. I thought it would be good to get some water into her mouth. She hadn't been drinking at all during the past few days. So I crushed up some ice cubes the way she liked, stuffing four or five cubes into a small plastic baggie and then smashing them with a large wooden mallet. I poised a few chips of ice on a plastic spoon and lowered them to her lips. A few slipped into her mouth.

In the kitchen, I could hear Jed rustling around for something. I left Bronnie there to let the ice melt slowly in her mouth and headed back to see what Jed was up to. When I got there, Jed was asking about batteries. Earlier I had replaced his VCR control with a new set of batteries, so I knew he didn't need them. My voice began to rise higher and higher as I tried to tell Jed the batteries were fine.

Then I heard something crash in the living room.

Bronnie's face suddenly flashed in my mind.

I ran into the living room and saw the bed was empty. She wasn't there.

I knew she couldn't get up on her own. She hadn't been able to do that for the past couple of days.

I rushed to the far side of the bed and found her there, lying face down on her covers and a pile of pillows. Bronnie had rolled out of bed. The ice chips had probably startled her awake and she had coughed, trying to swallow the small thimble-sized splash of water down her throat. She then must have rolled to her left and was unable to stop her fall or even cry out for help.

We had never put up the sides on the hospital bed. There seemed no need for this. Bronnie had always been peaceful lying there, always able to get up when she needed to and always willing to move about in the bed to keep the menacing bed sore on her tailbone from getting worse.

That all changed. Now she was utterly helpless, her body lying there on the living room floor, her muscles unresponsive to any commands from me, or worse yet, from her. I tried to lift her, but I stumbled badly. I almost fell on top of her.

I kept calling to her, "Bronnie, my God, Bronnie, Bronnie." I frantically checked to see if her IV line had been ripped out in the fall. It looked fine. I began to curse myself for, first, putting those damn ice chips in her mouth and, worse yet, leaving her and going into the kitchen.

I tried pulling Bronnie to her feet. But that was impossible. I then tried to lift her to her knees. It wasn't easy. I first had to get in front of her and that meant tiptoeing around the table and a stack of cardboard boxes that we had set up next to Bronnie's bed so she could reach tissues, paper and pens. A basket of photographs fell to the floor as I pushed my way to the other end of the bed where Bronnie's head still lay, thankfully on a pillow that had followed her when she fell.

I got around and pulled her shoulders up. That's when our two faces finally met.

Bronnie had a dazed look to her. And then, a childish expression filled her face. "Jiminy Cricket," she piped up in a voice filled with sparkle and air. It was as if she had seen the "Pinocchio" feature for the first time and had exclaimed out loud, in a little girl's voice brimming with innocence, "Jiminy Cricket." She kept repeating it as I tried to raise her from her knees to the bed.

She gazed deeply into my face as if she wanted me to answer her back. So I did. "Jiminy Cricket" was my feeble reply. But she didn't seem satisfied, and kept saying his name over and over, as if she wanted Jiminy Cricket to appear and grant her a wish.

I knew what that wish would have been, and it wouldn't have been to get her back to her bed. She wanted to be released. She wanted, as she had pleaded for earlier in the day, "to go."

I remembered an old fireman's carry that I was taught years ago in first aid training. I clasped my hands around her back, slipping my arms under hers and then I rose straight up, keeping my back as stiff as possible. It worked. But I missed my mark. Instead of the bed, I had to deposit her on the seat of the portable commode.

I was now panting heavily and sweat was sweeping down my forehead. Still, she kept repeating, "Jiminy Cricket." I then took a deep breath and lifted her again, this time pivoting as I did. I had never lifted so hard in my life. It was all I could do to move her, but it worked. We both collapsed on the bed, her voice emitting a sigh of relief as she exclaimed for the final time, "Jiminy Cricket."

The bars along the side of the bed seemed too easy to lift into place. Why hadn't I done this earlier? Why did I let her fall?

Bronnie lay exhausted on the bed. Her body was far down on the mattress, but I knew there was no chance of me moving her any higher up. So I piled pillows under her feet and let her rest.

I, too, rested as tears welled up in my eyes. My hands were shaking. I knew the end was coming. But not now. I still wanted to tell her I loved her, and for her to recognize me one more time. Was that asking for too much?

Yes, it was.

Sunday, October 29, 2000 — 13 days after Bronnie died.

Beloved

Bronnie and I met under the most unusual set of circumstances, incredible in fact. And it was imperative that I not — and let me repeat that again — that I not go in the *right direction*, but instead go *left*.

Let me explain.

Back in late May of 1973, I had just received — much to the dismay of my first sergeant — an honorable discharge from the Army. I served as a medical corpsman, and left San Antonio, Texas, with my Volkswagen bug stuffed to the ceiling with all my worldly possessions. I had only one goal in mind, to leave Texas as soon as possible. It's a very big state and it took two days but I finally got out of Texas and had made my way, along with a friend of mine, to the eastern edge of Colorado.

I had planned on taking some time off and then going back to Illinois — I grew up in Northbrook, a suburb of Chicago — and attend the University of Illinois' journalism school. I called from a pay phone at a deserted truck stop and got hold of my mother. I wanted to know when I had to head back home.

She had some bad news. The university had no room in its journalism school. They said I would have to wait until the winter term.

That's when fate stepped in.

Having nowhere to go, I asked my friend: Which way? We were literally at a crossroad, with one highway heading north and another heading west. To the north was Denver, the big metropolis. To the west, at the end of the highway was the small town of Durango. My friend said he had been through there once, and kind of liked the place.

That was good enough for me. I said fine. Let's go. So I took a *left* turn at the crossroad and headed west to Durango. How right that turn would prove to be!

Bronnie at her wedding on Aug. 11, 1979

Compared to Texas, Durango was like Shangri-La — with mountains, quaking Aspen, rivers, and even a newly opened ski resort. It also had a small college. Unable to finish my senior year due to Richard Nixon and the draft, I decided to enroll at Fort Lewis College.

One day while going to class, I noticed a poster that announced a casting call for "The Man of La Mancha." I love the play, so later that week I headed off to the tryouts.

When I entered the theater, there were a large number of people sitting in the center of the theater. So I settled into a seat off to the side. When my turn came to read my lines on stage, I belted them out with a ferocity that even surprised me. I think it woke the director up for he almost fell out of his chair.

Anyway, when I headed back to my seat, that's when I saw her, sitting there in the middle of this knot of people. A warm smile greeted me. But it was her hair that fascinated me. Stunning. It was the greatest 'do I had ever seen. The ultimate Afro. Beauty, in a word.

I knew then and there I had to get to know this girl "with the big hair."

A few weeks following the tryouts, I got my chance to spend some time with Bronnie.

But first let me set the scene for this date. Bronnie lived with three other girls in an apartment in Durango. It was a wild place. Remember, this was the '70s and it was a time for Bohemian lifestyles. There was always something going on at the apartment, and it often involved loud music and lots of people.

Well, one day at school, one of her roommates told me about a party they were having at their apartment. It was a most unusual party. A real ice-breaker of sorts. These young women had come up with the idea of having a "body painting party." Yes, you heard me right, body parts and paint.

Naturally, I wanted to go. My god, what red-blooded American male wouldn't.

It was a memorable party. Here's what I entered into my writer's journal about that night in the winter of 1974:

"I opened the door. It neither creaked nor groaned; it simply opened unto a man, bare-chested, and a woman painting his shoulder. Without removing my coat I headed straight for the refrigerator and from there retrieved the last of the Walter's. ... I sipped thirstily. B.J. (that was Bronnie's nickname back then) chided me, 'Is that all you came for?'

"What a vision? Her hair was teased nervously in every conceivable direction. This Afro-hairdo lent her a devil-may-care-attitude of moral decay.

"Her head tilted as I talked to one of her roommates. Bronnie's moist breath swarmed like bees buzzing into my ear. Her lips, marble smooth and glistening with delight, tacked from ear to cheek to chin to lower lip, sailing with the breezes, as my head pivoted, frolicking in the warmth. She kissed. I too."

Well, since we are in a church, we will end it there. Needless to say, I was infatuated with Bronnie, her hair, her smile, everything about her.

And so began our love story more than 25 years ago. You may call it coincidence, but I prefer calling it fate. Thank God for that.

☆ ☆ ☆

For the record, I want to say our marriage began with a bang, not a whimper.

It was on our honeymoon, and it was then that I realized there was another fascination in her life that, at times, far exceeded anything I could deliver. I'm talking about her love for fishing. She learned it at the side of her grandmother Gom, fishing for little minuscule perch at Kangaroo Lake, in Door County, Wisconsin, where her family's summer cabin was located.

I knew she liked to fish so on our honeymoon in Hawaii I decided to book a trip on a charter boat, and off we went, hoping just to enjoy the ocean spray along the beautiful Kona Coast. But I quickly realized that when you are fishing with Bronnie, it's never just a sightseeing cruise — you're there to catch fish.

After only on the water about an hour, two marlin hit the surface. One slammed into my lure but spit it out. The other hit Bronnie's and stuck.

Twenty minutes later Bronnie had reeled in this leviathan from the deep. It was enormous. It stretched nearly 10 feet in length. But how to land the damn thing? We had no idea.

While the huge marlin was pounding against the side of the boat, the captain yelled over to me, "Get that box." It was a rectangular wooden box with no distinguishing markings. I tried to hand it to him but he shook his head.

"Open it," he hollered. I flipped the latch and opened the lid. Inside was a loaded revolver.

Imagine now our surprise when the captain cried out to me: "Shoot it."

Now folks, that's the only way to start a marriage, with you holding a revolver in one hand and your wife holding a 480-pound marlin in the other.

✳ ✳ ✳

Our greatest adventure of all was raising a family.

For us, though, some things never come easy. We figured Andy was so eager to see the world, he decided to pop out and see what was happening. Unfortunately, he was 10 weeks early.

So on April 11, at 2:30 in the morning, after an emergency ambulance ride from Mount Vernon that took Bronnie to the University Hospital in Seattle, she gave birth to Spencer "Andy" Shannon Hatton Jr. He tipped the scales at a whopping 3 pounds 2 ounces.

It was from this moment, starting from Andy's birth, that Bronnie's love for family took on a whole new perspective. She would seek only what is best for her child. Of such was the love Bronnie had for Andy, and later, for Jed.

I mean here she is, just a day out of the hospital after undergoing a Caesarean section and she's out scrounging around Seattle for a breast-pump machine. She was determined that Andy would not be force-fed formula milk but would at least get some of her breast milk.

It didn't matter if she had to lug this heavy, bulky machine from the store to our car. And it didn't matter that she had to stay up hours on end extracting the most minuscule amounts of "mother's milk." She wanted it done, and by God it got done.

Her resolve never wavered as Andy left the hospital's incubator and headed off into manhood.

But the most difficult time came in 1992, when she was first diagnosed with ovarian cancer. Andy was 12 years old at the time, about the same age Bronnie was when her mother died.

She didn't want that to happen to her son. She didn't want to leave him motherless. She didn't want to miss his birthday parties and the night he went to his first prom or his graduation from high school and, in the deepest corner of her heart, the mix of overwhelming emotions, both of loss and triumph, when seeing her son Andy head off to college for the very first time.

She didn't want to miss any of that, so she fought the cancer. She went through the surgeries, all four of them, and the chemotherapy and debilitating effects of two radiation treatments.

She enjoyed eight more birthdays and was able to live through all that she had dreamt. What an extraordinary accomplishment.

And at the end, when all was lost and she knew the days would be fewer and fewer, she received the greatest gift a mother could ever get — that of her son whom she struggled so hard to live for, comfort her at the darkest hours of her life.

He stood by her, he knelt by her, he rubbed her feet with lotion and gave her the medications that would ease her pain, and serenaded her with music from his guitar.

During the two months that Bronnie was home, each morning he would greet her with the usual, "Hi mama-do," to which she would reply, "Hi Andy-do," and then he would kiss her on the cheek and say, "I love you."

Andy sketched this family portrait in elementary school

☆ ☆ ☆

Bronnie showed no less resolve with our second son, Jed. We expected our second child to be the "normal" kid. We had enough excitement with Andy's delivery.

And that's how it was for the first year or so after Jed was born on August 4, 1984. But his laughter soon turned to cold stares and his speech, once so searching and spontaneous, turned to monosyllables and, at times, nothing at all. Just before his third birthday, Jed was diagnosed with autism.

Autism is perhaps one of the cruelest of disabilities. It gives you a son and then takes him away. But Bronnie wasn't going to quit just yet. She knew we had a monumental struggle on our hands, and once again she proved to be more than capable of meeting the challenge.

There was one episode that best describes what Bronnie meant to Jed's life, and really to many parents of children with special needs. She proved you could get things accomplished, but you had to fight for them.

It took place at the time Jed was ready to leave preschool and head into his first year in the Yakima school system. School psychologists gave Jed the usual battery of tests. They were all verbal commands, none of which made any sense to Jed. He failed them miserably.

Bronnie knew he could do more. She remembered the time when he was three. Valentine's Day was approaching and he turned to us, and in a clear voice, said: "I ... love ... you." He said it only once or twice, but that proved to Bronnie her son was there — he just needed some coaxing to come out of his shell.

So we sat down with administrators and the school psychologist. We listened to their verdict: Jed would be better off in a multi-handicapped room with very limited academic work.

We were stunned. Bronnie got angry. "I want Jed in Mrs. Dilley's classroom," she told the special education director. We had visited Mrs. Dilley's special education classroom and found it was great, with lots of activities and academic challenges.

No, the director said, we don't feel he's ready for that. Besides, he said, Jed will need to have a fulltime aide with him and the district just can't afford that right now.

He really shouldn't have said that, but he did.

They waited for us to sign the education plan and end the meeting. That's when Bronnie delivered her ultimatum: "He's not going into the multi-handicapped classroom. He's going into Mrs. Dilley's classroom and he's also going to get his own teacher's aide."

There was a pause while she gathered her breath. "And I'm not leaving this room until he does."

Well, one look into her eyes told everyone there, including me, that she wasn't about to budge. So the special education director agreed. Jed got his own teacher's aide — an unprecedented move back then — and he got the classroom that we wanted, and that he needed.

Thanks to the district's support and the tremendous help from wonderful special education teachers like Mrs. Dilley, Jed has succeeded in school. His speech has improved and his smile has returned to his face. He's now a sophomore at Eisenhower High School, where he ventures outside the special education classroom most of the school day.

Yes, that's Jed, the kid few thought could do anything — except for his older brother, his dad and most of all, his mom.

✧ ✧ ✧

On Monday morning, Bronnie died.

Shortly before her death, she got a chance to wave goodbye to Jed as I put him on the bus that morning. I went back to the living room and sat down on the couch, just across from where Bronnie was lying in her bed. I could tell she was in some discomfort for she moaned softly after each breath.

Having been up most of the night with her, I began to doze off. I thought she was saying "hi" to me, so I answered back: "Hi, Bron. I'm just going to take a little nap."

That went on for a few more minutes, she saying "Hi" and me saying "Hi" back in return.

And then I fell fast asleep.

About a half hour later, the phone rang and I woke up. It was the wrong number. I hung up and noticed stillness in the room. I went to Bronnie's side and saw her face had changed. Gone was the look of pain. Calmness had spread across her beautiful face.

I shook her and a final breath issued up from her lungs.

I kissed her softly and said, "I love you, Bron."

Eulogy delivered at Bronnie's memorial service on October 21, 2000.

Let those lost lives live through us

A fish boil has all the makings of a Shakespearean drama.

Into a boiling cauldron goes whitefish, caught that morning in the clear, cold waters of Lake Michigan. Then a husky assistant, his thick neck looped with an apron that's cinched loosely around his waist, tosses in a heaping pile of red potatoes and onions and adds the only spice to the brew — salt.

But unlike Shakespeare's "Macbeth," the cauldron is never stirred and there are no haggard-looking witches offering grim incantations. Instead, the pot is left to boil, churned by a blaze of dried cedar logs.

Just when the bubbling becomes riotous, out comes the white-haired "master boiler." The clanging of a bell heralds his entrance. In one hand he carries a large metal container filled with kerosene. He nears the blaze and tips the contents onto the fire. Up rises a flash of flames and intense heat.

The famed "boil over" skims off all of the excess fish oils and leaves in its afterglow a near-perfect blend of whitefish, potatoes and onions, ready to be eaten by the ravenous onlookers.

It's just another night at the Viking Grill, where fish boils are dished out every night of the week. It's an aged, ham-and-egg restaurant that's the center of life in Ellison Bay, Wisconsin, a tiny town near the very tip of the Door County peninsula that separates the waters of Green Bay and Lake Michigan.

I was one of those watching the Grill's famed fish boil, congratulating the master boiler with a loud "well done." He smiled and headed back to the kitchen to prepare yet another kettle of fish. These are the sights and smells and tastes of a summer now fading into fall.

In late July, my two sons and I flew out to Chicago to be with my mother, sister and her husband. We drove up to Bailey's Harbor, a small town along the coastline of Lake Michigan. It is in the heart of Door County, the tourist destination for many suburbanites who drag themselves through the work week in Chicago's sweltering heat with only one goal in mind: to load up the car on Friday night and head up to relax for a day or two in the cool Wisconsin air and feast on fried perch, grilled bratwurst and such intensely Scandinavian treats as whitefish.

But for me, it was more than a summer's vacation spent devouring local cuisine. It held special memories of a time three years ago when I had last stood in line at the Viking Grill waiting for my serving of steaming hot whitefish. It had been raining that night, and we were forced to sit in a barracks-like shelter behind the restaurant. At my side were my two sons and my wife, Bronnie.

It was her last fish boil. Eleven months ago, after an eight-year battle with cancer, she died, never getting a chance to return to Door County, where she enjoyed so many summer trips as a young girl. Although my wife and I had first met in Colorado, we had both grown up in the Chicago area, with our two families building summer homes in Door County, hers along the shores of Kangaroo Lake and mine on the bluffs near Ellison Bay.

So I had to be there again at the Viking Grill, to stand and watch the boil over with my own eyes, to scan the flames as she would have, and feel the warmth of the fire washing over my face, as it surely would have over hers.

I had returned to Door County for a family reunion and a final memorial service so my wife's far-flung family of six brothers and sisters, aunts and uncles, and nieces and nephews could all say goodbye. We had flown there to be with others, but most of all, I had flown there to walk in the shadows of the past, to retrace the memories that my wife and I had shared in our 25 years together, and in a way, relive them as if she were at my side.

It's something I never would have considered had it not been for a dear friend who wrote to me after Bronnie had died. She wrote about the pain of losing someone whom you had loved so deeply. Her pain needed no explanation. She had lost a beautiful son in a horrible accident near Ellensburg. His seat belt failed and he was thrown from the car and died under the automobile's unforgiving weight.

In her letter, she included a passage from a book she had recently read, "Captain Corelli's Mandolin," written by Louis de Bernieres.

This summer, Hollywood came out with a movie based on the book. But in this case, the written word, far from any image a movie could possess, captures the feeling of those who have lost a loved one. Here's the passage my friend sent. The quote is from a doctor whose wife had died:

"When loved ones die, you have to live on their behalf. See things as though with their eyes. Remember how they used to say things. And use those words oneself. Be thankful that you can do things they cannot. And also feel the sadness of it. This is how I live without Pelagia's mother. I have no interest in flowers, but for her I look at a rockrose or a lily. For her I eat aubergines, because she loved them."

Like the doctor who finds himself gazing at a rockrose and feasting on eggplant, I too have taken up activities my wife had enjoyed so much. That's why I have now become the curator of her Beanie Babies. She adored her collection of these curious little creatures with names as "Pounce" and "Ewey," and had separated them into bags marked for specific seasons of the year.

I made light of her collection, but that all changed after her death. I knew then what I had to do. So when spring came around, out came the bag she had so carefully marked with the words, "Spring Beanie Babies." I arranged them on a table in our living room and there they sat, as the lilacs bloomed outside, their funny faces greeting me each morning. A friend among friends.

Now, I have taken it one step further. I give her Beanie Babies away as gifts. My wife was always the ultimate giver of gifts, doling out presents to friends and families and perfect strangers, in good times and bad.

Back in Door County, during the memorial service for my wife's family, I gave a Beanie Baby to Megan, a young daughter of one of her nephews. She had just been diagnosed with cystic fibrosis, a disease that infects the lungs and makes breathing painful and labored. I knew if Bronnie were alive, she would have done something special for that little girl.

So the blue bunny rabbit with the funny long ears went to Megan.

I may not have made sense of my wife's death, but I did ease the pain this summer by following the advice from "Captain Corelli's Mandolin."

Those of us, who have lost a wife or husband, father or mother, brother or sister, son or daughter, fill the void with sweet memories of a love fixed in time. If it means going to a fish boil or keeping track of Beanie Babies, so be it. No matter how tragic or painful, death will never claim these simple joys.

September 23, 2001

Tribute to a great Mom

Contrary to what Warner Bros. cartoons have portrayed, motherhood doesn't arrive on the wings of storks.

Nor are there the crashing of cymbals to mark the occasion, or college exams to cram for, or some angelic voice whispering in your ear: "OK, it's time now to be a mother."

What I've seen is something far more profound. It's as if the entire body and soul make a shift in a different direction, that the days of being a girl and sweetheart and wife wash away in a refreshing shower of clear, pure water and all that was once you, the kid with frizzed-out hair and flavored lip balm, suddenly becomes another you, the woman with someone else to care for.

That someone now depends on you not only for a kiss to the cheek but for the very basics of life, like food, and more food, and protection, the warm hugs and soft cotton things that wrap around this morsel of life you have now called "Kirsten" or "Eric" or, as in our case, "Andy."

I may not know what motherhood is all about, but I am somewhat of an expert on great mothers, and I got lucky enough to marry one, my late wife, Bronnie.

Boy, did she have to become a mother in a hurry, like about 10 weeks early. We hadn't even attended our first Lamaze class in the spring of 1980 when she was rushed to the emergency room after waking up in the middle of the night with a sharp pain, our bed where she had slept filled with a pool of darkened blood.

A frantic day followed, with lots of tests and ultrasounds that showed a beating heart beneath the thin, taut skin of a young woman not quite ready to be a mom.

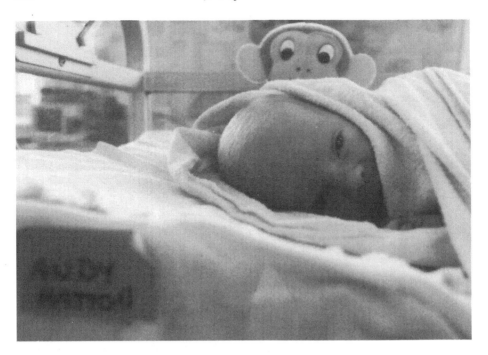

That changed rapidly as she took a 60-mile ambulance ride from Mount Vernon to the University of Washington Medical Center in Seattle. I tried to follow in our small Datsun, but the speedier ambulance zoomed away, leaving me alone and wondering what I would find when I finally reached the hospital.

What greeted me was a determined woman ready to have a child, regardless of whether the baby was 10 weeks early or not. I kept telling her the emergency would blow over. I even started to read to her about the Lamaze classes that we were signed up for, thinking we'd still get a chance. She glared at me, a look that cut my words short in mid-sentence. Get ready, she said, you're going to be a dad real soon.

She was right. At 2:30 a.m. the next day, our son, Andy, was born by Caesarean section. He weighed a mere 3 pounds, 2 ounces.

I was the only one to cheer his entry into the world. The one who suffered the most was fast asleep. The doctors had to sedate Bronnie moments before she gave birth. That was the last time she ever lost sight of her son.

The next morning she was all business, the kind that mothers do so well. She knew how good it was to breast-feed our newborn son, and that's what she wanted to get done. But that seemed impossible at the time.

Andy was a preemie. He lived in a small incubator and had little strength, certainly not enough to be breast-fed. And because the birth was so early — nearly three months — Bronnie's body was nowhere near the point of producing enough breast milk to feed even a tiny baby.

Did that stop her? No way. Motherhood stepped in, and it wasn't about to budge. She was determined to give our son breast milk, and that was that.

So a few days after undergoing major surgery — the kind that leaves your stomach muscles sliced apart and your ability to lift restricted to raising a gallon of milk and nothing more — Bronnie decided to call around in hopes of renting a breast-pump machine. She found one at a nearby medical supply distributor and, while I was back in Mount Vernon on an errand, she went to the store and hauled this 30-pound machine out to the car, a move that could have torn out her sutures and left her bleeding on the sidewalk.

Sheer grit prevailed.

She then drove out to my aunt and uncle's house near the hospital. There she camped out with the machine and started the long process of suctioning out breast milk, something the hospital nurses warned would be a nearly impossible task.

That only fueled her desire to get it done. With the breast machine going "ta-paka-ta-paka-ta-paka," Bronnie extracted a few precious drops of breast milk. It took hours to produce an ounce or two.

It meant everything to her, and she knew it would mean everything to our preemie son. Soon, that machine became Bronnie's constant companion, the newest member of our family.

That was the beginning of her motherhood.

Twelve years later, she would face another impossible task. She was diagnosed with advanced ovarian cancer, and instead of our son fighting for his life, she was fighting for hers.

After surgery to remove the cancerous tumor, while she lay in the hospital — the very same place where Andy was born — Bronnie vowed not to let her son face what she had to when she was 12. Bronnie lost her mother back then, and had to be raised by an older sister since her father had died years earlier.

So she fought, through three more surgeries, radiation treatments and a battery of chemotherapy regimens that stripped her of her hair and vitality, all with one goal, one purpose, to be there as a mother, to make his lunch in the morning, to cheer him on at ball games, and to celebrate his birthdays with banners and a homemade cake worthy of a crown prince.

At Andy's graduation ceremony from Davis High School in June 1999, it was sweltering in the auditorium. Bronnie was in between chemotherapy treatments at the time, having survived a nearly tragic reaction to a chemo drug earlier in the winter. The hot auditorium drained me, but I looked over at her and she was radiant.

After Andy received his diploma, we stood outside with hundreds of other graduating seniors and their families. I got Andy and his mom to stand together for a photo. I asked him to raise his arm in a gesture of victory.

Andy wasn't quick enough. Bronnie had already raised her fist, and exclaimed in a triumphant voice that swept through the Davis High court-yard: "I made it!"

Yes, she did, keeping her promise with the resolve and grace only a mother can offer a child.

I told you she was a great mom, and in the eyes of her son — the one who matters the most — she was the very best.

May 11, 2003

A PRIDE OF SONS

Andy greeted the world in the early morning hours of April 11, 1980, some 10 weeks premature. Despite the difficulties of his birth, Andy grew stronger. Four years later, Jed also took the same approach, arriving five weeks early. Though worried about his emergency delivery, doctors found no apparent medical problems. It took another two years before specialists would determine Jed's delays in speech and social interaction were the result of autism.

Two sons — with so many differences, yet so much in common. They cared deeply for each other and proved to those around them there was little they couldn't overcome, even during the worst of times.

Andy and his little brother, Jed

Silence is a part of college — for parents

Here's a hint for parents when they take their first-born to college. Hire someone else to do it. Because if you don't, expect the inevitable. You will leave with something you promised would never happen: tears in your eyes.

Our family went through this ordeal several weeks ago when our 19-year-old son, Andy, a Davis High School grad, headed off for his freshman year at Western Washington University in Bellingham. Preparing for his departure went smoother than anticipated, thanks to the friendly folks at Western who were kind enough to send along a checklist of what to bring and what to keep stuffed under the bed. Don't pack as if it's an expedition to the North Pole. Forget the labels on boxer shorts and socks. No one is going to steal your designer jeans, let alone the unmentionables. And skip the big stereo system and wide screen TV. Remember, these are dorm rooms, the brochure says, not penthouse apartments.

Despite this plea by university officials to keep our son's belongings to a bare minimum, we still ended up cramming enough into our sport utility vehicle to render the rearview mirror useless. How do you compress into a confined space such oddly shaped items as an iMac computer, a 15-inch monitor, and a steamer trunk? And being a past member of one of Yakima's hot rock'n'roll bands, my son could hardly leave behind his electric guitar and amplifier.

Fitting all of these into our car became my task. That's the role us dads play. We end up doling out money like human Pez dispensers, and assume the title of "The Packer of Things Both Large and Small."

The university warned us about the "day of unloading." This process is akin to the entire city of Sunnyside, roughly 12,000 souls, descending upon a patch of earth the size of a Walmart parking lot — all on the same day and with all their worldly possessions in tow.

It sounds crazy, but somehow the unloading all works out.

Sure there were delays. Our car idled for 10 or so minutes as we waited to pull into the circular drive leading to Nash Hall, my son's dorm, a miniature skyscraper that overlooks picturesque Puget Sound. But even that didn't seem so bad, especially for those of us parents who needed an early-morning jolt. On the corner across from the dorm, volunteers were handing out free cups of Starbucks coffee.

In less than an hour, my son had moved into his new home. We even found a spot for his guitar and amplifier. The process had been so casual, so routine, the fact that our son would not be returning to Yakima where he had lived since the age of 2 didn't seem to matter.

Later that afternoon, after we met his roommate and then strolled outside to say our farewells from a sidewalk outside the dorm, it struck me that this is no ordinary moment in time we had crossed. It certainly deserves something more than a free cup of Starbucks.

We are not alone. Thousands of other families who sent their sons and daughters off to college this fall also share in the joy. It took miracles, thousands of them, to bring their teenagers to the first day of college.

For our son Andy, the miracle took place 19 years ago, the very day he was born at the University of Washington Medical Center. An ambulance had taken my wife there on a wild 60-mile ride from a hospital in Mount Vernon. Doctors feared she was going to give birth prematurely. It was 10 weeks before her official due date, so there was good reason to be hyperventilating.

At 2 a.m. the day after the ambulance ride, doctors saw signs the baby was undergoing stress. In 15 minutes, the university's top surgeon had scrubbed and was ready to perform the Caesarean. He asked if I would like to join him in the operating room. How do you say no to witnessing the birth of your first child? So I went along.

I can't recall much about the operation. All I remember is my heart racing wildly and one of the attending physicians complaining about how badly the Sonics were playing. Then the chief surgeon announced, "Here he comes." Up popped a screaming baby boy from behind a shroud of white surgical linen. The surgeon showed him off to me and lowered him into the waiting arms of a nurse, who placed him gently on a scale to be weighed and measured.

Andy and Jed enjoy swimming at the YMCA's summer day camp

"He looks big," I said excitedly. The nurse stared at me in disbelief. "Not really," she answered back. Three pounds, two ounces. Fifteen inches in length. Just big enough to fit snugly into a shoebox.

For the next six weeks, Andy's home was in a hospital Isolette, a small incubator for premature babies where his every move and every breath were monitored. Even now I can hear the alarms going off telling the nurses my son's breathing had slowed or stopped. While it brought unspeakable horror to my wife and me, to the nurses it was nothing unusual. They would calmly go over to my son and reach in with their hands, rubbing the soft skin on the bottoms of his feet. The breathing would return and the monitor would be reset. That would go on again and again until, one day, the alarms stopped and our son finally came home.

Andy had survived being born a preemie, and now was standing there before me, a bit taller than I had remembered, saying goodbye.

At this time, you want to say the right thing to your son. But I came up empty, mumbling half-completed sentences and a farewell dotted with "I love you" and the painfully trite admonition, "Don't forget to call."

I guess I was too stunned to feel anything until we started to head out of Bellingham. As we entered the on-ramp leading to the interstate, I could see in the mirror our 15-year-old son Jed jostling around in the back seat.

It must have finally sunk in that he was now alone. His big brother Andy had been his constant companion this past summer, enabling him to attend a YMCA sports camp. Jed couldn't have gone without him for Jed is autistic and needs someone close by to keep him safe and to help him fill the days with fun things to do, whether it's swimming on a hot afternoon or playing catch with a baseball. Andy was always there, more than a mere aide, a big brother when it counted most.

Now it was over. Jed looked around and spoke from his heart, calling out the name of his best buddy: "Andy."

We listened hard, but there was no reply.

October 10, 1999

It's OK, I'm with the band

The High Dive is easy to spot in Seattle's Fremont district. Its long, slender neon sign reveals a svelte woman diving headlong into the abyss of nightfall.

On the sidewalk outside its front door, a chalkboard lists the bands playing inside. Last Saturday, there were four. Like its neon sign, the nightclub is long and slender with a bar that extends nearly three-quarters of the length of one wall. At the far end is a stage where the bands play.

It's 12:30 a.m. and the place is still crowded, with young professionals clutching pint-sized schooners of beer and chatting away incessantly, a few with cell phones clicking blurred photos of friends. Those closest to the stage have their eyes fixed on the musicians setting up their gear and going through routine sound checks. The bass guitar throbs to life.

I smile. I know that sound. I should. It's my son playing.

I hadn't planned on being in Seattle last weekend, but when Andy called to say his band — The Cast of Characters — was taking center stage in the Fremont district, how could I resist? I mean, how often does a white-haired 56-year-old get a chance to visit a hip, eclectic community that prides itself in its larger-than-life sculpture of Lenin, a "Pagan Hootenanny" called Trolloween and its annual World Naked Bike Ride (it's on June 11, if you're interested — I'm not).

When Andy called about the High Dive, I had absolutely no idea where Fremont was or why it calls itself the "Center of the Universe."

Last weekend's set at the High Dive was only the second time my son and his band have played in Seattle. A Davis High School alum and recent graduate of Western Washington University, Andy lives in Bellingham, where The Cast of Characters holds forth, playing mostly in nightclubs that are one step removed from bankruptcy and at house parties that can last until 4 in the morning.

Andy strikes the pose of a rock star   *Photo by Jon Brunk*

So I was excited about coming over to see him. I even enlisted the services of my cousin who lives near Seattle and his two daughters, both in their early 20s. My cousin would get me to the High Dive in one piece and his daughters would provide cover. A brilliant plan.

And, I must admit, my scheme was working flawlessly until I pulled out my video camera. My son's grin vanished into a frown. He gave me the slashing gesture across his throat that meant only one thing — don't do it, Dad.

Of course I did. What's the point of being a father if you can't embarrass your children?

I filmed for about 30 minutes before my cousin's two daughters hauled me out onto the dance floor. So there I was, the old man in a sea of young college students, hopping around on a beer-soaked dance floor and waving madly to my son, whose fingering on the bass kept in syncopation with the twirling lights of the band's portable disco ball.

Quite a sight to behold.

My bad dance moves, though, only marked the end point in a long series of events that began more than 12 years ago. It's odd how one small, seemingly insignificant decision can become, years later, so influential, or in the case of my son, so ear-shattering. It's how, I guess, we earn the rank of "parent."

That small decision happened in the spring of 1993, on the threshold of my son's 13th birthday. Like most parents, we had wanted our son to learn a musical instrument while growing up. Since I made a mess of my youth trying to produce something other than a squeal from my clarinet, I decided to steer Andy away from the woodwinds toward something nobler. Like the violin. Little did we know what destructive sounds that tiny wooden instrument could create in the hands of a restless fifth-grader.

Thankfully his elementary school orchestra teacher taught Andy and the other violinists a neat trick whenever they got lost in the midst of a performance. Instead of stopping cold, all they had to do was turn the bow upside down and fake that they were playing the music.

No wonder the fifth-grade orchestra's performance of Beethoven's "Ode to Joy" was so pleasing, and so inaudible. Out of 40 violinists in the orchestra, I bet only eight were playing. Andy wasn't one of them.

That's when we decided to make a change. So as his birthday approached, I asked him if he would like to drop the violin. His head bobbed up and down wildly.

What do you think about a guitar, I asked.

His eyes lit up.

It has strings and there's no violin bow to mess with, I noted. Hey, what about an electric guitar?

Suddenly, I noticed I was talking to myself. Andy was already in the car, waiting for me to take him to Ted Brown's music store.

That was 12 years ago, and how he has grown. No longer does he fake playing "Ode to Joy"; now it's strictly "Roll Over Beethoven." His first guitar has grown to four, and he owns an assortment of amplifiers, one of which could blow out most of the windows in Yakima's historic Larson Building.

Meanwhile, The Cast of Characters has been lauded by such venerable alternative publications as the Bellingham Weekly, which dubbed the band the best of the best, having "the ability to make a house party into a great house party. It's the stuff that drunk 22-year-old business majors can sway and sweat to, microbrew in one hand, pocket in the other."

While I don't mind participating in activities like Take Your Father To Work night at the High Dive, I realize there are more things to life than learning how to slap-string a bass guitar. That's why I look forward to seeing my son at his other job — taking care of autistic kids at the Nooksack Valley School District near Bellingham.

But at least for one night, I got a chance to see my son as a rock star, and witness what one small gesture, years ago, did to change both of our lives.

May 5, 2005

My wonderful son, Jed

Jed Hatton, a bright-eyed 18-year-old who brought his gentle touch of joy and love to everyone he met, died in the arms of his father on Tuesday, October 8, 2002, following complications from a seizure.

Jed was the younger of two sons born to Bronnie and Spencer Hatton. His older brother Andy came into this life as a three-pound preemie in 1980, and spent nearly two months in a tiny incubator before coming home.

So when Jed was born on August 4, 1984, the family hoped for a trouble-free beginning for their newest child. Although he arrived five weeks early himself, Jed received a clean bill of health from his doctors at Yakima Valley Memorial Hospital and off he went home, his mom and dad expecting a normal childhood.

And that was the way it was through the first year of Jed's life. His older brother would cuddle him and Jed would giggle, his angelic face aglow with an irrepressible smile. But then after his first birthday, Jed began to slip away. The usual imitation of sounds and words quickly stopped. His dad would go to his crib and there Jed would lay, quiet, alone, adrift in a room filled with riotous colors and loud noisemakers.

It took more than a year before a nationally renowned child psychiatrist at the University of Washington would tell the family Jed was autistic. Autism is a developmental disability characterized by significant delays in speech and social skills. Many afflicted with autism never speak while still others are savants, showing singular abilities in music, art, and mathematics.

Baby Jed in the neo-natal clinic with his Mom and Andy

There is one trait, though, that is constant — a cold aloofness. That's something his family would not accept. So they fought back with the only weapon they had — love. His world soon became a kinetic jungle of hugs, kisses, verbal jousting and armpit tickling. And he got his favorite gift of all, his own VCR, so he could replay his favorite tapes of Scooby-Doo and Winnie the Pooh, over and over again.

His mom, dad and big brother became his strongest allies, opening new worlds for Jed in the schools, which he attended, and in the community where he lived. But really, who could resist Jed's smile? He loved the joy of being with those who cared for him, and they soon numbered in the hundreds.

From his first days at the special education pre-school program at Hoover Elementary School, Jed found teachers and aides who loved him as if he were their son. Through this network of support, Jed began to take small steps forward.

His dad once sent a note to his very first teacher, Joyce McCormick, telling her about a wonderful thing that had just happened. Jed had said, in a clear, unmistakable voice: "I love you." That became a signal of the affection Jed would show the rest of his life.

He blossomed in Joyce's classroom. He continued these successes under the watchful eye and caring support of Mrs. Nel Dilley at Hoover. When he attended Adams Elementary School, he would always get a cheery welcome from the principal Rod Bryant, who made it possible for Jed to explore new challenges.

There, he took part in a Montessori classroom handled by a gifted teacher, Jon Osegueda, and enjoyed the companionship of two other special education teachers, Sherry Hallenbeck and Mary Wickstrom.

After overcoming the challenges of his early teen years at Wilson Middle School — where he continued to pursue academic courses through several regular education programs — Jed entered Eisenhower High School. For the past two years, his teacher, Mrs. Elaine Rovetto, helped Jed explore new subjects, including piano lessons, sewing, cooking, and typing, where he managed a very respectable 24 words-per-minute average.

It seemed like wherever Jed went, he opened new pathways for children with special needs. He was one of the first students in the district to have a one-on-one aide assigned to him. And they were all gems, including Maureen Booher, Shanna Simpson and Joy Froehlich at Eisenhower, who made no secret of the fact she had the best job in the district — taking care of Jed.

Beyond the classroom, Jed also pushed past the threshold of what a boy with autism could do.

Through the Yakima Family YMCA, Jed learned how to swim, how to ride a horse, how to take jump shots in basketball, and how to bed down with a cabin-full of teens at Camp Dudley where he once followed, with his dad at his side, other campers through a week of campfire songs, hikes, and a rousing game of capture the flag.

Jed also found another wonderful web of faithful friends at Children's Village. He couldn't wait to visit the dentist there (whom he affectionately called "Dentist the Menace"). He would rush into the secretary's office where he would slip his favorite tape into the VCR — "Scooby-Doo Meets Batman and Robin." Also at the Village he took part in Teen Club, which matches teens from various high schools with kids like Jed. He played volleyball and kickball games, and worked with others on arts and crafts projects.

Andy and Jed sit on a bench at Stanley Park in Vancouver, British Columbia. Photo was taken in May 2002, four months before Jed's death.

Special Olympics likewise played a big role in Jed's life. He captured several gold medals in track and field at the state games held at Fort Lewis near Tacoma. During the past few years, he expanded his activities to include soccer and bowling.

One of his greatest accomplishments in sports came this past winter. He and his dad traveled up to Whistler Mountain, British Columbia, and there he truly did the impossible — skiing down from the top of the mountain. With his dad skiing behind and pulling on long straps that were secured to the front of his skis, Jed weaved his way down the face of the mountain, to the amazement of all who watched.

For Jed, there were no limits.

Two years ago, though, he met a far different challenge. His mother died of cancer, after battling the disease for eight years. To help him at home while his dad was at work and his big brother was away at college, two caregivers came into his life — Lila Vincent and Jewel Noyes. They took him on walks, fed him favorite treats of Goldfish crackers, pizza and

Ranch dressing, and gave him the loving attention he so desperately needed with the loss of his "mom-mom."

Jed's death has brought a deep sense of loss among his many friends, especially his best friend — his big brother Andy.

Together they shared a love that is rarely felt between two brothers. They held hands, hugged, frolicked in the water while swimming, and spent long hours hunched over the computer as Jed would capture his favorite cartoon theme songs off the Internet. Andy never failed to kiss Jed on the cheek and repeat the very words Jed first spoke back in preschool: "I love you."

My son's obituary was published in the Yakima Herald-Republic on October 10, 2002

The most beautiful smile I've ever seen

I lost my son, my wonderful, beautiful son Jed.

The pain of his death has torn my heart into a million pieces, has sent me into near convulsions, has left me crying uncontrollably, has boiled my blood with anger I've never felt before, even when Bronnie died two years ago.

I will forever see Jed in his chair, a minute or two after his seizure had started, a moment or two after he violently threw up and I chuckled to him, saying what a mess he had made. I pulled his shirt off and looked at his face. The blood had rushed out, a chalky yellow complexion had spread across his once smiling face, that face I had kissed so many times before, kissing those chubby cheeks for no reason, just to tell him how proud I was of him and how much I loved him. I could tell his breathing had slowed. Had it stopped? I ran upstairs and grabbed the cordless phone and dialed 911. I hurried downstairs and pulled Jed up into my arms. I pounded on his back and turned him on his side. Vomit spewed out his nostrils and his mouth, his teeth still frozen tightly together, the effects of his seizure refusing to loosen its grip.

It wasn't supposed to be this way. Seizures don't kill. That's what Jed's doctor had told us weeks ago when we sat in his office — Jed sitting between Andy and me, his face placid, emotionless, oblivious to the medical terms being passed among us, the tones reassuring, the future still filled with hope. But there I was that night, yelling at Jed to breathe and seeing nothing but vomit fill his airways. I tried to breathe into his mouth, and suddenly mine filled up with vomit, too. I heard the sirens outside and cursed my life. I had forgotten to open the front door. It was locked. I ran upstairs and flung the door open, yelling at the medics to come downstairs.

It would take another 10 minutes before the medics could clear his windpipe. By now, they had fixed electronic patches to Jed's chest, which would give a readout of his heartbeat on a portable monitor. A medic said he couldn't get a heartbeat. The flat line on the monitor drove deep into my heart like a dagger. I pushed aside one of the medics, who was hunched over my son, and lowered my head onto Jed's chest.

"I love you Jed," I cried out as I clutched him in my arms. I could feel his life slipping away.

Then someone cried out: "We have a heartbeat."

I raised my head and stared down at Jed's chest. Over his heart where my head had rested a reddish hue appeared. Will he live? Tears blinded my eyes. A sliver of hope cut through the bleakness of that moment. But only a sliver.

Six hours later, death would claim my son, my wonderful, beautiful son, and all the world would come apart and tumble down, the sky, the moon, the sun, and that brilliant sparkle Jed would bring to me each day when he smiled and welcomed me with his familiar refrain, "Daddy is coming home tonight."

Daddy is home, but where is my Jed, my Jedi? I sit in his room, among the pillows and the Scooby-Doo dolls and the hundreds of sheets of yellow-lined paper on which he had written countless cartoon titles. I wait, the silence enveloping me, a shadow in the burnt orange of the afternoon sunshine, and I weep.

From my writer's journal — October 21, 2002

Touching the soul

I awoke in the middle of the night with an agony I had never felt before. My entire body flooded with despair. My breathing had slowed to a muffled wheeze; my heart had the shallowest of beats, as if I was in a suspended state, between sleep and death. "What's going on with me," I thought, my mind suddenly jolted with the stinging realization that Jed was dead, that there was nothing I could do.

Then the despair, which had coursed through my body, began to lift. The sensation came from deep, deep down inside of me, past my heart, past my lungs, past my gut, down to the very center of my spine, as if an indefinable part of my soul had been touched. A voice inside of me seemed to say, "It's over. You can move on."

I lay there for another 10 minutes or so, checking to see if I was all right, if the parts of my body were still ticking.

I imagined the feeling, which I had at this moment, was what Jed had felt when his body seized up, vomit rising up from his stomach, filling his lungs. I struggled to take a deep breath. I couldn't. I settled for slow, shallow breathing. I lay there wondering if this depression would be repeated night after night, a reminder of Jed's absence from my life and from the lives of his brother Andy and the scores of others who called Jed a loved one, a buddy, a friend.

I ran my hand across my chest and realized I was powerless to stop a repeat of this attack, just as I was powerless to save my Jed. I am so overwhelmed by all of this, by the sheer depths of despair that I have been plunged into. I know I must move ahead, to build a future among the shattered pieces of my life. But I know it will be a very long, tortuous path that

I must take, one that will bring me back to the panicked depression I felt last night. I can't escape it.

How I hate this life, and love it, too. This will be a constant battle, slipped in between every breath I take.

From my writer's journal — October 22, 2002

Journey to discover the truth

I took out my new pair of hiking boots and laced them up. Outside, high feathery clouds arced in from the west, a portent of storms to come.

I drove to Selah and turned onto a gravel road leading me closer to the Yakima River Canyon. Several miles later, I came upon a primitive parking lot that's near a trailhead leading into the L.T. Murray Wildlife Area. One of my hiking books mentioned something about a chemical toilet, and emphasized there was scant water available along the 12-mile Skyline Trail.

I indeed found the toilet. It sat on a small bluff and was riddled with bullet holes. An easy target for bored hunters. Not a good omen for a hike, I thought.

Beyond the toilet, I could see the trailhead. There was no sign as promised by the hiking book, but the trail seemed well established.

I could tell few had walked its rutted path in recent weeks. Tumbleweeds crowded the trail. I kicked some aside, hoping to clear a way for others. I took several branches of the light brown tumbleweed in my hands and hiked up the steep slopes. I passed by wild sage. To one side, a songbird called out, repeating its tender song as long as I would stand still. But I had to move on, and the song, so gentle to my ears, ended as abruptly as it had begun.

The air was now still except for the pounding of my boots on the dirt path and my labored breathing.

Path leading up the Skyline Trail

I'm not a hiker, but I like to take long walks to think things out. On this morning in early October, I had much on my mind. Despite growing older, I have come to realize there's little that has changed since the days of my youth and those of a white-haired man who's logged 55 years. Age-old questions still seem to evade answering, the very same questions that pushed me 30 years ago to take on a far different hike, deep into the Grand Canyon.

Released from my two-year commitment to the Army, I was adrift, trying to reconnect with who I was and where I was headed.

So my wanderings took me to the canyon's North Rim the day before Thanksgiving in 1973. For our three-day trek, a longtime friend and I had stuffed our backpacks with cans of apricots, olives, bread and wool socks. I wanted to fast on Thanksgiving, a test of my spirit and a way, perhaps, to shine light upon what lay ahead.

We left at sunrise, a whirlwind of snow and the swaying of pinyon pine to send us on our way. We had to cover two tough miles before reaching a desert plateau, walking through clouds of snow and mist along the South Kaibab Trail.

"The snow drifted along the path as our boots dug into the crushed rock seeking a hold, anything that would secure us from falling off the edge," I wrote in my journal. "Wind whipped itself into a fury, torquing through the deeply cut caverns and driving snow like sharply honed pins into our faces. It was nonetheless beautiful. Magical, like descending into a dream."

Our descent would take four hours, dropping us from 7,250 feet to 2,500 at the canyon's floor. There, we would camp, and on Thanksgiving, I would fast and watch the clouds skitter by overhead and the gin-clear waters of Bright Angel Creek stir to life. I would find, much to my surprise, mystery and meaning in the cold, dank chambers of the canyon.

"My hands are as numb as they were two nights ago in the car. But so what if my writing style becomes a bit cramped when I have been flying all day instead, soaring to be exact. I am turning into a different wave length, a frequency that surfaces with the river swells, that glistens green as the moss, that is as permanent as granite and as brilliant as the sandstone."

Despite going without food, I found strength in just being there, alone in quiet meditation.

"The night has clawed her way past day. I can barely make out the lines of this paper. The blue-black clouds have all gone home. Above the sky is blue. A fat robin fusses with her feathers and bounds in nervous leaps searching for bits of food."

"I am tired. My legs are tight and weary with the jarring climb up and down this valley of the underworld. Yet paradise could not be better, so here I will make my bed and dream about the other world that lies beyond the rim. Darkness and the abyss — tonight they are my bedfellows."

I left the wonders of the Grand Canyon and returned to a modern world filled with abundant food, chaotic motion and shrill sounds. I was no longer a "soul uplifted" as I wrote so eagerly in my journal, but as a lonely figure troubled by doubts, by the questions that still haunt me today: Who am I? Where am I headed? And, how do I get there?

"Nothing changes," I wrote a week after my trip to the Grand Canyon. "I am in a rut and yet last week I paraded myself around like I was a visiting guru from Orion's Belt Buckle. Face it. I am lost. Abandoned."

It's surely a human condition, this sense of loneliness.

You never expect to find someone else as adrift as yourself, and yet there are many. There's even a saint among us. On the threshold of her sainthood by the Catholic church two weeks ago, officials revealed Mother Teresa had also written about despair and a terrible separation, wondering if God had indeed abandoned her while she cared for the homeless and the dying in the slums of Calcutta.

When does it end, this questioning? When do the doubts fade like the storm clouds that once parted over the Grand Canyon?

That is why I took that hike two weeks ago. I felt lost again. Abandoned. It had been a year since my son Jed had died, and I needed time to heal, to be alone.

So I climbed the steep trail overlooking the Yakima River Canyon. I sat down on a bench made of rocks, and from my backpack — it was my son's — I took out a rock that I had found earlier this summer on a beach at Lake Roosevelt. It was a place my son had played on years ago.

I put that rock there amid the strewn stones of L.T. Murray.

I will return in the spring. And amid the blooms of buttercups, yellow bells and lupine, I will retrieve the stone. I will see then how far I have traveled, and no doubt, ask the same questions that troubled me 30 years ago.

For there is one thing that I have learned in all the miles I have walked: Truth comes in the asking. It always will.

October 26, 2003

Counting Crows: The long walk home begins with Step No. 1

Counting crows.

That's what we did years ago while taking long car trips. We would be wedged tightly in the back seat. My older sister and brother would be on either side of me as we watched outside for barn silos, picket fences and a row of crows on a power line. Each of us had what amounted to a bingo card filled with these highway scenes. Every time we saw one, we would move a yellow plastic screen over the square and inch one step closer to getting a winning row of five.

But always, the toughest was the dark line of crows.

Our wandering eyes scanned for them in the sky as we waited for the sound of the highway to end and the doors to open to the welcoming cry of, "We're here."

Decades later, I find myself counting again. This time the journey is much longer. Instead of crows, I count steps.

It started three years ago, shortly after the death of my son, Jed. Grief has a way of turning life upside down, taking the blue out of the sky and making it a struggle to walk, even to breathe.

Everything that had been familiar and routine suddenly was undone. I would stand there in my house, staring out the window at the school bus going by, and wonder why it didn't stop so I could send my son off to school as I had done for nearly 15 years.

Silence suddenly had become the blanket that comforted me, and believe me, it's no comfort at all.

Then there was the pain to deal with, a sickening depression, the kind that knots up your stomach and turns a 90-degree day into winter. I could always feel it coming, like a storm surge, a tidal wave sweeping over me. There was no way to fight it, though I tried. But I got smarter, and soon I let the wave take me. After an hour or so, I would find myself in a different place, my face dampened by tears and my gut burning hot with acid.

Experts say time heals even the deepest of wounds. So I looked to the calendar for help. But that was no good. Each day held what would have been — notes on doctors' appointments, a reminder about high school photographs. I now found myself staring at the calendar, cursing it, and all of those unmarked days and months that followed the 8th of October, the day my son died.

I knew I couldn't go on this way. I knew I had to start moving from where I was. Grief will eat you up, and it will for anyone. You don't have to lose a child. It can be a spouse, a parent, a grandmother, a favorite aunt, a college chum, a dog you reared from a puppy or a cat you once pulled out of a cage at the animal shelter.

That's when I decided to count steps. I figured that if I were able to take 100 steps, to move away from my grief in 100 different ways, I would be somewhere else, someplace other than the misery I was in. Some of the steps were just that, moving one foot ahead of the other.

That's the case of my first step, on October 18. I got into my car, drove to the Yakima Greenway parking lot at the end of North 16th Avenue and jogged for 33 minutes. I ran along the path that bordered Las Margaritas restaurant, and somewhere beyond Lake Aspen, among the burnt autumn leaves, I yelled at the top of my lungs. It was my version of a primal scream, a wild sound rushing up from my stomach where all the pain had settled.

It was a lousy run. But the fact that I got up and did something deserved a mark on the calendar. So I gave myself "1 Step."

Not all of the steps involved running, or walking for that matter. Going to the symphony earned a notch on the calendar. Even showing up at work made the grade.

But the most significant steps had to do with something we all take for granted — laughter. Back then, I figured I would never laugh again. I honestly couldn't imagine ever making a joke, or hearing myself laugh at someone else's.

So I didn't.

Until one day at Les Schwab. Yes, of all places, I made a joke at a tire store. I was paying my bill when the lady at the counter made a remark so utterly ridiculous I couldn't help myself. I turned it into a joke. She burst out laughing. I stared at her for the longest time, and then I realized I had made a step, a big step. I wrote it on the calendar: "Nov. 18. Joke at Les Schwab's."

At first, a step a week was all I could muster. Soon, though, things began to change. I guess I started to laugh more. Three-step weeks began to pop up. Now the hated calendar had become an ally, a source of pride.

I don't know what a professional therapist would have to say about my 100-step program. But it worked. Sure, I still have days when I can feel the wave of depression coming at me, but now I know the pain will pass, as surely as I know the tears will dry. The color blue has returned to the sky and my voice is now spiced with laughter.

I also do what grief counselors recommend: I water my house plants, tend to our family cat, Sylvester, and remain close to those whom I love.

So how many steps have I taken? I don't know. I stopped counting a long time ago. The actual number seemed unimportant; it was the act of counting that meant something.

I know there are others like me who have to count steps. I guess we all have to do it at some point. How much simpler, though, life would be if what mattered most were counting crows.

October 9, 2005

Memories vivid 10 years after ski trip of a lifetime

"So we beat on, boats against the current, borne back ceaselessly into the past."
— F. Scott Fitzgerald, "The Great Gatsby"

Fifty skiers were to our left and another 50 to our right. Together we formed a half circle, each skier poised to take the sudden drop down the hill into a bowl-shaped slope near the summit of 7,160-foot Whistler Mountain.

I stood directly behind my 17-year-old son, Jed. The front of his skis hung over the lip of the hill. I felt a sense of dread and could taste the bitter swill of adrenaline slicking my mouth. We are going to crash again, I thought.

I raised my hands and placed them on my son's back. We were ready to take the plunge. That's what dads do, right? Push their kids off a mountaintop. If I hesitated, all would be lost.

I shoved my son forward, and down we went.

The packed snow vanished beneath us. Wind blasted my face. Tears streaked my goggles. But Jed held firm, the snowplow wedge of his skis a mirror image of mine. I pulled back on the nylon strap, which cinched us together, and gained control of our free-fall.

For the next hour, we weaved our way down the slopes, attracting scores of onlookers who marveled at our tandem skiing. We eventually made our way back to a gondola station midway down the mountain.

Somehow we had conquered Whistler, future home of the Winter Olympics, and in so doing, made history.

This month marks the 10th anniversary of our trek to British Columbia. My heart still races when I think back to that day in March. We accomplished something no one had done before — skiing down Whistler Mountain using an adaptive ski device perfected by Outdoor for All Foundation, a nationally recognized, Seattle-based organization that provides year-round outdoor activities for children and adults with physical and developmental disabilities.

I confirmed our record-setting feat a few months after our trip when I met up with the foundation's executive director at a conference in Seattle. I asked him if anyone had skied down Whistler Mountain using the adaptive ski reins. He stared at me in amazement and replied, "Not that I know of. Who would be crazy enough to do that?"

I smiled back. "My son and I."

The device, which Jed and I used, consists of a pair of metal clamps, a long nylon strap that loops around the skier and a short bungee cord, which prevents the skis from crossing. By pulling to the right on the nylon strap, I was able to get my son to make a right-hand turn, and by tugging the strap to the left, Jed would turn left. Deceptively simple.

Though Jed was diagnosed with autism when he was nearly 3 years old, he never lacked for physical strength or agility. He loved to bounce on a trampoline and won numerous gold medals at Special Olympics track events. When the foundation held a clinic at White Pass Ski Area in 2001, I signed Jed up. He did great, so I decided to buy one of the devices.

Jed learns assisted skiing at White Pass in 2001

A year later we got our chance to use it when a college friend living in Iowa called and asked if we wanted to join his wife and daughter for two days of skiing at Whistler.

Our first day was a blast. Jed and I found an easy beginner's slope, where we performed a ballet of sorts — both of us cutting a path across the slopes with me tugging at the ski reins and Jed making graceful turns by forming a wedge-like V with his skis.

The next day, though, was a different story. My legs were stiff. I could barely bend my knees. But that didn't stop me from accepting a challenge posed by my friend: How about taking the gondola to the top of the mountain? Sure, let's do it, I replied, with a bravado that comes from growing up in the 1960s when no idea seemed too crazy.

To get to the gondola, Jed and I first had to ski down a short slope. I nudged Jed forward and we started our descent. I pressed down on my skis to make a wedge. Suddenly my legs tightened. Two turns later and my legs cramped up completely.

In a split second, I whizzed by Jed. He looked at me and I stared back at him. Up ahead, a bridge over a ravine was fast approaching. I had only one choice. I collapsed to the snow and locked my skis into the slope.

An eerie calmness set it. The ski reins lay on the snow, slack at my side as Jed zoomed past. I braced myself for the inevitable. Like a horsewhip, the nylon strap snapped loudly. I felt my shoulders strain as I absorbed the impact of Jed's 195-pound body slamming into the snow. His skis flipped wildly into the air.

After a few minutes of sheer panic, we calmed down and checked our body parts. No broken bones, no limbs hanging by a torn tendon. I decided discretion, not valor, was called for, so I picked up our skis. We slowly made our way to the gondola, beaten but not defeated.

No wonder I feared the worst a half-hour later when I pushed my son down that steep slope at the top of the mountain. What a frightening yet fabulous memory.

I'm still amazed it ever happened since two weeks before our trip, Jed suffered his first seizure and was taken by ambulance to the emergency room. I called my college friend, who's a doctor, and told him I thought we shouldn't go. He said Jed would be fine. "When are you going to get a chance like this again?" he added.

So I said "yes" to the trip and to that wild ride up the gondola.

My son would die seven months later following complications from another seizure. I don't have any photographs from that trip. It doesn't matter. How could I ever forget the sight of my son leading me down the face of Whistler Mountain, with his skis creating a perfect arc in the snow, and me holding on for dear life.

March 11, 2012

A gift of awkwardness

When raising two sons, I found Father's Day to be more of a myth than a reality. For me, it lasted about 30 minutes before my anticipated day of self-absorbed relaxation came to a grinding halt. If it wasn't an urgent plea to cut the lawn, fixing a leak in the bathroom sink came in a close second.

While fathers may receive few accolades from the one day of the year set aside for us to be showered with golf balls and bottles of barbecue sauce, I am thankful for one tradition that arrived courtesy of the Norman invasion of England in 1066. It's the right of primogeniture. Under this Norman tradition, the first-born son inherited the entirety of a parent's wealth, estate or title.

My first-born son, Andy, has already reaped the benefits of this inheritance. He had no choice. That's due to the genetic sludge I unloaded on my 32-year-old son. I certainly didn't hand off my macho good looks. It's probably because I never had any to begin with.

Andy reminded me, and thousands of others, of our inherited shortcomings when he posted a recent blog entry with this revealing title: "My gift of awkwardness."

Here's how he starts his posting: "As anyone who has seen me dance can tell you, I do not have moves like Mick Jagger. Rather, I have the awkward jerky movements of a marionette whose limbs and torso are controlled by invisible puppeteers who are seemingly both poorly trained and completely inebriated. Not only am I not an able dancer, I have also figuratively stunk up baseball diamonds, soccer fields and basketball courts."

What he described is a mirror image of me. My wife, Leslie, refers to my dance moves as "free form," which is another way of saying I look like a cheap imitation of Elaine dancing in a "Seinfeld" rerun.

"The reason that I couldn't pump the swing as high as other kids, the reason I couldn't make it up the jungle gym, the reason I couldn't make it across the accursed monkey bars — it was because I was different," Andy confesses. "And different was the absolute last thing I wanted to be (in elementary school)."

Time does not always heal wounds, nor does it alter the prospects of an awkward 9-year-old moving from third grade to high school. Once a klutz, always a klutz.

Andy's blog continues: "By the time I made it to high school, my self-confidence was practically nonexistent — to be fair, though, my physical awkwardness and lack of coordination were given key assists by rampant acne, braces and a perpetually cracking voice. In other words, I had the complete package."

He did leave out one more detail — eyeglasses. That's the same hand I was dealt back when I struggled through high school in the 1960s — the dreaded triple dose of acne, braces and thick-rimmed glasses. No wonder my self-esteem at the time had shrunk to the size of a subatomic particle.

Andy's awkwardness, though, had more to do with his birth than his birthright. He was born 10 weeks early and weighed just 3 pounds, 2 ounces. The premature birth caused him to suffer from the lingering effects of mild cerebral palsy, which hampers physical coordination.

"Although I never would become the power-hitting Cubs first baseman that my Dad might have secretly hoped for, I have had the opportunity to have a fulfilling and rewarding life thus far — even though I look pretty scary riding a bicycle," my son writes.

It's remarkable how some things turn out in life. Despite the frightening start at birth and the sometimes scary traits he inherited from me, Andy persevered. Best of all, he found a way to honor the memories of his mother and younger brother.

It wasn't easy for Andy. As an undergraduate at Western Washington University in Bellingham, he took time off from school to care for his mother. Despite undergoing chemotherapy treatments and two major surgeries for ovarian cancer, Andy's mom accomplished an improbable feat — she earned a degree as a special education teacher from Central Washington University.

In the fall of 2000, she died after an eight-year battle with the disease. Andy was at her side in those final months of her life, giving her foot rubs and warm hugs.

Andy holds his master's degree in speech language pathology

Then two years later, his younger brother died following complications from a seizure. Jed was 18 and had been diagnosed at an early age with autism, a disability that results in profound delays in language development.

Andy took inspiration from both his mom and brother. When he graduated from Western with a degree in English, he landed a job as a teacher's aide in a special education classroom, where he worked one-on-one helping kids with autism.

Then he decided to make a bigger difference in the lives of children with special needs. After nearly three years of challenging classes, Andy earned his master's degree from Western as a speech language pathologist. Imagine how proud his mom and brother would have been.

Andy now works as a full-time speech language pathologist at the Lakeside Center for Autism, a private facility in Issaquah, Washington. Each day he sees young boys and girls trying to overcome speech delays caused by autism. His entry about growing up awkward appeared a few months ago on the Lakeside Center's blogsite, where it was warmly received by families raising children with developmental delays.

"I am not so insecure now that I need to pretend that I am completely 'normal,' although we live in a world where the concept of normalcy and normative development is becoming more difficult, if not impossible, to define," Andy writes at the end of his blog.

"What I do know is that the difficulties I faced as an awkward, uncoordinated, scrawny kid helped turn me into the slightly less awkward, uncoordinated, and scrawny — yet successful — man I am today. And I wouldn't trade that for dance skills."

I hope other fathers today take pride in their awkward sons and daughters. It's not what they do on the dance floor that really matters. It's what happens when the music stops.

June 17, 2012

DIFFERENTLY ABLED

In the world of children and adults with developmental disabilities, there are no easy solutions. Each day is a challenge, and each success a moment to cheer about. As a father of a son with special needs, I found myself seeking the smallest of miracles — a word uttered without prompting, a hug given freely.

Despite the odds, these miracles continue to happen thanks to Dads and Moms, sisters and brothers, teachers and specialists refusing to give up hope.

Inflammatory words overshadow need for respect

Thomas McCormick regrets the words, not the anger.

He never should have threatened the Yakima school superintendent. Nor should he have threatened to harm school board members.

But McCormick was angry. And it wasn't simply about losing in his perennial race for a seat on the school board. He had lost five times before. It really had to do with being put down, about being placed on the outer margins of life and being forgotten, excluded.

You have probably seen Thomas McCormick around Yakima. The 46-year-old with thinning hair and bushy sideburns is a frequent bike rider, pedaling down the streets in his red windbreaker, traveling to his part-time job at the library in downtown Yakima.

Thomas McCormick is a person with developmental delays. The most noticeable effects of these delays are in his speech. He talks with a heavy nasal resonance, making his words hard to understand especially when he becomes excited.

He's also someone on a mission, and that's protecting others like himself who are on the outside looking in. He particularly wants to save others who are struggling through a school system that he sees harming those with disabilities by further reducing programs in special education.

McCormick knew he shouldn't have written that letter to the Superintendent of Public Instruction in Olympia. On November 5, the day after losing at the polls, McCormick wrote to the state's chief educator about "getting very upset" with losing the election and about what he believed were unfair cutbacks in special education.

He also wrote about how he wanted "to take some form of disciplinary action" against the Yakima school superintendent — "to kill him and the other school board members."

To those who know McCormick, that threat of violence is hollow. But McCormick had to pay the consequences for what he had done.

When he appeared in Yakima County Superior Court last Tuesday, Judge Robert Hackett had no other choice except to grant the Yakima School District's request for a restraining order. It will be at least another six months before McCormick can attend a school board meeting or go onto school property. It will be at least another 180 days before he can even be seen within 500 feet of the school superintendent.

Before the ruling was handed down, McCormick told the judge he had been screened by a panel of psychiatrists. They told him he wasn't a threat to anyone.

"I don't think you are either," said Judge Hackett, who has known McCormick since the early 1970s.

But to those who don't know Thomas McCormick, to those who have not taken the time to talk to him or who step aside when they see him walking down the sidewalk, he may indeed be seen as a threat. Perhaps not to their physical well-being, but to their sense of who makes up a free society. His appearance begs the question to those who are afraid to ask: Where do these people who are different fit in?

McCormick has never wanted the world handed to him on a silver platter. He said he just wants to be treated like a person, with respect and dignity, not as an object reserved solely for scorn and derision.

When people say things that are mean to him, it "makes a whole life bad," McCormick confessed.

He told me that at public meetings when he gets up to speak, it seems like no one cares. It's as if "I wasn't even there," he said.

Those who see the Thomas McCormicks of the world as a nuisance or, even worse, as a threat, had better wake up. They are not going away. McCormick represents a burgeoning class of people who are fighting to be recognized in society. Those with special needs are demanding to be included in regular school classrooms, in government offices, on public buses and inside public facilities. They no longer want to be on the outside. They want to be included, like everyone else.

The struggle for acceptance hasn't been easy. And McCormick's inflammatory letter will not make that process any smoother.

Offering apologies might help. At least that's what the judge thought last Tuesday when he asked McCormick if he might consider sending an apology to the Yakima school superintendent. I asked him what he thought about that idea. McCormick said he was going to do it.

I then wondered what he thought about others apologizing to him for what they had said and done to him over the years because of his special needs.

He thought that, too, would be a good idea.

November 11, 1997

It takes a village like this

Parents of children with disabilities know the routine.

They've been through it before. They have traveled from clinic to clinic, from city to city. They have repeated their child's bleak and disturbing medical history a hundred times to a hundred different clinicians, have stared blankly down linoleum-lined corridors with nowhere to go, waiting for hours for tests that prove nothing.

They, too, have heard the "death sentence," the decree that their child's future is without hope, a declaration uttered with cool precision by a specialist they'll never see again, given in a language they've never had a chance to understand.

I have a child with special needs. And like so many parents before us, my wife and I have gone through the misery of early diagnosis where specialists refused to look at us, instead gazing at a spot on the ceiling so they didn't have to see the tears running down our faces.

One of our more troubling experiences happened early in the process of determining why our son, at nearly 2 years old, had little or no language. After hearing and speech tests in Yakima proved negative, we sought help at University Hospital's child development clinic in Seattle.

We arrived at 8 a.m. for the first in a daylong series of exams that began with a battery of tests to be given by a trained child psychologist. The appointment, though, started late. The psychologist rushed into the room. I could tell she was flustered and a bit on edge. Apparently she had missed a ride to work. She also complained that, since she was only working on a part-time basis, she had not been given enough time to prepare for our appointment.

The session went downhill from there. After giving her our child's medical history, repeating what we had told a half-dozen other specialists during the previous two months, she began to give our son a series of developmental tests. Although we told her our son would not respond to verbal commands, she proceeded anyway with the exam.

After completing the series of questions and tasks, she stepped out of the room for a few minutes. When she returned, she went quickly through the results of her exam. I remember hearing the phrase "significant delays." Then she went beyond the test results and offered her own conclusions. We should prepare for the worst. Perhaps institutional care for our child.

Stunned by that pronouncement, we were then led out of the room into a crowded corridor of the medical clinic where we sat, waiting for the next appointment and wondering what the future would hold for our son.

It took another year before a doctor in child psychology would finally diagnose our son with autism, a birth defect characterized by significant delays in language development and social skills. And the dire warnings did not come true. Our son has progressed into middle school thanks to the wonderful support from teachers and other specialists in Yakima.

I don't think the callous treatment we received years ago by that part-time psychologist was her fault. She was caught up in a process that functioned on an adult time-schedule, with little leeway for the shifting idiosyncrasies of children with special needs. When our 40-minute appointment was over, she no longer had to deal with us … ever.

But that enslaved process is turned upside down at Children's Village, Yakima's latest and most innovative of approaches to collaborative medicine.

When Children's Village opens its doors this Friday to the public for the first time, visitors will enter a building graced with a childlike touch: warmly painted walls, trees in hallways, rooms notched with windows at a height just right for a 2-year-old.

Forged by one of the Yakima Valley's most successful private donation drives ever, which netted The Memorial Foundation more than $4 million, Children's Village creates a kingdom where the center of the universe is the chronically ill and disabled child, around whose outstretched arms gather the pediatric experts, physical therapists and doctors.

For those who have dreamed this dream of bringing the clinics and the physicians to the child in a setting friendly to groping fingers and wandering feet, Children's Village thunders out across the health-care community like an impassioned sermon where the central article of faith is that the purest of spirits is the child facing the greatest of disadvantages.

Those entering Children's Village will find a simple message etched in a massive stone that stands in front of a bridge spanning the world of adults to the world of children: "It takes both the sun and the rain to make a rainbow."

Those families with special children know all about the rain. It's the sun that Children's Village brings forth. Under one roof more than 13 different agencies will work together, from Yakima Valley Memorial Hospital to the Yakima Valley Farm Workers Clinic.

When families take the wooden bridge to Children's Village, they will be asked to fill out one and only one medical history for their child. And when a diagnosis is given, families will be provided the latest information about their child's illness or developmental delay.

Outside, there's even a secret garden where wheelchair-bound toddlers can scoop up dirt and get all messy, the way children should. They can also paint on a special water-coloring wall and trace animal tracks across a cement pathway. The building offers a therapy pool, along with exercise rooms and an always-open community center where support groups can meet.

Children's Village is where the sun never sets. Its light shines through the hallways that are brightly colored, creating a friendly neighborhood where both children and adults can be seen together, hand in hand. Its light shines even into an elevator where a make-believe mine shaft draws the child's attention away from the closing doors toward a hidden treasure of shining emeralds and diamonds.

It's a miracle that Children's Village ever got built. But its true magic is yet to come. That will begin unfolding when the first child crosses the bridge and scans the faces of those on the other side, searching for a rainbow.

October 5, 1997

POSTSCRIPT: Since its opening, Children's Village has undergone a major expansion of its facility and, in 2011, received a national charitable service award. "This program is a jewel in the community," said the chairman for the awards committee. In November 2011, Memorial Hospital also held its first-ever Promise Awards to honor those who contributed to the success of Children's Village. I served as master of ceremonies for the event.

Picture it, then go out and do it

State wildlife agents have obviously never met Temple Grandin. At the very least, if they had read her book, they wouldn't have made such a colossal public-relations mess of last Monday's roundup of elk on the Hanford Nuclear Reservation.

Grandin is no lightweight when it comes to the business of getting animals to move from point A to point B. One third of all cattle and hogs in the United States pass through facilities that she has designed.

How does this remarkable 52-year-old woman create such animal-friendly designs that enable cattle to calmly lope, one after the other, into a slaughterhouse? She does it with pictures, in her mind.

Grandin says she actually reacts as an animal would to new sights and sounds, where fear of the unknown — such as entering a pen or chute — causes cattle and sheep and hogs to balk.

"When cattle learn that a certain area is safe, they become reluctant to move to a new area, which may contain danger," Grandin writes in her book, aptly titled, "Thinking in Pictures."

The goal of the recent elk roundup was to funnel 100 or so wild elk down a quarter-mile-long V-shaped entrapment and get them to pass through a tiny eight-foot-wide gate. Then the elk were to enter an enclosed corral, where trucks would eventually take them far from the Hanford Nuclear Reservation where they had enjoyed, for nearly three decades, a rather hedonistic life, foraging on the grass of the pristine shrub-steppe lands with no predator, either human or otherwise, to bother them.

Wildlife agents planned to coax these fat and sassy elk toward the V-shaped chute by using a helicopter.

So when faced with the whirling blades of the helicopter and the minuscule opening at the end of the chute, you can imagine what direction the elk chose — freedom. Some even jumped over the eight-foot-high plywood fencing. Anywhere but the place where agents wanted them to go.

I don't know if Grandin would have laughed at this. She confesses she doesn't always laugh at the appropriate times. Handling emotions is not her strongest skill.

You can grant her that shortcoming. Temple Grandin isn't your ordinary genius. She is autistic, and proudly says she wouldn't have it any other way.

"If you get rid of autism, you'll probably get rid of people like Einstein," she said while delivering the keynote address last month at the state's autism conference in Bellevue.

After hearing Grandin speak that morning, I still shake my head in bewilderment at her accomplishments. She indeed is a kindred spirit of Einstein.

She grew up as most children with autism, alone and frightened. As she describes it, her disability is linked to immature brain development. Those afflicted with autism, as is my 15-year-old son, have enormous difficulties with speech and with social interaction. For Grandin, this meant an especially hard time understanding what adults were talking about when she was young.

"If adults yakked really loud, I thought they were speaking in a foreign language," she says.

With the combined strength of her family, who believed in her and teachers who forced her to overcome the "yakking" rattle of language, Grandin succeeded in school. She did so not by learning the intricacies of word usage, but with the vision of a film editor, all seeing and all knowing. To her, visual symbols, not syllables, are the cues to memory.

"I think in pictures," Grandin admits simply.

This videotaping approach to thinking propelled her through the University of Illinois, where she earned a doctorate in animal science. Her persistence then carried her even further, opening a career in designing livestock facilities that are the marvel of efficiency, and most importantly, of humane treatment. The curved chutes that she creates draw cattle toward their natural tendency of circling away from danger.

Grandin did this all by picturing what animals see, and by getting inside their skins and sensing the fear of the unknown that is all too familiar for someone who's autistic.

No wonder a youthful Einstein, much like Grandin, had to overcome his own innermost fears and nearly pathological shyness. In Grandin's estimation, if it weren't for the possibility of being imperfect, there never would have been a genius like Albert Einstein.

"Genius may be an abnormality," she says.

That's not an easy concept to swallow, but just look at the life of the person Time magazine called the supreme human being of the 20th century.

Einstein grew up an outcast. He showed no inkling of a high IQ. His teachers saw little in him that would raise even an eyebrow of recognition. The intellect that turned the comfortable world of physics upside down barely passed mathematics and flunked his entrance exam to engineering school.

There was that spark, though, in Einstein that shone through. It's the same fire that burns within Grandin, who sees nothing wrong with being labeled "abnormal" if that also embraces the concept of "genius" so remarkably played out by people like Einstein.

It's nice to see this same kind of brilliance shining through in Yakima, too.

That happened several weeks ago at the Capitol Theatre during the seventh annual Yakima Youth Awards, when Michael Murray walked to the podium to receive his award. In the audience stood his mother Linda, her face wet with tears and her smile probably the biggest in the universe.

Her son Michael had overcome many heart-wrenching times before putting his hands on that award for "personal achievement."

He is autistic, just like Temple Grandin. While he has no doctorate degree like Grandin's, he has been able in the past few years to live independently and to take part in a youth group at Holy Family Church in Yakima. So impressed were his youth leaders that they nominated him for one of the youth awards.

Although Michael was surprised by the honor, Temple Grandin wouldn't have been. She has learned there is nothing you can't accomplish. You just have to picture it in your mind.

March 12, 2000

POSTSCRIPT: A professor of animal science at Colorado State University, a best-selling author and subject of an award-winning HBO movie, Grandin has earned yet another honor. In 2010, Time magazine listed her among the 100 most influential people in the world for being "an extraordinary source of inspiration for autistic children, their parents — and all people."

Endless frustration in quest of autism cure

There's nothing worse than seeing a desperate parent, who's raising a child with autism, believe a cure is at hand.

But in the world of autism, disappointment quickly follows hope as cures vanish, wasting precious time and money.

The anguish parents suffer while caring for sons and daughters tormented by this baffling disability make the yearlong vitriolic debates over President Obama's health care reform seem like, well, like child's play.

With autism now being diagnosed in 1 out of every 110 children in America, its impact on families is profound. Costs are astronomical. A recent study by the Harvard School of Public Health showed that direct medical and nonmedical expenses — for such things as special education, prescriptions, occupational and speech therapy — could total $3.2 million over the span of an autistic person's lifetime.

It's clear autism is a national health care crisis unto itself.

When psychiatrists first came up with the diagnosis of autism in the 1940s, they blamed the child's self-absorbed behavior on a cold, reclusive "refrigerator mother." That, of course, is not the case. Experts now define autism as a disorder of neural development linked to abnormal biology and chemical interactions in the brain. The disorder appears during the first three years of life and impairs social interaction and communication.

Why the diagnosis of autism, with its wide spectrum of severity, has grown to such an extent in recent years remains a mystery. Is it solely the province of better skills in the medical profession? Or is there something more sinister at play?

In the 1980s, a miracle drug promised a possible cure. Called fenflu-ramine, it reduced the level of serotonin in the blood — a chemical that affects the brain, which autistic children tend to have in higher amounts. But studies failed to prove the drug had any beneficial effects.

Then came megavitamins and special diets; injections of secretin, a pancreatic enzyme extracted from pigs; and hyperbaric chamber therapy. Swimming with dolphins even became the rage. All held promise; all were proven false.

The cure du jour of the early 1990s was Auditory Integration Training. My late son Jed took the treatment when he was 7 years old. It consisted of listening to specially modulated sounds through headphones. By doing so, an autistic child's super-sensitivity to sounds would be controlled and, as a result, improve the child's erratic behavior.

So we traveled to Vashon Island near Seattle and spent $2,000. While our son appreciated being the center of attention, the training didn't "re-wire" his brain. Another cure; another flop.

Equally as frustrating have been the failed attempts to divine the root causes of autism.

Most provocative on the list has been the MMR vaccine. Incidences of autism began to rise sharply at the time the vaccine to fight measles, mumps and rubella was introduced in 1971. Also, those children who are later diagnosed as autistic tend to display delays about the time the MMR vaccine is administered — around age 2.

Adding fuel to the worries over childhood vaccines was the much-her-alded research study published in 1998 by the British medical journal The Lancet that claimed there might be a link between the MMR vaccine and autism. Many parents suddenly stopped vaccinating their children.

Fear over childhood vaccinations continues to this day. A recent study released by the journal Pediatrics revealed one in four parents think vac-cines cause autism in healthy children — despite also believing that these same vaccines help prevent diseases.

Like so many aspects of autism, fear gets in the way of facts.

No credible study has found any link between vaccines and autism. Then came the stunning announcement last month that Lancet was retract-ing its 1998 report. It was riddled with faulty assumptions. It also turns out the lead researcher was paid nearly a half million pounds by lawyers who wanted to prove that vaccines indeed cause autism.

So has the search for cures and causes of autism reached a dead-end?

Far from it. Another study, released online a few weeks ago by the peer-reviewed medical journal, Current Opinion in Pediatrics, offered this provocative claim: Toxins in the environment may be linked to autism.

According to the New York Times, the study noted the "likelihood is high" that numerous chemicals "have potential to cause injury to the developing brain and to produce neurodevelopmental disorders." If babies are exposed to harmful chemicals in the womb, the end result could be brain defects lasting a lifetime — in other words, autism.

Though the debate continues in Congress over health care reform, I have heard no mention of autism. Coming to terms with its far-reaching impacts on our society won't be easy. Parents of children with autism know that.

They also know it's a disability that's not going away anytime soon.

March 14, 2010

POSTSCRIPT: The diagnosis of autism continues to rise. A study released in March 2012 by the Centers for Disease Control and Prevention states the chances of a child being diagnosed with autism or a related disorder increased by more than 20 percent from 2006 to 2008. In 2008, one child in 88 received one of the diagnoses, known as autism spectrum disorder. That's compared with about one in 110 two years earlier and one in 155 in 2002.

Warm heart extends tradition of Santa visits

It must have been quite a spectacle, Santa descending from the heavens in broad daylight.

He would have been a mere speck in the sky, a dot growing larger and larger. Then suddenly, he would have been upon them, the helicopter swaying and the rotary blades whipping up leaves and dust and commotion among the throng of children.

That's how Jerry Henderson, back in 1969, brought Santa Claus to the students at Yakima's Hoover Elementary School. By then, he already had two years of work under his belt as the school's whimsical Mr. Claus, portraying the immortal Saint Nick for Hoover's young special education students. He was the complete Santa Claus, with bells dangling from his belt loop and a bag filled with magical fairy dust he would scatter atop the tousled heads of children.

For 25 years, Jerry's Santa routine never broke stride, not on the first day when he showed up to hand out gifts to children in wheelchairs, nor when he landed on the Hoover playground in that borrowed helicopter (he did those theatrics for three straight years), nor the times he would line up the entire student body to do the Conga dance, the kids bubbling with excitement, their hands on the hips of the kid in front and their feet kicking out wildly in mad pandemonium, with Santa leading them out the gymnasium door, his red cap swaying to the beat of the swarm of students snaking behind him.

While Jerry liked playing for Conga lines and big crowds, his first love has always been the small special education classrooms.

"I fell in love with those kids," Jerry said, his voice warmed by the many memories of past Christmases.

Jerry reasoned that the other "regular kids," as he called them, always had a chance to see Santa at a department store where steep stairs often led to a disinterested Claus. That department store trip wasn't possible for most of the special education students, whose fragile health or behavior problems made it a logistical nightmare.

So that's why Jerry's Santa came to them, at their level. Jerry never sat in an overstuffed, high-backed armchair. He got down to the kids' level, down to the linoleum floor if necessary, so they could gaze into Santa's eyes and know he was for real. He found that out during the very first time trying to portray Santa. Little kids cowered at the sight of the plump guy in red.

"When you are sitting face to face, there was no fear," said Jerry.

Imagine, then, the excitement they felt when Santa called them out by name. That's another added feature to Jerry's Santa. He got to know the kids' names because he kept coming back for repeat performances to the same classrooms, the same schools. In a sense, Jerry grew up with the students as he moved from elementary school to elementary school, first Hoover and then on to Adams, Barge-Lincoln and Gilbert, eventually hitting all eight in the Yakima School District. Jerry's Santa made trips to the Headstart program and to EPIC's crisis nursery center. He even made surprise visits to Davis High School where he always found a way to get the former choir director, Deb Wagner, to sit on his lap, much to the delight of the entire student body.

In every way, Jerry was the ultimate showman.

Except for this Christmas. For the first time in a quarter of a century, Jerry Henderson no longer played the role of Santa Claus for the special education students at Hoover, or for that matter, any student in Yakima. Like those kids with special needs whom Jerry came to love so much, he now finds himself facing his own battle with a debilitating illness. Several years ago, diabetes forced him into a motorized wheelchair that now comes with an oxygen tank just in case he gets too winded.

That doesn't mean Jerry has slowed down at all. For years, he still kept up an array of volunteer activities, from resurrecting the Yakima trolleys to auctioneering at church fundraisers. But this holiday season, his doctor advised Jerry it might be time to hang up the Santa suit. Getting down on your knees, Jerry was told, was not allowed. And Jerry knew, if you can't get down to the kids' level, what's the point of being Santa?

Jed hugs Santa (aka Jerry Henderson)

That doesn't mean, though, Jerry's Santa is forgotten. Far from it. With the help of the Yakima Kiwanis Club, which years ago came to Jerry's rescue with a fancy new red Santa suit, Ol' Saint Nick is alive and well and playing for packed classrooms at Martin Luther King Elementary School. Earlier this month, Roger Bell, a Kiwanian, donned the red cap and bulging midriff of Santa and welcomed onto his lap some 38 students from the school's special education classrooms. They all got their photos taken with Santa.

What a treat it is to see the face of a young girl with Down syndrome come to life when Santa takes her in his arms and asks, "What do you want for Christmas?" With a candy cane and a small gift in hand, she pauses as she is led away by her teacher, her eyes still fixed on the bearded Santa as another child, who arrives in a wheelchair, poses for a Polaroid. Smiles fill the room as fairy dust sparkles down upon the bobbing heads of the young students.

It's nice to know Jerry's Santa is still around. That's the way it should be. Gifts that come from the heart have a way of living on, even if the man behind the beard goes by a different name.

December 16, 2002

POSTSCRIPT: Jerry Henderson died on February 3, 2005. His wife asked me to organize a memorial service for him. Eight days later I was the first to speak at his service at Englewood Christian Church in Yakima. Three years earlier, Jerry had been the first to speak at my son's memorial service. It was held at the same church.

Singing the joys of Camp Prime Time

The pontoon boat meandered across the calm waters of Clear Lake. It was 100 degrees in Yakima that day, but here along the east slopes of the Cascades, the coolness of the stream-fed lake made for a pleasant boat trip for our small band of campers.

With a setting like this, the last thing you would expect to hear is someone singing. But often in life, the unexpected is the rule.

I was sitting across from her. The young woman's mom, Fran, politely asked: Do you mind if my daughter sings?

How could we say no?

I expected the worst, of course. Whenever a mother claims her daughter can hold a tune, no less sing a cappella on a lake in the middle of nowhere, you gird yourself for a sickening serenade akin to fingernails inching down a blackboard. Ah, misery for the ears and delirium for the mind.

When Ever Fecske hit the first note, though, it was pure joy. Her delicate voice brought bright smiles to everyone as she breezed through the 1930s classic "Pennies from Heaven" that Bing Crosby had made famous: "Ev'ry time it rains, it rains pennies from heaven/Don'tcha know each cloud contains pennies from heaven?"

Perfect pitch, I thought.

"You're fantastic," I exclaimed when Ever finished with a flourish, the concluding line: "There will be pennies from heaven for you and me." The boat rocked with applause.

"You should be in movies," I beamed.

That's when her mom answered with measured nonchalance: "Oh, she has been."

It turns out Ever, who's 22 and lives in Southern California with her family, had a starring role in the popular television series, "Boston Public." She played the character of Ester Guttman in four episodes in 2003 and, yes, even sang on air, before millions of viewers.

And then the unexpected happened. Her life took a turn no one had anticipated.

Everyone — her dad and younger brother included — had all assumed Ever would continue with her promising singing career. She had even been accepted into the prestigious performing arts program at Berkeley. Success seemed to follow her every step, and so too had nagging sore throats, bronchitis and sinus infections.

So off she went to see doctors and specialists. They ran her through a battery of tests and fed her a diet of densely sounding medical terms that she would later search out on the Internet.

Then, on February 27, 2005, Ever became a member of an exclusive club who all had one thing in common: PIDD, or primary immune deficiency disease. Her body, which had produced such a sparkling singing voice, also had a damaged immune system that, through a rare genetic flaw, was in short supply of a key element to good health: immunoglobulins. It's the stuff that keeps our immune systems ticking and keeps sore throats a rare occurrence.

The disease runs the gamut of extremes, from Severe Combined Immune Deficiency (the boy-in-the-bubble disease) to what Ever has, Common Variable Immune Deficiency, a far more treatable disease.

The maddening aspect of PIDD is its difficulty in being diagnosed. Often, it may take years for doctors to finally fix the right diagnosis to the symptoms, but by then the damage to a person's organs, especially the lungs, may be too severe to be responsive to treatments.

These remedies are not a walk in the park. For those like Ever, treating immune deficiencies means long hours undergoing intravenous injections of immune globulin, a substance extracted from human plasma that helps to rebuild the body's immune defenses. Her treatments can last up to four hours and are given every two weeks. More severe cases may require daily treatments.

The grim news doesn't end here. Proposed cutbacks in Medicare may have some families scrambling to pay for these life-saving treatments.

That's why the Immune Deficiency Foundation began nearly three decades ago to help advocate for those in need, and to improve the diagnosis and treatment of PIDD through research and education.

The foundation also brings families together like Ever and her mom who decided to travel up from California several weeks ago to spend the weekend at Camp Prime Time with a group of other families afflicted with primary immune deficiency.

The 50 or so people who showed up were newcomers to Camp Prime Time, a camp near the shores of Clear Lake that offers a no-hassle, three-day weekend for families of children with special health-care needs and disabilities.

Besides being in the outdoors, the camp is also free for those who stay, thanks to generous donations from businesses and families, and to a veritable army of volunteers who cook, clean and organize such adventures as excursions on the camp's pontoon boat.

While scrubbing pots and pans in the kitchen, I was struck by how well everyone in this group got along, even though many had never met before. A few families had come from as far away as Florida. They laughed together, signed letters to send to Congress to protest the Medicare cutbacks, toasted marshmallows on an open fire, and yes, sang familiar camp songs. Even though a small infection could spell a trip to the emergency room, they happily swatted mosquitoes and played roughhouse with each another, as if the unexpected had never happened in their lives and that the wheeze in their lungs was not really permanent but something passing, like the Frisbee that someone had just tossed in their direction.

At the Saturday night camp fire, Ever and her mom sat together, chatting with others. They smiled often. For Ever, keeping a positive frame of mind is essential.

That's one of the messages Ever wrote in the June-July edition of I.G. Living!, a publication devoted to the community of immune-globulin patients.

"It is through my experiences that I am learning about people and about behavior, and about fear and love," she wrote. "It is through all of this that I have learned the will to survive."

No longer able to continue her singing career, Ever told me she was going to study music therapy.

Helping others — not a bad way for Ever to spend those pennies from heaven that came raining down on her the day she was told her dream of singing to the world was over.

August 8, 2006

Birth of the Fathers Network

"Fathering is the single most creative, complicated, fulfilling, frustrating, engrossing, enriching, depleting endeavor of a man's adult life."
— Kyle Pruett, "In the Nurturing Father"

James May remembers the day in vivid detail. It was 10 on a Saturday morning. May entered the family home and saw his father pacing back and forth, like a caged animal.

This meeting between father and son had come about in a most unusual way. May was there on an assignment from graduate school. Then in his early 30s, May had decided to stop teaching and become a counselor. In one of his classes, the professor had asked the students to interview a parent about a traumatic event that had happened to their family.

That was an easy one for May. And it had a name, too: juvenile rheumatoid arthritis.

When he was 14 years old, May had noticed his arm hurting after tossing a baseball around. The problem worsened. At summer camp, he woke up one morning and realized he couldn't get out of bed. Arthritis had attacked his body. It changed his life, and those around him, forever.

Soon the arthritis spread to 30 joints. For the next three years — when most high school boys are spending their time playing sports, cruising with buddies and chasing after girls, May was in and out of hospitals. There were limited options for treatment back then.

He popped aspirin as if they were candy, taking up to 25 a day. This regimen eventually ate holes in his stomach, causing internal bleeding and more misery. To provide relief, doctors would put his limbs in plaster casts. But that only ended up withering away his muscles.

His mother took on the role of full-time care provider. Her life plunged into a daily struggle to assist her son. Desperate for support, she once visited her minister and was devastated by what he had told her: Your son's disease was God's way of saying you had sinned.

Now abandoned by her church, she was also deserted by her friends. Depression filled the void.

May's father moved in a vastly different direction. A successful salesman, he was soon on the road seven days a week. "I sort of lost my dad," May said. Never once did his father ask about the disease that was destroying his son. Never once did he visit his son's doctor. And only once, when he got the news of his son's diagnosis, did he ever say the words "juvenile rheumatoid arthritis."

And now, some 20 years later, after his mom had died much sooner than she should have and after battling the disease to a standstill, May was there, face to face with his dad, this tormented man who had turned his back on his family during the very worst of times.

Filled with anger, May asked the question that had haunted him for years: Where were you when I was sick?

What happened next shocked both of them. May's dad cried, and cried, and cried. This tough-as-steel man, who couldn't bear to see the sight of his son in pain, sobbed from the very depths of his heart.

"I'm sorry. I failed you as a father," he confided to his son. Feeling helpless and realizing he couldn't fix his son and make him normal again, May's dad walked away from the pain by walking away from his family.

The two men, so distant for so long, talked for eight hours.

May had finally discovered his father again, and at the same time, discovered a new calling. He realized that if his father had become this isolated, what about other fathers of children with special needs?

So his journey began.

In the years that followed, May took his immense skills as a counselor and a teacher and created a program for fathers — the Washington State Fathers Network — that has touched countless lives across the nation. He pursued this new passion despite battling arthritis everyday of his life, becoming what he jokingly refers to as "the bionic man" after being fitted with five artificial joints.

A nonprofit program of the Kindering Center in Bellevue, the Fathers Network began with a small group of dads meeting with May once a week.

Now there are more than a dozen chapters throughout the state holding regular meetings, including one in Yakima, which I and another dad of a son with special needs help to coordinate. The Fathers Network sponsors state and regional conferences, publishes a regular newsletter and maintains a website packed with testimonials from fathers and links to information about resources and disabilities.

It wasn't easy in the beginning. First May had to break through the male stereotype of what it meant to be a man — always in control, supremely self-sufficient, able to fix problems without seeking help.

He performed this task in a deceptively simple manner. He brought men together and allowed them to share their fears, their pain, their loneliness, and best of all, their love for their children. They had only one thing in common — they all played a vital role in the lives of children with special needs.

"To finally openly talk about one's child, to know we have many of the same fears, angers, and frustrations as well as the joys of personal accomplishment, is an incredibly powerful experience," the 64-year-old May once wrote. "The isolation slips away as the commonalities become supremely evident."

Last October, James May retired after nearly 19 years of leading the Fathers Network. In a room in downtown Seattle filled with friends and fathers and the children whom they loved so dearly, May and his father stood side by side, arm in arm, a symbol of strength forged by pain and regret and nurtured by a deep, enduring affection for each other.

On Tuesday, after rallying his strength during the past few weeks to hear his son's voice one more time, May's dad died. He was 93. Though he will be deeply missed, the love he shared with his son James will be long remembered and cherished by those who knew them.

And it all started at 10 on a Saturday morning with a son searching for his father, and a father sharing his innermost feelings and doubts with his son.

June 19, 2005

Remarkable father sees good in life

Hogan Hilling stands tall.

Sure he's got height, sort of like an NBA player, with long arms and a willowy frame. When facing him, I get the odd feeling I'm eye-level with his belly button.

He's a gentle giant, though. Soft-spoken, and with a smile that never fades entirely from his face. His thinning hair is the only sign of aging that I can see. He's pleasant and agreeable, in sharp contrast to the personality you would imagine from someone who's a bulldog when it comes to his family.

Hogan is on a mission that has taken him far from the humdrum routine of hanging wallpaper for a living to the heady atmosphere of nationally televised shows, state awards and speaking engagements. That doesn't seem to faze him. He's got a great story to tell and he has taken it far beyond his hometown of Irvine, California. It's all about how great it is to be a dad.

With three sons, one of whom requires 24-hour care due to his profound disabilities, Hogan has eagerly accepted the mantle of stay-at-home dad, sending his wife off to succeed in the world of dollars and decimal points.

Since he started staying home with the kids more than 11 years ago, Hogan has accomplished more than keeping a tidy house or reading nightly to his sons. He's helped to start several dads' organizations, one for expectant parents at a local hospital. In 1995, the honors started rolling in, with a national parents' magazine declaring him "parent of the month," and the former governor of California, Pete Wilson, handing him a highly sought-after Courage To Care Award.

Last Father's Day, Hogan sauntered onstage for the "Oprah" show and was handed the keys to a new wheelchair-lift van specially constructed for Wesley, his now 12-year-old son who has a rare genetic disability that has robbed him of both his ability to speak and to walk.

This year he published a book, "The Man Who Would Be Dad," and is developing a national workshop program titled, "Proud Dads."

Who would have guessed Hogan would have traveled this far in such a relatively short time? Well, I bet Hogan did. The guy emits positive energy.

That's what a roomful of dads and I found out several weeks ago when Hogan spoke at the annual Washington State Fathers Network conference in Seattle. It's an organization of dads — we have a chapter here in Yakima — who play vital roles in the lives of children with special needs, from autistic sons like mine to those battling cerebral palsy and a dizzying array of genetic abnormalities. Though the 80 or so dads in the conference room varied in size, shape, age and occupation, there's one thing we all had in common, and it's something we share with Hogan — an abiding love for our sons and daughters with disabilities. It's an affection mixed with hope and the acceptance of a crushing, bittersweet reality. That's what makes it lasting, a bond that's often unspoken and virtually unbreakable.

Hogan spoke about that affection for Wesley, the blond-haired boy who will never get to play basketball or even say the word "Daddy." It was devastating to Hogan when the gravity of Wesley's disabilities was discovered. But that didn't stop Hogan from rolling up his sleeves and trying to make the world, in which Wesley found himself trapped, a place where he could thrive. When he tried to get Wesley enrolled in the preschool that his older brother Grant was in, administrators balked. They didn't want to take him.

"That sent a message to Grant that his brother is not good enough to be in this world," Hogan said.

Hogan continued on. He didn't succeed through embittered tirades or with a team of lawyers. Instead, Hogan said he kept a positive attitude and forced administrators to focus on what Wesley could do, not what he couldn't accomplish.

It's this positive approach that has carried Hogan and his family through the long days when seizures would imprison Wesley with unremitting frequency. It's the same positive attitude that drew the producers of an ABC-TV special, "Fathers and Sons," to his house several years ago.

How they got there, of course, is another classic Hogan Hilling tale. The ABC producers showed up in California with absolutely no idea where to find dads for their special. So they made what they thought was a logical move: They started calling around to golf courses asking anyone who picked up the phone if there was a dad out there on the back nine who might make a good interview. A ludicrous approach, but it remarkably netted a great dad. They happened upon a caddy shack where the pro had just read a newspaper article featuring none other than Hogan and his son Wesley.

A phone call to Hogan resulted in an initial interview. The producers were oblivious to the fact that Hogan was already a strong voice for dads, having co-founded a Fathers Network chapter in Orange County and having received a governor's award. No, the highly paid television producers knew none of this. What they did discover, though, was a touching story unfolding before their eyes of a loving dad and his son.

So they filmed. After a long day of interviewing at home, Hogan decided to take a break. He walked outside and stood at the railing of his deck. Wesley followed, crawling along the wooden planks that led out to his dad. The cameraman saw what was unfolding and started to roll the film even though both Hogan and Wesley had their backs to the camera.

It's lucky the cameraman shot from that angle. The scene is remarkably poignant, with a son, unable to walk, crawling toward his dad, one painful move at a time, and finally pulling his twisted body up to the railing and there, draping his arm around his dad's shoulder, an embrace that seemed to last forever.

Against this silhouette of father and son, the producers later dubbed in the voice of Hogan reading the lines from a poem he had written about Wesley when his son was only 18 months old:

Instead of walking with you,
I will crawl with you.
Instead of talking with you,
I will find ways to communicate with you.
Instead of focusing on what you cannot do,
I will reward you with love for what you can do.
Instead of isolating you,
I will create adventures for you,
Instead of feeling sorry for you,
I will respect you.

Through Wesley, Hogan wrote about discovering the untold truth within a father-child relationship, that it "is more than just a dad's genetic ties to his child. It's about the soul."

From wallpaper hanger to philosopher, Hogan has many callings, but the one he will always list first is dad. For Wesley and his two brothers, that's the most important of all.

June 16, 2002

POSTSCRIPT: Hogan has written two more books, "Rattled: What He's Thinking When You're Pregnant" and "Pacifi(her): What She's Thinking When She's Pregnant." In November 2010, Hogan appeared with his wife, Tina, for the second time on Oprah. During the interview, Oprah showed a segment from the ABC documentary in which Hogan recites his poem about Wesley. That clip can be seen on YouTube by searching for "Hogan Hilling" or "Inspirational Dad Video."

Bragging has its virtues

What we need to see are more fathers as braggarts and fewer as lazy bums. You know the drill — in the TV advertisements, the plump papa is mired deep in his leather lounge chair rooting for his favorite football team with a beer in one hand and a greasy buffalo wing in the other.

Why cheer for overpaid athletes you'll never meet when someone much closer to home deserves the attention? What's wrong with being labeled a "braggart" anyway? Is it a crime to be the family's ultimate cheerleader — without the pompoms, of course — heaping accolades on a son or daughter with an arsenal of fist-bumps and high-fives?

For fathers raising "typically developing" children, the bragging comes easy. Driving children to athletic practices may be a pain, but the exhilaration of seeing them kick the winning goal in soccer or drive a home run over the fence in Little League more than makes up for the hours spent behind the wheel. Then comes academics, the honor roll, perhaps entry into the National Honor Society and a scholarship to a prestigious university. No problem bragging about those accomplishments.

What happens, though, when a doctor tells a father, who had always hoped to see his son throw a touchdown pass or his daughter play Chopin at a piano recital, that his child has a lifelong disability? What happens next?

Shattered dreams, lots of them. The diagnosis of a disability, whether it's Down syndrome, autism or a life-threatening genetic disorder, tears apart the known world for a father and draws him deep into a labyrinth of isolation, where he becomes a stranger to his friends and even his family.

This is not a new revelation by any means. I have seen it played out many times before in my capacity as regional coordinator for the Washington

State Fathers Network, a statewide organization devoted to reasserting the vital role of fathers and men in the lives of children with disabilities.

While raising a son with autism, I found myself on the outside looking in after his diagnosis back in 1987. I wanted an easy fix. Face it, men are fixers. Give us a power tool and a little time, and we can build a village. But give us a disability that defies a cure, and we lose our way.

Getting dads to understand their crucial role in raising a child with disabilities isn't easy. How the medical community treats fathers doesn't help, either. It happens at a time when dads are the most vulnerable — when they walk into a doctor's office or a clinic with their wives to talk about their child's disability.

Invariably, the doctor or therapist will only look at the child's mother. They avoid the angry, brooding man sitting next to her. It may take place only once, but that's enough. During parent workshops and conferences that I have spoken at, I ask fathers for a show of hands if this has ever happened to them. A moment later the room is filled with waving hands.

That's why bragging is so important. Think of it. When do fathers of children with special needs get to brag about their kids? Not at the doctor's office, that's for sure. That's why at the Fathers Network, whenever fathers get together, we give everyone a chance to brag about their kids.

Success at potty training? That's cause for a round of high-fives.

A 12-year-old daughter gets her first invitation to a birthday party? Cheers for dad and daughter.

A son who requires 24-hour care goes for a month without a seizure? A well-deserved pat on the back for the single dad.

It was more than 20 years ago when I first heard a group of dads brag about their kids with disabilities. We were huddled inside a classroom at Hoover Elementary School in Yakima.

When asked to boast about his 13-month-old daughter, a young father told of a miracle that had happened a few days earlier. As he was cradling his very sick daughter in his arms and whispering a lullaby in her ear, the father noticed something he had never seen before — a smile.

For more than a year, his daughter had never shown an emotion, never revealed an expression until that night when the corners of her mouth arced upward into a smile.

Those tender words still echo today and reinforce what James May, retired program director for the Fathers Network, once told a room crowded with dads: "Hug your kids everyday; tell them you love them, and then do it again. Always brag about and share your child's accomplishments."

That's when being a braggart takes on new meaning for a dad. It becomes a badge of honor.

June 20, 2010

IN SEARCH OF ANSWERS

When I knelt down on the concrete floor of a lonely stretch of highway in North Dakota and tried to breathe life into a stranger who had collapsed minutes earlier, I realized that what I was doing made little difference. I was powerless. I felt lost, utterly alone.

Nearly two decades later, I'm still asking: What's it all about?

Up a cliff of no return

Before there were gravity-defying heroics in movies like "Vertical Limits" and those endless vignettes on cable television where sinewy mortals scamper catlike up sheer rock facings, there once were guys like me, in cut-off shorts and floppy Converse tennis shoes, who hung by our fingernails with only a bed of boulders to cushion our fall from grace.

Climbing didn't come to me naturally, if at all. I arrived at my vertical angst by sheer folly and fate.

Blame it all on Kierkegaard and the U.S. Army.

Let's go back to May 1973. I had just been discharged from the Army after spending the last year of my two-year hitch at Fort Sam Houston in San Antonio. Having no desire to stay in the land of swarming mosquitoes, hostile rattlers and road-kill armadillos, I pointed my intrepid Volkswagen bug westward and, two weeks later, ended up in Durango, Colorado. It was there I wanted to test my newfound freedom.

Often I would daydream while in the Army of a time when I could live as an existentialist should, in the manner embraced by philosophers like Soren Kierkegaard and Martin Heidegger — "to live as if you were floating over 7,000 fathoms of water."

Well, that's a rather poor translation of existentialist philosophy, but that's about all I could remember from my college classes. I was not the brightest of students, but I did fix on certain ideas, and that was one of them.

Since 7,000 fathoms of water seemed a bit far removed from the scrub oak and mountain valleys of Durango, I decided to try my hand at free climbing. No ropes and clanging pitons to get in my way, just sheer grit and determination.

To my meager mind, it seemed the ultimate test of a budding existentialist would be to drink deep from the cup of life and taste the bitterness of sheer terror. That's what Kierkegaard would have urged. Besides mankind being invested with the greatest of gifts — the freedom to choose — the 19th-century Danish philosopher also saw that God drew us to our ultimate calling through the depths of despair and anxiety. Dread, in a word. That's for me, I thought. Scaling impossible rock cliffs with no footholds, no hope.

So off I went one morning to explore a river canyon north of Durango. I bid farewell to my friend who headed upriver for a long hike into the mountains. Alone, I found my way to the river's edge and began scanning the rocky cliffs for a suitable warm-up climb. There, that looks good, I thought to myself, as if I had any experience in vertical climbing. Having none, I concluded the slope was perfect for my purposes.

The rock wall I was to scale jutted out from the river canyon's high walls, which rose some 200 feet from the boulder-strewn stream below. The wall started low at the river's edge and angled impressively to the top of the canyon — or at least that's what I thought. But at that moment, I had no intention of climbing the rock wall to its peak. I just wanted to climb straight up a 20- or 30-foot section and practice some maneuvers, since I had none to begin with.

Completing a few deep knee-bends, I grabbed hold of the rock and up I climbed, merrily humming to myself, quite unlike any existentialist that Kierkegaard had ever envisioned. Perhaps I was a new breed, I thought, one who laughed in the face of adversity.

At about the 20-foot mark, I felt exhilarated. This isn't so bad. The adrenaline, no doubt, had fogged my brain for I soon realized that going up is far easier than going down, a maneuver I tried to do. On my third step down, my gym shoe slipped out from a thin outcropping. Maybe venturing a little higher wouldn't be such a bad idea after all, I surmised.

So up the slope I went. Suddenly the firm climbing-rock vanished. I gasped greedily for air as my mouth sucked in dust from the clumps of rock that were being pulverized in my hands. Not an encouraging sign.

I looked down once, but realized that was a bad idea. Dizziness set in. I also noticed a twitching sensation in my knees. Was I hyperventilating,

I wondered? My stomach churned. I felt queasy, not unlike the nausea that Jean Paul Sartre, another famed existentialist, had once written about. It comes when you confront the random pointlessness of the universe and realize that freedom, though intoxicating, greets you at every moment with no point of reference to ultimately tell you whether your choices were right or wrong.

I decided to forego the lesson in nausea and slow my breathing. I looked up and found what I thought was my salvation — the top of the ridge.

A few minutes later, I took in the scenery. It's not what I had expected at all. Nothingness lay before me. There was no gentle slope rolling down from the ridge's knifelike edge. In fact, it curved inward. A cliff within a cliff.

Now, sheer panic set in. Get to the top of the river canyon, a voice cried out inside of me. My eyes trailed up the ridge's spine that led to a soft blanket of grass atop the canyon. Yeah, I could do that, I mumbled to myself.

My hands clutched at the sharp rocks that studded the ridge like so many spikes. I had lost all sense of heroic intent and was now audibly grunting as I frantically pursued terra firma.

Disappointment, the nectar of existentialists, greeted me — again. I was a few feet away from reaching the canyon's top when I realized the ridge ended abruptly, a full body-length away from pine and aspen trees that were my sanctuary.

I moved to the edge of the ridge and reached out. My right hand came within a few inches of an exposed root of a tree that clung resolutely to the outer-most edge of the canyon wall. It seemed like a big enough root. But was it sturdy? Was it firmly fixed to the tree or was it one of those phantom roots, the kind you pull at and off it comes, throwing you to the ground — a comedic pratfall waiting to happen?

My brain tried to conjure up some semblance of rational thought. Nothing came out — except fear.

Leap, you fool, leap and take hold of the tree root. With no other thought left in my dazed brain, I tensed my legs and lunged forward, the only direction that could save me from my own folly.

In my right hand, I gripped the root. It held.

With my other hand, I clawed away at the wet sod and dragged my body onto the hilltop. The dread, which had filled every fiber of my being, washed away. I stared greedily at the sun as it sparkled through the aspens.

It's strange how certain episodes in a person's life can always be there, to be relived at the flick of an eyelid or, as in my case, the mere sight of a rocky cliff. I still feel the panic to this day, some 27 years later. The existentialists were right. The dread never leaves.

I can't say I'm still a huge fan of Kierkegaard. I haven't read him since then. No need to. Living to the fullest is always the preferred route to take, even if it does lead you up a cliff of no return.

February 4, 2001

A chance encounter

It's not something you expect to see while driving through the Badlands of North Dakota — a man on the floor of a rest area bathroom, his legs buckled under and someone at his side calling out, "I can't find a pulse."

Disbelief, that was my first reaction. Only minutes earlier I had been checking out the map to see how far it was to Bismarck and suddenly I found myself kneeling down on the cold tile floor, trying to breathe life back into someone I didn't know.

What are the odds of encountering a life-and-death emergency while driving 2,100 miles from Yakima to Green Bay? A few minutes either way would have made all the difference. If our family hadn't driven around Billings that morning, searching for the perfect cinnamon roll, we never would have come upon the stricken man.

We did and our day was no longer routine. Sometimes a situation offers you no choice but to act. To do otherwise is really not an option, unless your heart is a lump of coal. You act and worry about the consequences later.

It was a cloudy August afternoon, about 3 p.m. We pulled over at Exit 32 along Interstate 94 that leads to the Painted Canyon Visitor Center, one of the few "viewpoints" in North Dakota. It lies on the south unit of the Theodore Roosevelt National Park near the state's western border.

My wife, Bronnie, walked on ahead to the restrooms while my two sons and I strolled over to take in the sights of the park's forbidding landscape of serpentine ravines and bizarrely shaped spires of rock. We scanned the horizon for buffalo herds that were promised in the tour book, but saw only a labyrinth of canyons. At that moment, Joe Kanski, the chief maintenance man for the Painted Canyon Visitor Center, was finishing up his work for the day. He had been employed by the park service for the past 19 years and, for the last 12 years, had been assigned exclusively to Painted Canyon, responsible for keeping the restrooms clean and the sewage system running.

Joe had arrived to work that day with a pounding headache. He had complained about it to several people and was thinking about leaving early. But Joe wasn't a quitter. He rarely, if ever, called in sick. So he told a fellow worker he would "tough it out."

And he did. Shortly before his shift was to end at 3:30 p.m., Joe made one last check of the women's restroom. Before going inside, he told a woman standing there that he would take only a minute or two. That woman was my wife.

Moments later, Joe passed out. Hearing a commotion inside, Bronnie opened the door and found Joe on the floor, his head bleeding from a fall. She screamed for help. At first, no one responded. The door opened several times but closed quickly. Only a young child paid heed to the plaintive call for help.

Soon into the darkened room arrived another park employee and three or four travelers who also had responded to the emergency. The young park employee had radioed for assistance, but was told it could take awhile before trained medics would arrive. North Dakota is a big, lonely state, with the nearest hospital 26 miles away in Dickinson.

When my sons and I reached the restrooms, a small group of people was blocking the way to the women's bathroom. I overheard a woman say an ambulance had been called.

Not seeing my wife, I pushed through the milling crowd and stepped into the restroom. I found Bronnie crouched over Joe. Several others were also tending to him, tugging at the buttons of his shirt and trying to comfort him.

I moved closer and could tell the situation was desperate. Joe's lean body lay motionless on the floor, his pants soaked by urine. His face had turned a sickly pale, purplish color.

We knew there was little time to waste. We certainly couldn't stand around. It was up to us, a collection of passers-by who had wandered unwittingly into this unfolding drama, to provide first aid and try to keep Joe alive.

Though no one would utter the words, we knew it might already be too late.

"Do you want to begin CPR?" a fellow traveler asked. Several of us replied, "Yes." The short, white-haired man, who sported a neatly trimmed goatee, hunkered down and began to give mouth-to-mouth resuscitation. He pinched Joe's nose and breathed deeply into his mouth. Joe's chest rose slightly and fed the air back into the man's face. The traveler groaned and backed off.

I offered to help. Together, the man with the white goatee and I went through the CPR drill. He applied compressions to the chest while I gave mouth-to-mouth.

Despite repeated chest compressions, we could not feel a pulse. But we kept at it, knowing once you begin CPR you are not supposed to stop. I continued breathing in between the rounds of compressions, my blast of air whistling through Joe's throat. But the only hint of life was Joe's left eye that remained open, gazing up at me, the darkness of the pupil as inky black as any moonless night I'd ever seen.

The minutes passed slowly. Still no ambulance.

We decided to give Joe a pep talk. "Come on, Joe, you can breathe," we pleaded. "Come on Joe, you can do it."

Then something remarkable happened. I backed off the mouth-to-mouth. Immediately his lips pressed together and his tongue pushed forward. Was he breathing? We all cheered.

"I still can't find a pulse," said the man with the white goatee.

We would cheer no more. We resumed the CPR routine. Another traveler came forward to help with the chest compressions.

When the medics arrived, we were emotionally drained. The medics ripped open his T-shirt and patched him up to a defibrillator, which jars the heart back to life through electric shocks. The portable machine had a computer-generated speech simulator that coolly called out instructions in a soothing, feminine voice. It sent an electric jolt that lifted Joe's body into the air.

Still no pulse.

Later in the ambulance, and again at the hospital emergency room in Dickinson, medics were able to get a faint pulse following several electric shocks. But always the heart failed to sustain a beat.

There were to be no miracles that day in the Badlands of North Dakota. After less than an hour at the hospital, doctors pronounced Joe Kanski dead.

Cause of death is unofficially listed as an aneurism, or a broken blood vessel. That might explain the terrible headaches he had experienced earlier in the day.

Joe, who was in his early 50s, left behind a wife. They had no children.

At his funeral, scores of friends filled the Ukrainian Catholic church in Belfield, just nine miles from where Joe had worked. The superintendent at the national park said the outpouring of affection didn't surprise him. He said Joe was always "real personable" and would often welcome into his home volunteers who were assigned to the park during the summer months.

Looking back at the incident, there wasn't much we could have done. I sensed that minutes before the medics finally arrived. Cradling Joe's head, I pressed an open palm against his cheek. "Everything's OK now," I whispered in his ear.

His left eye never blinked. But it seemed to follow me as I leaned back. Was he listening? Could he see the sorrow in my face?

I passed my hand across his forehead and gently closed the eyelid. He never looked up at me again.

September 14, 1997

The ephemera: A fleeting emblem of life

Sherry Engebretsen. Patrick Holmes. Artemio Trinidad-Mena. Julia Blackhawk. Paul Eickstadt.

All five were strangers except for one critical detail — late on a sunny afternoon, August 1, they were together on the same bridge span in Minneapolis. One of them had made a point of telling her family she hated going over the bridge because of the heavy traffic. But that day she decided to take a chance.

Her car was one of about 150 on the span when it collapsed at 6:05 p.m. It took only four seconds.

All five died. None of the five had reason to believe they wouldn't be home that night, having dinner with family and friends. Tragedy knows no boundaries.

Jillian Lee Ward. Becky Lynn Fife.

Two names, two separate lives, both from the Yakima Valley. Ward, a 26-year-old with an infectious smile, worked at St. Paul Cathedral School. Becky, an 11-year-old who attended Ahtanum Valley Elementary School, loved to play soccer.

They had gone into the water to have fun. Neither assumed anything bad would happen.

Ward was rafting in the Wenatchee River with friends last Sunday. They decided to free themselves from the raft, untying their inner tubes. She tried to help when one of her friends was pulled under a logjam. Ward became entangled in a branch and drowned.

Becky had gone swimming in the Naches River two days earlier. She made it out to the middle of the river before the swift currents overwhelmed her. No one could reach her in time.

On Wednesday their pictures appeared together in our newspaper. On the obituary page.

I read of these deaths and recalled, with bitter sadness, the tragic deaths that have filled my life. Though it happened 15 years ago, how could I ever forget that phone call from my mother telling me my older brother had died of a heart attack. He had sat down in a chair after playing tennis and collapsed. He was 45. It was his birthday.

Surely my brother never thought he wouldn't be alive for another hour, another year, another decade or more. We have expectations; we make plans. When tragedy strikes, life suddenly seems so short, death so fickle.

I remember reading in my high school English class a whimsical essay written by Ben Franklin in the late 1770s. While living in France, a country he loved as much as America, Franklin penned a series of essays, what the French call "bagatelles" or trifles. One of those trifles was titled "The Ephemera: An Emblem of Human Life."

The story is about Franklin's chance encounter with the ephemera, a tiny mosquito "whose successive generations, we were told, were bred and expired within the day."

Noting he is an expert on the languages of inferior animal tongues — a reason why, he jokes, he has trouble with the charming French language — he's able to decipher what the ephemera are saying. While listening to several chatter, he is struck by their impassioned debate about a trivial topic. They are discussing the merits of two musicians, trying to divine who is better, "seemingly regardless of the shortness of life as if they had been sure of living a month. Happy people!"

Franklin ends his "bagatelle" by recounting the soliloquy of a much older ephemera who, though in still good health, expects to live no more than seven or eight minutes more. Having lived for so long and having seen entire generations of ephemera come and go, the venerable fly acknowledged his fame, as surely as Franklin had recognized his own at the time. "But what will fame be to an ephemera who no longer exists?"

Back when I first read this, I cared little for Franklin's jabs at the fleeting nature of governments and the shallowness of courtly vanities. Instead,

I felt sorry for the unlucky ephemera cursed with the life span of a mere 18 hours.

We cannot always live as if we are allotted a single sunrise. But we can behave differently, and we surely must remember that the people dearest to us may not be there at the end of the day — whether that day is indeed measured in hours or in months or in years.

For the families and friends of those in Minneapolis and here who have lost so much in the recent tragedies, regrets are many and the future, once so bright, has grown bleak. When my brother died, I took comfort in knowing that when I got the chance, I told him how much he meant to me.

It was an hour before his wedding. "You are my very best friend," I said to him. We parted with a hug. And then the moment was gone, so fleeting, so ephemeral.

August 12, 2007

Forgetting victims would be a crime, too

For Elie Wiesel, the act of remembering is not meant to heal wounds or to make sense out of the chaos of losing loved ones.

It's an obligation.

As a Holocaust survivor who lost his mother, father and little sister in Adolf Hitler's death camps, Wiesel came to realize that memory was the only pathway to salvation for those who had escaped the incinerators of Auschwitz.

"For us, forgetting was never an option," Wiesel said in a lecture prior to accepting the Nobel Prize for Peace in 1986. An author, teacher and gifted storyteller, Wiesel received the prestigious award for his efforts to help oppressed people around the world.

"Remembering is a noble and necessary act," he said. "The call of memory, the call to memory, reaches us from the very dawn of history. No commandment figures so frequently, so insistently, in the Bible. It is incumbent upon us to remember the good we have received, and the evil we have suffered."

The need to recount the misery and the senseless, systematic slaughter of nearly an entire race of people became for Wiesel the only way out of the rubble of civilized society where all of mankind's accomplishments had seemingly vanished, rising as shadowy vapors from the smoke-stacks of crematoriums like Treblinka.

"Each one of us felt compelled to record every story, every encounter," Wiesel said. "Each one of us felt compelled to bear witness. Such were the wishes of the dying, the testament of the dead. Since the so-called civilized world had no use for their lives, then let it be inhabited by their deaths."

And there were so many stories, from those who were starving to death in the Warsaw ghetto to even the members of the Sonderkommandos, "those inmates forced to burn their fellow inmates' corpses before being burned in turn."

Survivors of the death camps chronicled the killers and the methods of their slaughter, and told timeless tales of children like "the little girl who, hugging her grandmother, whispered: 'Don't be afraid, don't be sorry to die. I'm not.' " She was 7, that little girl who went to her death without fear, without regret.

Wiesel has seen the face of death, the same mask that the two killers wore who stalked and gunned down students at Columbine High School in Littleton, Colorado.

It was the same mask that Barry Loukaitis wore more than three years ago when he walked into a fifth-grade algebra class at Frontier Junior High School in Moses Lake, Washington, pulled out a deer rifle that he had concealed underneath a long black coat and opened fire, killing a teacher and two students.

One of those murdered students was Arnie Fritz. His mother, Alice Fritz, has kept his memory alive since the day — February 2, 1996 — when her world came crashing in around her.

When she speaks of that day, her words are so clear, so graphic you can almost see the horrifying scene being replayed in slow motion, the bullet spinning in the air on its deadly path toward her son.

"The bullet passed through his arm, his right lung, his heart, his left lung and exited his lower back. Although his wounds were mortal, he did not die immediately."

Alice wrote these words in a story published on the third anniversary of Barry Loukaitis' killing spree. It was part of a three-day series focusing on safety in schools that our newspaper and other daily newspapers across the state printed.

When it comes to making public appearances, Alice rarely declines an offer to talk about her son and the many lost opportunities of saving the emotionally disturbed Barry Loukaitis. I heard her speak to a room full of journalists as we prepared for the statewide series on school safety. When she had finished, tears not only flowed from her but from us as well.

Although separated by geographic and cultural barriers, Alice arrived at the same crossroad that Wiesel reached after he settled in Paris following the war. Forgetting the past is no option. Memory is the only way to escape despair and rekindle hope.

Alice urges us to "fight the natural inclination to move on and put this behind us before the full truth is known, and the grieving process completed. Let's all share what we have learned. It's the least we can do."

Wiesel is not so naive as to think memory alone will provide the answers to the continued threats posed by racism and fanatical beliefs, by prejudice and demagoguery.

"There may be times when we are powerless to prevent injustice, but there must never be a time when we fail to protest," Wiesel said. "The Talmud tells us that by saving a single human being, man can save the world. ... Mankind must remember that peace is not God's gift to his creatures, it is our gift to each other."

For Alice Fritz, her goals may not be so lofty as world peace. But to prevent another Barry Loukaitis from killing children such as hers, that is a noble goal indeed.

In Littleton, if there had been an Alice Fritz around, imagine how much better our world would be today.

May 2, 1999

Tribute to a moral compass for our times

A voice was missing last Easter Sunday.

For more than four decades, he spoke with eloquence and steadfast conviction, easily angering those in power and, in the same breath, just as easily kindling hope for those in despair.

His was a voice of passion and peace, and for his beliefs he was jailed and, at times, reviled. His presence, though, always demanded attention.

But now the Rev. William Sloane Coffin is gone.

Four days before Easter, the 81-year-old Coffin died of congestive heart failure in a small town in Vermont, ending a lifetime of civil disobedience that placed him on board the "Freedom Rides" in the South and in the forefront of the anti-war movement in the '60s when he served as chaplain at Yale University.

For aiding young men to turn in their draft cards as a protest against the Vietnam War, Coffin was indicted by the federal government in what became known as the Benjamin Spock conspiracy trial. For his outspoken criticism against the spread of nuclear arms, he became president emeritus of SANE/FREEZE: Campaign for Global Security.

And for being in the national spotlight, he earned this distinction: being permanently inked in the comic strips of Doonesbury as Reverend Sloan.

Though his career also took him to the pulpit of the influential Riverside Church in New York, I wonder how many here even knew his name, or the profound effect he had on the lives of an entire generation of Americans who were enriched by his moral teachings and by his undiminished faith in a loving God?

Sadly, our newspaper didn't mark his death with a story. So I figured, in this absence, it would be fitting to share a few quotes from his life. These are words that stir the emotions. You may not like what Coffin has to say, but that never stopped him from saying it.

"In life you can either follow your fears or be led by your values, your passion."

Challenging yourself, that's the key.

"All of life is the exercise of risk."

In fall 2003 at the World Communion Sunday at Riverside Church, Coffin continued to spread his sermon of peace at a time when U.S. troops were being killed and wounded in Iraq and Afghanistan.

"Patriotism at the expense of another nation is as wicked as racism at the expense of another race," Coffin said, his words slurred by several strokes he had suffered. "Let us resolve to be patriots always, nationalists never. Let us love our country, but pledge allegiance to the earth and to the flora and fauna and human life that it supports — one planet indivisible, with clean air, soil and water; with liberty, justice and peace for all."

He never failed to urge those in power to address what he saw as the real axis of evils — "environmental degradation, pandemic poverty, and a world awash with weapons."

What also troubled Coffin was our failure to accept responsibility for the world's decline.

"It's clear to me, two things: that almost every square inch of the Earth's surface is soaked with the tears and blood of the innocent, and it's not God's doing," the Presbyterian minister said in an interview two years ago. "It's our doing. That's human malpractice. Don't chalk it up to God."

Coffin had a gift for the sound bite, for the chiseled phrase. His quotes had more bite than sound, and were always layered with deeper meanings, turning the listener into a miner of sorts, drilling for hidden diamonds, greater truths.

"Hope arouses, as nothing else can arouse, a passion for the possible."

The foundation for these thoughts and for his actions was his faith. While today we focus on the differences within the principal faiths of the world, Coffin saw only what they have in common.

"The impulse to love God and neighbor, that impulse is at the heart of Judaism, Islam and Christianity. No question about it — we have much more in common than we have in conflict."

What I find refreshing about Coffin is the fact that he never wore his faith on his sleeve, but in his heart and through his actions. Despite his fame, he never forgot that the message, not the messenger, was what mattered most.

And I will never forget the moving eulogy he gave at his son's funeral in 1983. Words of hope spoken by a father with a broken heart. His faith carried him through, a faith in a God whose love never falters, never dies.

"God gives all of us — minimum protection, maximum support," Coffin said during the eulogy at Riverside Church after his 24-year-old son Alex died when his car skidded off a rain-soaked road and sank into Boston Harbor.

"For some reason, nothing so infuriates me as the incapacity of seemingly intelligent people to get it through their heads that God doesn't go around with his fingers on triggers, his fists around knives, his hands on steering wheels. ... The one thing that should never be said when someone dies is 'It is the will of God.' Never do we know enough to say that."

"My own consolation lies in knowing that it was not the will of God that Alex die; that when the waves closed over the sinking car, God's heart was the first of all our hearts to break."

Coffin knew that for his son — "when Alex beat me to the grave" — the finish line was not the watery tomb in Boston Harbor. "If a week ago last Monday, a lamp went out, it was because, for him at least, the Dawn had come."

Now for William Sloane Coffin, the Dawn has come, too.

April 23, 2006

Sermon of hope, faith still resonates

He stood there, his back straight and eyes intense. He was not a big man, but his booming voice filled the small stone church that had endured so much in the 100 years since it had first taken root in Yakima — world wars, the Great Depression, poverty, gang shootings in the neighboring streets. He knew what he had to say because he could feel in the church an almost palpable sense of determination from those who had accomplished what seemed an impossibility, not as individuals, but as a community of friends, of family, of the faithful.

Stillness filled the space between the pews.

"How did you do it?"

That's how his sermon began and ended. For the next 45 minutes, Bishop John Richard Bryant kept repeating it as he held sway over the 100th anniversary of the Bethel African Methodist Episcopal Church. Though his words echoed more than two years ago in that hallowed church at Sixth and Beech streets in southeast Yakima, what he said still resonates today. Who could have imagined back then the ascendancy of Barack Obama to the presidency of the United States? But somehow in the bishop's message of hope and resilient strength, he foretold that one day there would come a time when an African-American would be sitting in the White House, a home built by slaves more than two centuries ago.

"How did you do it," Bryant asked again, wondering aloud how this tiny church in such an immense universe had ever survived.

But it did. And he knew why: They did it on faith. A faith based, not on the ingenuity of mere mortals, but on a greater power.

"How did you do it," he asked, his salt-and-pepper beard framed around a toothy grin.

I sat there in the church, transfixed by his speech. The celebration took more than three hours, and who cared? It was more than a celebration of a building, more than a celebration of families who had grown up together. It was the celebration of a covenant of faith.

My wife and I were a distinct minority among the blacks who surrounded us. Though we had never been in the church before, we were given a warm welcome and later joined others in singing familiar hymns while outside the early summer sun poked through the clouds and birds danced among the trees.

When the bishop had finished his sermon, I couldn't imagine anything more could be said. And I was right.

The Rev. Juliet Hemphill, pastor of the Bethel AME Church, was the last to address the celebrants. I wondered what more she could say. She didn't have to. Instead, Hemphill picked up a microphone and sang a hymn, without accompaniment. It was beautiful, capturing in song what the bishop had spoken in words.

So this past week I called Hemphill and wondered what she thought about Tuesday's inauguration of Obama as this nation's 44th president. What does this moment in time mean to her church that has survived so much, and especially to the older members who had suffered so much discrimination in the past — their right to vote restricted, their opportunity to buy a home denied, even their ability to drink from a public water fountain blocked by three despicable words — "for whites only."

"I'm excited," she said.

When Obama won in November, Hemphill wrote her next sermon around the theme of "God can do anything." It was a message of belief in God that she says extends to everyone, from those sitting in the pews of her church in Yakima to Obama sitting in the Oval Office.

It is also carried along by the dream of undiminished hope and faith that Dr. Martin Luther King Jr. once spoke of more than four decades ago. For Hemphill and her church that now enters its 103rd year, King's message lives on today, a seed that has borne fruit in the presidency of Obama.

So, too, do the words of Bishop Bryant: "How did you do it?" Today he could ask this same question of Obama.

And his answer would be, as it has been for the members of the Bethel AME Church — through humility and faith in a better tomorrow.

January 18, 2009

Reaching out to our extended family

"... for I was hungry, and you gave me food, I was thirsty and you gave me drink, I was a stranger and you welcomed me, I was naked and you clothed me ..."
— Matthew 25:35-36

Jim Silsbee has had tough assignments in the past. In his 26 years in the Army, he served in Vietnam, France and three times in Korea. He rose to the highest rank for a noncommissioned officer, sergeant major.

Since moving to Yakima, he has taken on a host of challenging tasks, once running a food bank. For the past three years, he has been the lead director for a men's homeless shelter at Englewood Christian Church.

The 70-year-old Silsbee knew the path he had chosen would require long hours with little reward and no pay. But he said he's inspired to help others by following in the footsteps of another.

"To walk in Christ's shoes," he said.

That's not easy for anyone, even a sergeant major. A few weeks ago, Silsbee did just that. I know. I was there.

It was a Friday night, in late February, when the temperature was sinking to the teens. It's the kind of bone-chilling cold that can kill if you don't have a roof over your head. Last year, 29 died among the more than 1,000 who are homeless in Yakima County.

My wife, Leslie, and I were asked that night to stand outside the side door leading to the church's homeless shelter and direct people, who were arriving for a special performance by gospel singers, toward the main entrance.

A little past 6:30 p.m. a van showed up at the side entrance. Fifteen men stepped out into the frigid air and walked toward us. But we didn't turn them away as we did the others. Instead, we opened the doors and greeted the men with smiles.

For these men, the common bond that drew them together was their homelessness. They stepped into the church and knew what waited for them: a home-cooked meal, a clean mattress to sleep on, newly washed socks and hot coffee in the morning.

By 7 p.m., I was standing alone. I had sent Leslie into the church to save me a seat for the gospel singing.

That's when I noticed a man walking toward me. He wore a thin jacket and had his hands shoved deep into the pockets of his jeans. I blocked his way and told him he couldn't enter. He said he was supposed to be there. I figured he was one of the volunteers. So I let him pass.

I was wrong.

Inside the hallway, Jim greeted him and told the young man the shelter was at its 15-man capacity. Those are the rules, he said. Besides, each man has to arrive on the van. There are no exceptions.

That was the military side of Silsbee speaking.

The man pleaded with him to reconsider. He confessed to Silsbee that he had messed up again. This time he failed to report to his parole officer. For that infraction, authorities had put him back in jail. They set him free that evening, but it was too late for him to reach the van in time. That didn't stop him. Despite the cold, he walked to the church at the corner of 44th and Englewood avenues — a distance of four miles.

Silsbee knew what had to be done next. How could he turn this man out into the cold, without food and nowhere to go? That's not what Jesus would have done when, during his life, he cared for the downtrodden, the sick, the unwanted.

"We will find a place for you to sleep," Jim told the man.

With the gospel song "I Will Dance Like David Danced" echoing down the hallway, the man sat down to a hot meal. He had found a home, finally.

Last week, the five homeless shelters in the county closed for the winter after being open every night since early December. Coordinated by the Sunrise Outreach Ministries, in collaboration with the Homeless Network of Yakima County, these shelters have a 70-bed capacity, mostly for men. Organizers hope one day, in the not-so-distant future, to create a permanent homeless shelter in northeast Yakima.

Silsbee is among 500 volunteers who keep the shelters in full operation. With the Rev. Dave Hanson at the helm, Sunrise Outreach relies on a steady supply of donated food and clothing: fresh green salad, Ranch dressing, instant oatmeal, breakfast bars, thick socks, boxer shorts, gloves and hats. Warm meals are prepared by a vast network of volunteer cooks, many from churches dotting the Yakima area.

Leslie and I have also donated clothing and food, including a spiral ham that the men ate the night we stood as sentinels outside the side door. Once when Leslie stepped inside to warm up, one of the men approached her. "Thanks so much for the ham," he said.

Silsbee noted these kinds of compliments are common.

"They are very grateful for what we provide," he said.

It helps that these men are treated like neighbors, like family, for that's really who they are. How far removed are any of us from being homeless, to be in need of a warm meal and a friendly smile?

Witness the tragedy that is now unfolding in Japan where, in a matter of minutes, entire cities were swept away by a tsunami, leaving thousands dead and thousands more without homes.

Really, what better way to make sense out of a world that, at times, seems spinning out of control than to open the doors to a church with the promise of a sanctuary from the cold. To say to someone in need, as Jim Silsbee has done countless times: "Welcome. We have been waiting for you."

March 20, 2011

Lost loves of all kinds can cause heartache

She's in her late 60s and lives alone. She rarely gets two hours of sleep. She's like so many who stubbornly fight the past, unable to make peace with what has been lost.

A soldier returns from the war in Iraq and suffers through the post-traumatic stress of combat. He has lost his sense of balance and must find his way in a world that is suddenly strange to him.

Teachers enter their classrooms, and are filled with anger. They have lost the passion for their one true love — teaching. They feel it's been taken from them by the tedious requirements of state testing standards and the federal No Child Left Behind Act. Gone are the days of creativity and shared discovery. Now it's all about teaching to the test.

A man's wife dies a few weeks after he retires. They had planned on traveling to the farthest reaches of the world. Now, instead of visiting Italy or the Caribbean, he holds yard sales, selling off the remnants of his past.

Lost loves.

Martin Howell has dealt with all of these, and more. He knows all about lost loves. But so do we. The older we get, the more lost loves we endure.

That's why with Valentine's Day only a few heartbeats away, I decided to sit down and talk with Howell.

I'm not alone. A lot of people have already done that. He's the Dr. Phil of the Yakima Valley. Actually, he's much better. His life experiences alone qualify him for some kind of medal for courage and compassion.

He has cared for those dying from AIDS. He has counseled those in hospice and those with broken hearts and shattered souls. He has traveled to Kenya and Addis Ababa where he reached out to the world's poorest.

He arrived in Yakima in 1991 and for the past eight years has worked as a senior consultant with LeMaster & Daniels, a Yakima accounting firm. It's a strange place for someone with a master's degree in social work. In fact, he's probably the only one in the nation with an MSW after his name serving alongside a bunch of CPAs.

When he's not helping nonprofit organizations like the Yakima Family YMCA with strategic planning, he's conducting workshops on how to deal with changes in life and at work, inspired by the writings of Spencer Johnson, author of "Who Moved My Cheese?"

Howell knows why Valentine's Day can be such a difficult time for many of us. It has to do with the way we handle our lost loves. We don't. We try everything to avoid confronting them.

And lost loves, Howell points out, are not restricted to the loss of wives and husbands, family and friends. Lost pets, lost jobs, lost youth, lost health, lost honor, lost freedom. We grieve for all of these.

Especially lost intimacy. It is one of the great losses in our wired society. With the popularity of text messaging, e-mails, cell phones and iPods, we are no longer truly in touch with others. We no longer see their smiles, their frowns, their bodies speaking to us. Nor do we hear their voices quake with fear or sadness or joy.

That's why Howell is not surprised that so many relationships are in conflict. The moment intimacy and openness arrive, someone falls apart. We are not ready for the consequences, nor do we welcome the pain that may follow.

Even worse is the way our culture commands us to love ourselves. The bigger the ego, the better. We take pride in the Donald Trumps of the world and see material wealth — the trappings of a super ego — as the ultimate goal.

What a waste of humanity, Howell would argue. Humility, and not a Hummer 3 parked in the driveway, is the road to riches. With humility comes gratitude — for the lost loves that have graced our lives.

For this reason, Howell recommends doing something significant, especially for what he calls the "heavy-duty losses." In honor of my late wife, I started a scholarship fund for special education teachers at Central Washington University. For his part, Howell chose to plant aspen trees in his backyard. He planted 17 for the dear friends whom he lost to AIDS. The stand of aspens now has spread to more than 50.

© 2012 Peanuts Worldwide LLC

Artwork courtesy of Peanuts Worldwide

Under several of the trees, the 60-year-old Howell has buried the ashes of his beloved pets, including Farnaby, a floppy-eared Springer mix he retrieved from a shelter run by the "Dumb Friends League" in Denver.

A tree was almost planted in Howell's memory last year. Weakened by a long bout with the flu, he arrived at the emergency room scarcely breathing. One of his legs had swollen to what he described as the size of a balloon. A blood clot blocked his lungs. He was minutes from death.

Tough times. That's why gratitude and humility are words Howell uses often.

He also recommends the following exercise to ease our earthly burdens. It's his Valentine's gift to everyone.

It's really simple. Just remember Charlie Brown's trusted beagle. Throw your head back, raise your arms in the air ... and do the Snoopy Dance.

Keep dancing until you smile.

February 10, 2008

POSTSCRIPT: Martin suffered an apparent aneurism and died at his home on July 22, 2011. One of Martin's close friends asked if I could help lead his memorial service, which was held at the Yakima Valley Museum on August 8. To close the service, I stood before more than 250 of Martin's friends and family members and performed the Snoopy Dance. It worked. We all laughed till we cried.

Simple things bring joy to life

What is the key ingredient to life?

It's a question that has haunted the world's greatest philosophers for centuries. Is it vast wealth, good health, a loving and blissful relationship with another? Or is it something less obvious, like getting 3 million hits on a YouTube video?

The answer is quite simple — Ranch dressing.

Let's face it. Everything really does go better with Ranch dressing. On salad it's a natural, but try dredging a Doritos Nacho Cheese chip through a vat of creamy white Ranch and you're one step removed from a religious epiphany.

Ever tried it with a fresh banana? Sounds disgusting, but when it comes to Ranch dressing, there are no limits.

So how did I arrive at this startling discovery? I learned it from a gifted teacher — my late son Jed. Though he didn't know it at the time, my 18-year-old son taught me everything about enjoying life to the fullest each and every moment of the day. He also showed me that the simplest things in life can be the very best — like Ranch dressing.

Jed was fearless when it came to dragging food through the buttermilk-laden dressing. Yes, including bananas. A slice of pepperoni pizza? A good dunking of Ranch made that culinary treat even tastier. The same holds true for hamburgers. Though he preferred the flame-broiled flavor of a Whopper, he would never consider it palatable until it was dripping with a good helping of the white stuff.

Diagnosed after his second birthday with autism, Jed exhibited the typical delays associated with this baffling disability — limited speech and an inability to move comfortably in social settings. Children with autism also have crazy diets. I know of one family whose son for years lived on a daily regimen of potato chips.

Luckily for us, Jed was attracted to a colorful array of food, even hummus. It became a motivating force during his youth. We used food to expand his language skills by writing out detailed sentences on paper that he would later recite in order to get what he wanted. Soon, he was able to sift through a stack of these scripted sentences to tell his schoolteachers and us what was on his mind: "I would like crackers, please."

Jed was born August 4, 1984, at Yakima Valley Memorial Hospital and died there 18 years later following complications from a severe seizure.

When his birthday was fast approaching last summer, I wanted to do something different since he would have been 25 years old. I never did much in the past. Instead, I had focused on October 8, the day he died, by taking long, brutal hikes in hopes of convincing myself I could move past the pain of his death, one step at a time. It made no sense, but little does when a child dies.

So in the early morning of that darkest of dates, I would head off into the L.T. Murray Wildlife Recreation Area north of Selah and trek up the Yakima Rim Skyline Trail, which overlooks the Yakima River Canyon. It captures picturesque views of Mount Adams and Mount Rainier, but I was there for the sheer torture of the three-hour climb. I would return home exhausted, my feet blistered.

I got to thinking last summer, what's the point of adding agony to misery? Why not celebrate his birthday? We always did when he was alive. It was a 24-hour blowout where Jed ruled as a benign dictator. He got everything he asked for, even unlimited access to the computer with the help of his older brother, Andy.

That's when I came up with the idea of using food, which had always motivated Jed, to help others find a way to celebrate and remember Jed as he had always been — a smiling, affectionate young man who had overcome so much in so little time.

So I sat down at the computer and wrote an e-mail listing Jed's favorite foods, ranging from Goldfish and turkey bacon (he would always pronounce it "gacon") to soft vanilla ice cream from Dairy Queen. I sent it out to his brother, aunts, uncles, cousins, former teachers and friends of mine.

A few days after Jed's birthday, the messages came flooding in from Boston, Chicago and California. Jed's menu was a smash hit. Some even tried the banana routine with Ranch dressing. The verdict: not bad. A dear friend took photos of family and friends eating Jed's treats. Each photo prominently displayed a bottle of Ranch dressing along with a photo of Jed smiling. It had the inscription: "This is for you Jed!"

Too often we try to move as far away as possible from the pain of losing a loved one. We shut out the past, take the clothes to Goodwill and rearrange the room in hopes of blocking out the sadness that fills the empty spaces left in our hearts.

It doesn't work. So why fight it? It's better to find ways of capturing and keeping the memories you never want to lose.

That's why I will be in line at a Burger King restaurant this Wednesday putting in my order the way Jed would have: "I want a Whopper with cheese, please."

Then the ritual dunking will follow. Really, everything does go better with Ranch dressing.

August 1, 2010

EXIT LAUGHING

A belly laugh, big and bold. That's how Nikos Kazantzakis ends his 33,333-verse epic poem, "Ulysses: The Modern Sequel."

Though considerably shorter in length and far less lyrical in scope, my book comes to the same conclusion: no flowery speeches, no gaudy gestures. End it with a laugh, or two, or three.

So breathe deep and prepare to exit laughing as my life plays out in of all places a clinic where I undergo a colonoscopy, and later, in a classroom where I enter wearing bright yellow ballet tights. What more can you do at this stage in life than to laugh at yourself? If it's good enough for Ulysses, it's surely good enough for me.

Injury casts new light on daily life

Let's blame it on the Mariners. Why not, their season can't get any worse.

The team didn't actually cause the mishap. But watching Bret Boone pop out with the bases loaded didn't help, either.

I was distracted. I looked up at the television and muttered a curse as Boone trotted back to the dugout.

That's when I dropped the hunk of cheese.

As if caught in an ESPN slow-motion replay, the freshly cut square of extra sharp cheddar floated in the air, bounced off the kitchen counter and down into the opening of my full-leg cast. I could feel it slide into the abyss, settling in between my leg and the fiberglass cylinder that held my right leg rigidly in place.

Utter despair, that's what I felt. I knew the next time I'd be seeing that cheese chunk would be in another 15 days when the orthopedic nurse would cut open the cast, freeing my leg and that morsel of decaying cheddar. Not a pretty thought.

Somehow I persevered. Or rather, the cheese somehow disintegrated, for when the nurse indeed removed the cast after the allotted 15 days, only gold dust remained. Even the odor was not unpleasant. Moderately disgusting, but not putrid.

"You should see when people get pennies stuffed down their casts," laughed the nurse. From what I hear, the skin beneath the coins turns a purplish black. I'll take cheddar cheese any day.

The reason for my cast is all too familiar for us 55-year-olds who think the only way to stay young is to play young — and I'm not talking about frequenting karaoke bars. Playing racquetball, which will keep your heart pumping. It's a fiercely competitive game that requires numerous starts and stops, all calling into action one key element in the body: the Achilles tendon.

I never thought that when I pulled up lame one day while playing racquetball at the YMCA, the injury would put me on crutches, lead to a full-leg cast for seven weeks and then two smaller casts for six more. But that's what you get when you tear your Achilles tendon.

It turns out a ruptured Achilles is worse than even a broken leg. It's one of the most difficult injuries to recover from, taking at least six months. In the movie "Troy," Brad Pitt's Achilles proved to be fatal. Mine just got to be a pain.

Though I'm not recommending everyone should rupture their Achilles (though I wouldn't mind the company), I believe the injury has shed new light on everyday living that may prove beneficial to those who prefer to keep playimg racquetball and end up having only one ankle in working condition.

So here are a few words of advice from someone who now, thanks to my crutches, has the strongest armpit muscles in all of the Yakima Valley:

• Don't go outside.

If you think negotiating a bathroom is tough with a leg cast, try puttering around your garden. It's hopeless. Even sitting out there amid the sweet peas and marigolds can be a challenge.

One sunlit morning, I hunkered down in a lawn chair to enjoy a little peace and quiet while reading the newspaper. Midway through the editorial page, I felt something skittering across my skin. I spied down to see one of the most feared pests in the garden: an earwig. The insect's minute but menacing claws were crossing over the expanse of my thigh, heading straight where the hunk of cheese had gone.

Only a whack with the rolled up end of the letters-to-the-editor page saved the day.

• Yes, coat hangers do work.

I never had much of a problem with itching, even on the hot summer days in July. But leave it to friends and to perfect strangers to change all of that. Instantly when someone would ask the inevitable question — "Hey, I bet that cast really itches during the summer?" — an itch would immediately take hold.

But getting to the itch is no easy task. You can sneak a finger a few inches past the edge of a full-leg cast, but you can't get anywhere close to the Mother of All Itches — at the crook of the knee.

Thank heavens for coat hangers. By creating a loop at one end of an outstretched hanger, you can shove it down — gently — to the backside of the knee. Then pulling the metal hanger with a back-and-forth motion, you can get the blunted loop of the hanger in the right spot. One more twist and, magically, you are transported to the Land of Oz.

• A salute to garbage bags.

Taking a shower in a cast is not a vision anyone, even a trained nurse, should behold. So make sure the door is securely locked before sudsing up.

Next take out one of those large 32-gallon black garbage bags you use for autumn leaves and stuff your leg and cast into it. With a short piece of clothesline you have retrieved from the garage, tie it around the open end of the bag that's covering the uppermost part of the cast. Cinch up the rope until the blood begins to back up around your hip. At last, you are ready to take a shower. See how easy that was?

• Don't be a blabbermouth.

OK, let's set the record straight. Be honest with your doctor, especially if he's a surgeon wielding a very sharp scalpel.

However, the doctor's office isn't a confessional, so there's nothing written in the U.S. Constitution that requires you to divulge trips that you may — or may not — have taken to the White Pass Ski Area. This is especially true if you went between the time of the injury on the racquetball court and the moment when the doctor first said, "I think your Achilles is ruptured."

Let's face it, skiing is permitted under almost any circumstance short of military insurrection, and even then it's fine if it means your escape.

And really, what are the chances of injuring your Achilles any further? Your ankle is rigidly secured in a ski boot. The only harm that could come is if you slammed into another skier, and that happily didn't happen the day I ventured onto the slopes.

So when the doctor asks — "How long has it been since you injured your Achilles?" — my advice is simple.

You study the calendar tacked to the wall and answer in a calm, but firm voice: "Long enough."

August 8, 2004

I will go lightly into that good loosening

It's sold under a more clinical-sounding name, "Colyte." But to those of us choking down the foul-tasting liquid to prepare for a colonoscopy exam, "GoLightly" is the code word. Believe me, it's anything but.

When I turned 50 and again at 55, I underwent a less intrusive search for cancer-causing polyps by getting a flexible sygmoidoscopy. Why they need to refer to it as "flexible" is beyond me. Do you really want a "nonflexible" exam?

Anyway, the sygmoidoscopy, with its happily flexible scope, only goes about a third of the way up the lower intestine. What lurks in the other two-thirds of that dark and dreary chamber is anyone's guess. That's why for my upcoming 60th birthday, I treated myself to the full-meal deal.

Getting a colonoscopy requires what is called "the prep." And that, my friends, leads us to GoLightly. A full gallon of the stuff. When you pick it up at the pharmacy, it looks innocent enough — a pile of powder at the bottom of a plastic jug. But when mixed with water, the substance turns nasty. Its goal is to clear out all living and dead matter from your bowels. Once GoLightly starts priming the primordial pump, there's no stopping it.

I decided to keep a writer's log of how I fared. I guess that's why I'm a journalist — jotting down details that would otherwise go unnoticed. Or in this case, go down the tubes.

The prep starts with three little pills to get you into the swing of things. Here's my first entry at 2:17 p.m.:

"Though I know the stuff couldn't possibly be working so quickly, I do feel a sudden urge to trot over to the toilet. Am I that weak? Where is my resolve?"

As you can see, self-doubt had already crept in.

Thankfully, someone at work told me to mask the terrible taste of the GoLightly with Crystal Light flavoring powder. I chose lemonade. I took my first glass of GoLightly at 3:05 p.m. Thanks to the Crystal Light, "the GoLightly went down easily," I noted. "I doubt, though, I will be saying that an hour from now when the stuff supposedly kicks in."

An hour later, at 4:14 p.m., the inevitable happened: "I made my first pit stop. Nothing too awful to report, but I can certainly feel a jiggling in the stomach and a certain — how shall I call it? — loosening effect. Not a pleasant sensation. I'm sure it will get worse, and then worse and then suddenly, there will be nothing left. What fun. ... Uh-oh. I felt an urge. Yikes. I still have two more quarts to go."

The trips to the bathroom finally subsided about an hour before my noon appointment the next day. I knew the worst was over. Everyone who has a colonoscopy tells you that, and they are absolutely right. It may be one of the few things on this planet that everyone agrees on.

After arriving at the gastroenterology clinic and being treated to a small sedative, I was lying on the exam table when the doctor showed up. He was all smiles. Now that's the way to approach a colonoscopy.

On the small television screen in front of me, I could clearly make out what was going on behind me. Tethered to the flexible scope, the doctor was spelunking through the twisting caverns of my large intestine. Quite a sight. There I was, or rather my colon, in living color.

Suddenly the flexible scope stopped. The doctor had reached the opening of my small intestine.

That's when he started to back out. I guess this is how you do colonoscopies — going in reverse.

"Oh, look at that," the doctor exclaimed, again with a cheerfulness that unnerved me. He came across a small indentation in the lining of my colon. It's what the medical world calls diverticulosis, a common disorder that, on rare occasions, may lead to infections. Nothing to panic about. The doctor found several more of what I now refer to as "my divots," an endearing term golfers use when they scuff up the turf with a pitching wedge.

Then came the polyps. Two of them. That was the whole reason for the colonoscopy — to lop off these polyps before they turn cancerous. The doctor snipped them off and continued on his merry way.

Just as he was about to call it quits, the doctor made one final observation: "Looks like you have a small hemorrhoid here."

Great, I finished the exam with what amounted to a colonoscopy trifecta — divots, polyps and a 'rrhoid.

Colonoscopies are serious business, especially if you are at high risk of getting colon cancer or are 50 or older and have never been tested. The stats aren't good. Nearly 150,000 Americans will likely be diagnosed with colorectal cancer this year, and almost 50,000 are likely to die from it.

So if you have a family history of colon cancer, suffer from such maladies as colitis or Crohn's disease, or have hit the 50-year mark and beyond and have never had a flexible scope visit your inner sanctum, then stop reading this and call your doctor.

Don't wait another minute. Colon cancer is preventable, but only if you act.

And don't worry about the GoLightly. It could end up being your very best friend.

August 3, 2008

A journalism career full of colorful characters

It's a colorful list: gamblers, convicted felons, Pulitzer Prize winners, devout Christians, dog lovers, chain smokers, sociopaths and at least one Elvis impersonator.

In my 35 years as a journalist, I have crossed paths with all of these, and more.

It does help to be a little off kilter. Really, what person in his or her right mind would actually seek out a profession that pays little, forces you to work weekends and nights and then requires you to write a correction every time you screw up? The daily grind is relentless; the search for truth elusive.

No wonder retirement has finally lured me away. On Monday, I will begin my first week without a deadline staring me in the face.

My wife Leslie says I'm not really retiring. I'm graduating. Not a bad way to look at it. I'm also getting back the freedom I lost when I became a taxpaying adult. "You can be a kid again," a friend wrote me last week.

I landed my first full-time job in the spring of 1975 when I began working for the Wyoming State Tribune in wind-ravaged Cheyenne, Wyoming. I was named sports editor and chief photographer, and for these twin titles I received the kingly sum of $2.50 per hour. That was minimum wage at the time.

I learned early on that journalists could one day gain fame, but don't count on a fortune to go with it.

One of the more memorable people I ever worked alongside was Kirk Knox, the newspaper's veteran police reporter. He was crusty, profane, and yes, endearing. When he appeared in the morning, he looked as if he had slept in his car overnight. His sports jacket and pants were always wrinkled and hung like a drop cloth over his skeleton-like frame. He wore a tie stained by coffee and singed by cigarettes, which he smoked constantly.

Whenever he sat down at his typewriter, he would wedge one of his hand-rolled cigarettes between his two front teeth. As he jabbered away on the phone, the cigarette would bounce wildly up and down causing a shower of ash to cascade onto his typewriter and lap. It was quite the spectacle.

Kirk was so cheap he would park his car outside the newspaper building and feed the parking meter with just enough money so he could finish his story without spending a penny more.

One day, though, things weren't going well for Kirk. He was following up on a murder that had happened the night before and his interviews were taking longer than he had anticipated. He kept getting up from his desk and scurrying down the stairs to feed coins into the parking meter.

On about the fifth trip to the street, the editor exploded out of his office. "Where the hell are you going," he thundered. When Kirk mumbled something about the parking meter, the editor reached into his pocket and hurled a handful of coins at Kirk.

"Get your damn story done!"

What drama, I said to myself. I can't believe I'm getting paid for this. It's so much fun.

Such were the delusions of a young journalist.

When I arrived at the Yakima Herald-Republic in the fall of 1982, I had the good fortune of working with Charlie Lamb, the night reporter. Charlie was a talker. I can't remember a conversation that didn't last at least 15 minutes. He could talk your ear off about anything, especially if it had to do with growing fruit or raising cattle. In his heart, Charlie was an old farmhand who just happened to be working at a newspaper all his life.

What made Charlie so fascinating was how he handled assignments. He would head out of the office in utter disarray, invariably forgetting to bring along a notebook to write on.

One night he went to cover a Chamber of Commerce event featuring a high-powered speaker. The convention center was packed with a who's who of Yakima. Before the speech began, Charlie could be seen going from table to table asking if anyone had a matchbook they could spare. Back then smoking in public places was still allowed so matchbooks were plentiful.

Charlie wasn't there for a smoke. He needed the matchbooks so he could have something to write on.

Attending this event was the Herald-Republic's recently hired editor. He had never witnessed Charlie in action. Naturally he panicked when he saw the reporter hunched over a matchbook scribbling notes. So after the speaker had finished, the editor rushed back to the newsroom and started to write his own version of the event. Could you blame him?

But Charlie was a journalist, a seasoned veteran in a profession that thrives on an individual's talent to turn the mundane into something meaningful. Such was Charlie.

With only three matchbooks to rely on, Charlie banged out a story on his antique Olivetti typewriter. It ran the next day on Page One.

After that, the editor never worried when Charlie rushed out of the office empty-handed. He knew Charlie would return with the goods.

What I learned from Kirk and Charlie is this — never make assumptions about people.

And always keep spare change and a matchbook within reach. You never know when they will come in handy.

September 4, 2010

Stepping back on stage a wakeup call

Certain words have a way of triggering fear in an actor who has just left the stage.

"Hey, man, didn't you drop a few lines?"

"No way," I replied. "That couldn't have happened."

That, of course, wasn't the case. I did indeed mangle my long speech, leaving out a key section where my character, Mark, confesses he's "a bozo, a yutz, a jerk."

This gaffe wouldn't have been so bad if it had happened two weeks before opening night. But my screw-up came less than 24 hours before the curtain would rise on the world premiere of "Dinner/Music," a play written by veteran actor and director Kurt Labberton, a well-respected Yakima dentist.

As I drove home that night from the Warehouse Theatre, I could feel my chest tighten as I struggled to catch my breath. What if I do it again and freeze up completely, standing there in front of a packed house, my lips trembling as I utter the only word left in my addled brain: "Help!"

Being gripped by terror and fear, I have come to learn, are key elements to acting. It makes parachuting out of an airplane at 15,000 feet seem like a walk in the park.

And I had good reason to be terrorized. When Kurt told me I was in the play, he neglected to mention I had to memorize a six-page speech. It's twice as long as Hamlet's celebrated "To be or not to be" soliloquy.

It also didn't help that I had taken a brief hiatus (35 years) from acting. Sure, I have been a master of ceremonies at various events, but that never required memorizing hundreds of words — all in sequence.

I could never find the time to be in a play since moving to Yakima in 1982, what with raising two boys and working at the Yakima Herald-Republic. But when I retired last fall, the idea of trying out for a part crept into my mind. It had to be the right play. Something special.

So when I got word that Kurt had written another play and was going to produce it this spring, I decided to take the leap. His previous work, "Bookbound," was brilliant and became the first original play to be staged at the Warehouse.

I wanted to be a part of history when he unveiled his second masterpiece.

"Dinner/Music" is a deliciously ingenious play that revolves around a group of friends attempting to recreate a dinner party that Cole Porter, songwriter and fabled socialite, once hosted in 1947 for King Edward VIII and his American divorcee, Mrs. Wallis Simpson. It offers lots of Porter music, laughter and even a kazoo chorus blaring out a Four Seasons hit. During the dinner, guests reveal secrets about themselves, delivering intricately woven speeches about faith and friendship.

When Kurt called to tell me I had a role, he exclaimed on the phone: "You're perfect for it. Just play yourself."

Only later did I find out that my character, an orthopedic surgeon, is stuffy, self-absorbed and kind of full of himself. Nonetheless, I chose to take Kurt's words as a compliment. Why argue with the playwright, co-director and lead actor? He has far more "street cred" than I do.

And let's be clear about this: Acting is a full-time job. We started practicing our lines in late February and maintained a steady schedule of four or five rehearsals a week. The workload is immense, even for a retiree. For the rest of the cast, I honestly have no idea how they did it. Most have 8-to-5 jobs.

I'm also sad to report that over the course of the nine weeks leading up to opening night, I managed to butcher every line Kurt wrote.

Gradually I got to feel more confident. That's thanks to the cast around me. What a phenomenal troupe of pros. Most are regulars at the Warehouse Theatre and many have performed at the annual Christmas cabaret shows at Gasperetti's restaurant.

Together, they have more than 100 years of theatrical experience. They know how to get the most out of a written line, and most importantly, how to get out of a mental "tar pit" when you come up empty on stage. Their advice for when this happens? Keep talking. In theatrical terms, you can't hit a moving target. Stay in character and work your way through it. The audience won't know you're dying on stage — just your fellow actors — and they will be there to toss out another line and snap you back to life.

Still, that advice gave me little comfort after I flubbed my big speech on that final rehearsal before the April 29 premiere. I suffered through a sleepless night. The next morning I could barely keep my eyes open. I chugged down what seemed like a gallon of coffee in hopes of waking up. Nothing worked.

I pushed on. I went over my part with a very demanding line coach, my wife Leslie, who cheered me on. "Flawless," she said, lifting a word from the play.

Somehow, everything came together on opening night. I said all of the lines Kurt had written. At the end, the audience treated the cast and our gifted playwright to a standing ovation.

Saturday night brought down the curtain on three weekends of performances, many to a sold-out theater. What an experience. Thrilling and terrifying, all at the same time. Again, that's live theater.

A friend asked me after one of the performances if I would try out for another play. Recognizing what I had sacrificed over the past three months, I quickly responded, "Are you crazy?"

But if something special comes along, like another "Dinner/Music," who knows? As the Bard once wrote, "The play's the thing."

As I came to discover, it's everything.

May 15, 2011

Edward the Elf delivers Christmas joy to special kids

Paul stiffened his back as I placed a red Santa's hat on his head and slipped on a pair of Elvis sunglasses, which slid down his slender nose.

"I now proclaim you an Elf of the First Order," I said in a solemn tone.

The young students in the special education classroom at Hoover Elementary School erupted with laughter and applause.

As an assistant elf, Paul helped Santa hand out stuffed animals. The 4-year-old quickly warmed up to the task, giving high fives to his classmates as they eased onto Santa's lap.

"Awesome," Paul exclaimed.

He then gave a thumbs-up and paused to mug for photographs with a smile that could easily melt the coldest of hearts — yes, even that of Ebenezer Scrooge.

Such are the miracles of being an elf. I know. For the past six years, I've dressed up as Edward the Elf, doling out candy canes and appointing Elf of the First Order to excitable boys and girls.

In what amounts to a "rock concert" tour, Santa Claus and I travel to elementary schools within the Yakima School District and visit each special education classroom, including the preschool classes at Hoover. We turn routine school days into a near riot and spread Christmas the way it should be — with a bag full of stuffed animals and a briefcase crammed with candy canes.

The Kiwanis Club of Yakima makes possible our visits, paying for Santa's elaborate suit and the 178 stuffed animals we handed out this December.

The visits continue a tradition started by the late Jerry Henderson, a longtime Kiwanis member and renowned community volunteer. In 1967 he began showing up in classrooms dressed as Santa, bearing gifts and telling goofy stories about mischievous elves and the redeeming powers of Christmas magic dust. Often, his arrival would be heralded by the sound of sleigh bells over the school intercom.

And Jerry insisted on going to special education classrooms. He figured children with special needs rarely, if ever, get a chance to see a department store Santa. Too scary. So Jerry brought Santa to the classrooms where the young students felt safer.

After Jerry's death in early 2005, Kiwanis continued to dispatch Santa to several classrooms. I tagged along, helping with the stuffed animals. Wearing a tie and dress shirt, though, didn't seem right. Why not shake it up a bit, I thought to myself. So I rented an elf suit from a party store in

Yakima. It was made of flimsy green felt and came with floppy leather elf shoes, which slipped off when I attempted to prance around the classroom.

A year later I pulled out my credit card and committed fully to my newfound Edward-the-Elf persona. I bought, off the Internet, a new green elf suit with a pointy hat. For leggings, I added a pair of camouflage long underwear and then "elf-ified" a pair of old loafers by spraying them with green paint and fastening a big bell on each shoe. Now I entered classrooms the way Jerry once did, with the sound of clanging bells echoing across the floor.

Still not satisfied with my attire, I put Edward the Elf through another serious upgrade for this Christmas season. Gayle Wingerter, a retired Yakima teacher and skilled seamstress, agreed to transform my suit into a replica of Will Ferrell's outfit in the hit movie, "Elf."

I have to admit the result is stunning, especially since I've tossed away the camouflage long underwear and now sport a pair of bright yellow, performance-grade ballet tights.

Eat your heart out Will Ferrell.

I even use the "Elf" flick to my advantage. When introducing myself to a new classroom of boys and girls, I tell them that Edward the Elf is really a movie star. That's when I pull out a DVD case of Ferrell's "Elf" movie. His face, though, is not on the front cover. It's mine — thanks to a skillful cut-and-paste job performed by my wife, Leslie.

The DVD is a showstopper.

That's only part of our classroom routine. It starts out with yours truly doing an Irish "Riverdance" around the room, much to the delight of the kids and utter dismay of the teachers. I ramp up the energy another few notches by urging the kids to yell as loud as they can for Santa Claus.

Suddenly the door flings open and Santa swaggers in, an impressive sight at 6-foot-5 (Full disclosure: Santa is Jay Carroll, a fellow Kiwanis member and Yakima attorney who has a heart of gold and a commanding voice, which can turn a Christmas story into a theatrical treat).

I then perform a magic trick with a silk scarf that turns a stack of papers in a battered briefcase into brightly colored candy canes. The kids scream with joy when I flip open the lid of the briefcase.

Not to be outflanked by Edward, Santa jumps into action with a song. He favors "Rudolph the Red-Nosed Reindeer." Next Santa tells a story about the time when Edward applied super glue to the bottom of Santa's sleigh. Only with a generous sprinkling of magic dust is Santa able to free the sleigh and save Christmas. At this point in the story, Santa pulls out a bag of magic dust and sprinkles the glitter upon the children's outstretched hands. A sense of awe fills the room.

Finally, we select a helper — an Elf of the First Order — who assists Santa in doling out stuffed animals to the boys and girls. If necessary, Santa gets down on his hands and knees, leveling the playing field between Saint Nick and a child who may still find him a bit intimidating.

Then it's over. Santa and Edward the Elf head out of the room, giving kids "high fives" and wishing them a merry Christmas.

Not a bad way to spend the holidays. Or in the words of Paul, an Elf of the First Order: "It's awesome."

Yes, simply awesome.

December 25, 2011

You know you're retired when honey-do list is a spreadsheet

Retirement has nothing to do with a sunny frame of mind. It does, though, have everything to do with "honey-do" lists.

When I retired from the Yakima Herald-Republic last month after 27 years, I had no idea what to expect. But my wife Leslie certainly did. I had made a strategic mistake of earlier putting off projects around the house with the offhand comment: "Oh, I'll take care of that after I retire."

So when I started receiving Social Security benefits, Leslie reminded me about what I had promised. How about painting the garden shed, she asked. And what about the kitchen sink? It's still leaking, she noted dryly.

Put it down on paper, I replied. I handed her a yellow legal pad and went back to the computer to update my Fantasy League football team.

But Leslie didn't start writing. Instead she flipped open her laptop computer and began typing away. In 15 minutes the printer belched out a sheet of paper.

Out came a neatly lined sheet with columns and rows. Leslie had done the unthinkable. She committed the "honey-do" list to a Microsoft Excel spreadsheet.

Under the heading of "action" items, she listed nearly 30 projects including putting new grout in the shower and placing more paving stones in the garden. At the end of each row she noted the "status." In the event I actually finished one of the chores, she would then type in "Done."

I noticed at the very bottom of the spreadsheet the initials "SB." I asked what that meant.

To Do List: After Retirement
Bold = Important

Action Item	Status	Date Completed	Comments
Fix Kitchen sink	Done	Oct. 10, 2010	Either fix this or call the plumber!
Fix toilet seat			
Unplug sinks-big bath			
Grout shower -big bathroom			
Fix towel hangers			
Change furnace filter			Allergies!!
Wash windows-outside	Done	Aug. 25, 2010	Thank you for doing this before your retirement
Wash windows-inside			
Clean out vent-laundry	Fire Hazard		911
Paint shed			
Clean garage			
Hang pictures			
Clean Pantry			
More paving stones			
Fix Sliding Door			
SB	Or else!		Daily Delivered Starbucks

"Starbucks," she replied. "I want an espresso." Then she paused for dramatic effect.

"Now."

At a recent fundraising event, I told several husbands about Leslie's Excel spreadsheet. One of the husbands had a horrified look on his face. No doubt he was guilty of failing to fix a towel rack in the master bathroom for the past two years.

"Whatever you do," he said, "don't ever introduce your wife to mine."

The real problem with retirement is you never get a day off.

It can also be bad for your health. That's why having a ready supply of antibiotics is sometimes more important than enjoying a robust 401(k).

That's what I needed following a recent eye infection. It wasn't pretty. My left eyelid looked like it was sprouting a Red Delicious apple. I could barely see out of it. What's happening here? I barely begin to reap the joys of retirement and I can't even see to play golf.

Leslie and Spencer   Photo by Jon Brunk

Actually just reaching retirement can be a life-and-death struggle. I found that out a few days before my farewell party last month. I was heading to the newspaper office in downtown Yakima as usual, turning off of Summitview Avenue and onto a short side street leading to Martin Luther King Boulevard. I had driven that piece of pavement for nearly three decades without mishap.

That morning, though, was decidedly different. A speeding motorist was approaching on my right from another street. He had a stop sign; I didn't. But did that matter? He blew right through the stop sign and was on a collision course with my retirement plans.

I hit the brakes, muttered a curse under my breath and waited for the inevitable sound of metal hitting metal.

A miracle intervened. I had swerved to the left at the last second and escaped being hauled off to the hospital by a mere two inches.

Still, joining the 53.5 million other Americans receiving Social Security benefits does have its perks. A Tuesday matinee movie is one of them. No one is there. It's like having a private screening — with fresh popcorn.

Then there are the mid-week trips you can take without the hassle of packed hotels and crowded tourist attractions. We returned recently from a five-day trek to the Oregon coast. It was a pleasant change of scenery, though Leslie failed to consider what it would mean to her sleep patterns.

"What's that racket outside," she asked, awakening me in the early morning hours of our first day.

It's the ocean, I explained. Our hotel room in Lincoln City was only a few hundreds yards from the rolling surf of the Pacific Ocean.

"Could you tell it to shut up," came her crisp reply.

I decided not to ask if this was going to be added to my spreadsheet. Why invite more trouble into my life?

When we returned home, I got another Excel update. I actually got around to fixing the leak in the kitchen sink, so that got marked as "Done." But what's this at the bottom of the page?

Good grief, the letters SB were back again, now in boldface print.

So back I headed to Starbucks for another espresso. This time, though, I ordered it on the rocks — just like my retirement.

October 24, 2010

Afterword

Proceeds from the sale of "Counting Crows" will be donated to a scholarship fund in honor of my late wife, Bronnie. The fund helps aspiring special education teachers at Central Washington University, where Bronnie earned her diploma.

If you wish to make a contribution to the scholarship fund, please write your check to: CWU Foundation — Bronwen Hatton Endowed Scholarship.

Mail the contribution to:
Central Washington University Foundation
400 East University Way
Ellensburg, WA 98926-7508

✫ ✫ ✫

A few months after I retired, I found an opportunity to write about Bronnie's scholarship. The column in the Yakima Herald-Republic ran under the headline: "A scholarship winner holds promise for the future."

Sometimes in the most unlikely of settings, something wonderful happens.

Take, for instance, a winter's night last year when my wife, Leslie, and I attended the Zonta Club's "Murder Mystery Dinner Theatre," which raises money for a host of service projects.

As with most fundraisers, being grouped with strangers is common. Such was the case that night at the Yakima Convention Center. I struck up a conversation with a young lady sitting next to me.

"So what do you do for a living?" I asked.

She said she was a special education teacher. How nice, I thought — my late wife, Bronnie, was also a special education teacher.

"Where do you teach at?"

"Adams Elementary School," she replied.

Wow, I said to myself. Not only did our son, Jed, attend special education classes years ago at Adams, but a few months earlier I had made a visit to the school as part of our Yakima Kiwanis Club's Santa Claus program. Each December, Santa Claus and I go to special education classrooms throughout the Yakima School District. Our goal is to bring Santa to children with special needs who rarely, if ever, get to see "the big guy in the red suit."

I could understand why she didn't recognize me at first. When I go with Santa, I arrive dressed up as Edward the Elf, Santa's rather talkative helper who's decked out with a pointy hat, Elvis sunglasses, yellow ballet tights and old loafers, splattered with green paint and adorned with huge gold bells.

"I hope I didn't scare the kids too much," I said.

She laughed and shook her head. She said her students loved Santa, and yes, even Edward.

Then I asked her where she had earned her degree. She said Central Washington University.

"What a coincidence," I exclaimed. "We have a scholarship there in my late wife's name — Bronwen Hatton."

That's when she started to blink away tears. Did I say something wrong?

She smiled and said she had received one of our scholarships.

"I couldn't have made it through without it," she confessed.

Who could have imagined meeting Sharol Parry-Hodgson, one of only nine CWU graduates to receive our scholarship, over a plate of tossed salad in the middle of a packed convention center? Rarely do you ever see the consequences of a good deed.

Then there are those moments of serendipity when a stranger, sitting next to you, says in the most heartfelt of voices, "Thank you." That's when you know how powerful the force of giving can be. It can change lives, not only for the person receiving but also for the one giving.

The need for college scholarships has never been greater given what's going on in Olympia where lawmakers are, once again, taking a sledge-hammer to higher education. Reduced funding means another cycle of annual double-digit tuition hikes. Since 2008, tuition rates at CWU have increased by more than 70 percent.

Larger research institutions like the University of Washington are better prepared to handle these cutbacks by admitting out-of-state students, who pay upwards of three times the amount of tuition that an in-state student does. But CWU doesn't have that option. The university in Ellensburg is a magnet for in-state students, with some 95 percent of its enrollment coming from the Evergreen State.

And getting a college degree isn't cheap. Last year, the average annual cost for an undergraduate at CWU — tuition, room, board, books and fees — reached $19,041.

This underscores how critical giving to endowment funds at universities and colleges has become these days. It's no longer a luxury to receive a scholarship; it's now a matter of financial survival for students. Gifts through CWU's foundation amounted to more than $10 million in 2010. Among the university's 10,447 students, 83 percent received some form of financial aid, totaling $120 million.

When Bronnie was diagnosed with ovarian cancer in 1992, she had entered her second year of special education studies at CWU. She had earned a teaching degree earlier in Colorado but wanted to work in special education after raising our son Jed, who was autistic. Even though she underwent two surgeries and a grueling regimen of chemotherapy during that final year of classes, she still received straight A's and earned her degree.

Shortly after she died in 2000, I sat down with CWU administrators and established a scholarship in her name. I couldn't imagine a better way to honor her determination than to ease the financial burden for young special education teachers like Sharol.

I never mentioned to Bronnie the idea of creating a scholarship while she was fighting cancer. I knew she would have vetoed it.

I think, though, she would have had a change of heart after seeing what the annual $1,000 gift has accomplished over the years. Through her scholarship, she will continue to be an inspiration, helping others earn their diplomas as she did hers — against all odds.

April 18, 2011